SCHADENFREUDE, BABY!

SCHADENFREUDE, BABY!

A Delicious Look at the Misfortune of Others
(and the Pleasure It Brings Us)

Laura Lee

The Lyons Press
Guilford, Connecticut
An imprint of The Globe Pequot Press

> To buy books in quantity for corporate use
> or incentives, call **(800) 962–0973**
> or e-mail **premiums@GlobePequot.com**.

Copyright © 2008 by Laura Lee

ALL RIGHTS RESERVED. No part of this book may be reproduced or transmitted in any form by any means, electronic or mechanical, including photocopying and recording, or by any information storage and retrieval system, except as may be expressly permitted in writing from the publisher. Requests for permission should be addressed to The Globe Pequot Press, Attn: Rights and Permissions Department, P.O. Box 480, Guilford, CT 06437.

The Lyons Press is an imprint of The Globe Pequot Press.

Designed by Sheryl P. Kober
Photography throughout © Shutterstock

Library of Congress Cataloging-in-Publication Data
Lee, Laura, 1969-
  Schadenfreude, baby! : a delicious look at the misfortune of others (and the pleasure it brings us) / Laura Lee.
    p. cm.
  Includes bibliographical references.
  ISBN 978-1-59921-235-7
  1. Embarrassment. 2. Embarrassment—Humor. 3. Self-consciousness (Sensitivity) 4. Failure (Psychology) 5. Fortune. 6. Fame. I. Title.
  BF575.E53L44 2008
  081—dc22
                                                    2008006034

Printed in the United States of America

10 9 8 7 6 5 4 3 2 1

CONTENTS

Introduction VII

    I. Ego and Vanity 1
   II. Do as I Say, Not as I Do 21
  III. Excuses, Excuses 43
  IV. The Secret World of Children's
        Television 53
    V. Just Deserts 59
   VI. Nature's Revenge 79
  VII. Publicity Problems 93
 VIII. Incompetence 111
  IX. Bureaucracy and Other Legal Madness 131
   X. Department of Homeland Insecurity 147
  XI. Cartoonish Accidents 155
  XII. Embarrassing Moments 169
 XIII. Unappreciated Ideas 181
 XIV. Really Bad Days 185
  XV. The Joy of Gawking and Other
        Weirdness 195
 XVI. How Will You Be Remembered? 205

Bibliography 209

Introduction

"Every time I'm on ABC, I crash," Vinko Bogataj once said after suffering a minor fender bender in a hotel parking lot. He was on his way to be interviewed by ABC's Terry Gannon.

Poor Vinko Bogataj. By all accounts he was a highly accomplished athlete—you have to be to get to the World Ski Flying Championships, as this Slovenian ski jumper did in 1970. If only that was how the world remembered him.

Instead, Bogataj became famous for what happened next, on his third jump. The snow in Oberstdorf, West Germany, was heavy, and part way down the ramp the skier realized too late that the conditions had made the ramp too fast. He attempted to lower his center of gravity and stop his jump but instead lost his balance completely. He rocketed out of control and crashed in a stunning, dramatic fashion but fortunately walked away with only a concussion. It is said, though, that he never fully regained his confidence on the slopes.

Perhaps Bogataj would have a nobler legacy, were it not for the fact that his painful spill took place right in front of ABC Sports cameras. ABC's editors thought this particular accident would be a perfect opening for their *Wide World of Sports*, an ideal illustration of "the agony of defeat."

Throughout the show's long history, various images were used for the other parts of the opening, including for the triumphant "thrill of victory," but Bogataj's fall always illustrated "the agony of defeat." It became something of a catch phrase in America, thanks to a rather overly dramatic narration.

Here in the United States, we fell in love with the Agony of Defeat Guy. Let's face it, we all have more in common with that guy than with the one collecting his third gold medal on the Olympic platform. Vinko Bogataj stands—or falls—for all of us. Back in Europe, however, Bogataj was unaware that he had become an icon for bad luck. Given his less-than-memorable career, he was surprised when he was invited to participate in an anniversary special of the *Wide World of Sports* in 1991—and wouldn't you know, he had a crash on the way to the studio.

The Germans have a word for joy over the misfortunes of others. It's called *Schadenfreude*.[1] Because English lacks German's nifty ability to stick nouns together and call it a new word à la "Fahrvergnügen," we've gone ahead and adopted this great import. This is not to say that we didn't have the concept. It's really just a more economical version of the English expression, "One man's pain is another man's pleasure." The Chinese have a comparable expression: *Xing zai le huo*. It is a universal guilty pleasure and a central ingredient in humor.

Take slipping on a banana peel . . . please. For some reason this personal injury is a real knee-slapper. It's been a visual punch line since the music hall days. Why? It evokes the same *Schadenfreude* instinct that gets us to turn on *America's Funniest Home Videos* and watch a bunch of saps getting accidentally whacked in the privates with ill-placed rakes and shovels. (We may just enjoy the spectacle of people who are willing to stage humiliating "accidents" just to have a moment on television. Either way, it counts as *Schadenfreude*.)

One of my dear, sweet mother's favorite pieces of comedy was from *Laugh-In*, and it involved a guy in a rain slicker riding a tricycle, crashing into things and falling down. (You have to see it.) And who among us has not seen a friend injure himself in a way that unfortunately struck that *Schadenfreude* funny bone? You know the guy's really hurt, but in spite of your better instincts, your eyes well with the tears of repressed laughter as you call the ambulance.

Is it a sense of superiority, the leveling effect, pity, or painful empathy? Whatever the reason, we keep laughing when the clown gets a pie in the face. If you've ever read scholarly analyses of what makes humor funny, you know that it's best to enjoy it and not to think too much.

Incidentally, people do sometimes slip on banana peels. In real life, they call personal-injury lawyers. During a 1992 excursion to a U-Save Supermarket in Palm Beach County, Elvia Soriano slipped on a banana peel. Evelyn Owens was shopping in 1995 at a Publix Supermarket in St. Cloud, Florida, when she slipped on one. You're not laughing? It must be how I told it.

Schadenfreude has other manifestations. It has become most closely associated with reveling in the woes of someone who seems too

---

[1] Germans capitalize all their nouns. While it is gaining currency in English, *Schadenfreude* is still essentially a German import. Thus *Schadenfreude* appears with a capital "S" throughout the book.

big for his britches. The people we elevate the highest seem to be the ones we most want to level.

It's interesting that in a nation where we're so politically correct that we changed "and the winner is" to "and the Oscar goes to" to avoid hurting celebrities' feelings, we're terribly quick to relish in their downfalls. In the spring of 2007, CNN, the 24-hour cable news network, became the 24-hour Anna-Nicole-Smith's-death-is-a-soap-opera and Britney-shaved-her-head network. Before that it was the all-Michael-Jackson-Trial-all-the-time network, and before that the watch-Martha-Stewart-go-to-jail network, and long before that it was the all O.J.-Simpson-Bronco-chase network.

Don't blame the media; they air what we choose to gawk at. If we had more interest in the economic structure of the European Union than in "The vice president shot a guy in the face" or "The girl from *Different Strokes* robbed a video store," you can be sure that's what they'd air. (We sure do love those child-stars-gone-bad stories.)

While some people argue that celebrity gawking is the ultimate meaning of *Schadenfreude,* my personal feeling is that most of it doesn't quite qualify. When we're gossiping about who JLo is dating this week, or when our eyes pop at a scandal like Woody Allen's choosing his girlfriend's adopted daughter (the sister of his own children) for a lover, I believe we're enjoying the spectacle as a living soap opera. It's not *Schadenfreude,* baby. It's gossip.

Gossip plays an important role in human society, and it has since the days of our tribal ancestors. In nineteenth-century China, women had a novel solution to the problem: professional gossipers. Wealthy Chinese women of the time, by reasons of social mores and bound feet, did not travel much. Elderly women, usually widows, supported themselves by going from home to home getting and spreading tales about the people of society.

Our feet may not be bound, but modern Westerners are just as cut off from the majority of people in society. Our populations are simply too large for everyone in a major city or even a medium-size town to know everyone's business. To fill our need for gossip, we turn to entertainment, sports, and television to provide common reference points—individuals we all know whether we are from the same "clan" or not. A person from Manhattan can discuss the Michael Jackson legal case with someone from Iowa or even England. Tom Cruise's engagement becomes our common currency.

On the other hand, when Winona Ryder is arrested for shoplifting, the emotion *is* what I would call *Schadenfreude*. You get all of the reality-television drama, of course, but you also laugh because she brought it on herself. "Why is Johnny Depp's ex-girlfriend stealing stuff from a store? Can you show me that mug shot again? Wow, Reality Bites." Then again, bringing it on yourself isn't the key to *Schadenfreude* either. For example, the spectacular downfall of televangelist Jimmy Bakker in a sex scandal in the 1980s produced a *Schadenfreude* effect. There's nothing more satisfying than seeing hypocrisy exposed. Yet Catholic priests caught molesting altar boys are also guilty of hypocrisy and brought their misfortunes on themselves. We do not feel *Schadenfreude* when hearing their stories.

Being deserving isn't the key either. We didn't know enough about our bad luck hero, Vinko Bogataj, to take glee because he deserved to fall off his skis. We just relished the spectacularness of his tumble. In fact, we feel an odd affection for the man. (There must be a German word for *Schadenfreude* mixed with empathy. If there's not, I'm sure there are a few nouns they can push together to make one.)

In 1964 Supreme Court Justice Potter Stewart tried to explain pornography by saying, "I know it when I see it." He could just as easily have been speaking of *Schadenfreude*. It's not something that is inherent in a particular misfortune. It's not out there in the world; it exists in our reactions. One person sees Martha Stewart's legal troubles as a crying shame; another person, who always felt Martha's kitchens were a little too perfect, feels glee. When the hotdogging U.S. snowboarder Lindsey Jacobellis lost the gold medal at the Turin Winter Olympics in 2006 because she wanted to impress the crowds with a showy toe grab on her last run, it was a great *Schadenfreude* moment for everyone in the world . . . except the Americans.

This book is full of missteps and downfalls of the famous and not so famous. What they have in common is that if you put yourself in the central character's shoes, you'll find a misfortune, but from the comfortable distance of your armchair (or perhaps that porcelain chair in the smallest room in your house), you can't help but smile.

There can be an odd comfort to *Schadenfreude*. So you didn't quite manage to scale Mt. Everest, you never won a Pulitzer Prize, and you failed to become a rock star. What began as a dream of being the next Donald Trump got scaled down to the dream of being a contestant on *The Apprentice*, and finally the dream is just to avoid hearing "you're fired" before the mortgage is paid off.

When it seems you are not getting the credit you deserve, it may help to remember the people who have come to represent the accidents, crashes, and agonies of defeat of life. As the folk singer Arlo Guthrie (who became famous because he was arrested for littering) once put it: "During these hard days and hard weeks, everybody has it bad once in a while. You know, you have a bad time of it, and you always have a friend who says, 'Hey, man, you ain't got it so bad. Look at that guy.' And you look at that guy, and he's got it worse than you. And it makes you feel better that there's somebody that's got it worse than you. But think of the last guy. For one minute, think of the last guy. Nobody's got it worse than that guy. Nobody in the whole world. That guy . . . he's so alone in the world that he doesn't even have a street to lay in for a truck to run him over." No matter how bad it seems, you can take comfort in the fact that "that guy" is out there—the last guy—the one who has it worse than you. These are the people who woke up not only on the wrong side of the bed, but in a burning house the day after the insurance expired.

So here's to the spectacular pratfalls of life. Get ready for some roadside gawking, some petard hoisting, and satisfyingly smug grins. *Schadenfreude*, baby!

I.
Ego and Vanity

There is an interesting contradiction in human nature: While we're attracted to people with confidence, we don't want them to have too much confidence. We like someone who stands tall but not someone who paces like a peacock. We like to see a person well dressed but not overly so. When someone crosses the line between speaking firmly and boasting, between acting proudly and posturing, we spring forth to bring them down to a more human scale. When the world does it for us, we feel *Schadenfreude*.

Don't Hate Me *because* I'm Beautiful

Do you hate how you look? Who doesn't? Americans went through 4.6 million cosmetic-surgery procedures in 1999, according to the American Society for Aesthetic Plastic Surgery. That's a lot of folks who don't like their noses and double chins. If you manage to catch on to the latest fashion at about the time grandmothers are fishing it out of the bargain bin, this is the chapter for you. There are a lot of people who just can't get their look together. So when we see those perfectly coiffed fashion plates at a runway show, or the kid in the high school who sets the trends, we secretly want to see that person's perfect façade torn down.

If you're average, you see between four hundred and six hundred advertisements each day. One out of every eleven is selling something to make you more attractive. They feature women who look very little like us. Some of them look suspiciously like Barbie, a doll with an anatomically impossible figure. These women may well be from other planets. And that's really the key—if they looked like everyone else, we wouldn't need to *buy* anything to try to look like them.

There's just something about Kate Moss that makes an average woman in her size-16 dress seethe. So when we read that she was fired from lucrative modeling contracts after she was videotaped snorting coke, many of us secretly snicker. (Why drug use by a model who was described as personifying "heroin chic" would shock us is a question for another day.) It's easier to hate the models than to admit we're jealous.

The *Schadenfreude*-beauty connection does not apply only to women. Male models especially bring out some sort of primal emotion. We can't help but relish it when their perfectly coifed and managed images take a beating. Don't believe me? Let's look at two headlines. First, "Roller-Coaster Passenger Injured by Bird Strike." Second, "Supermodel Fabio Hit in the Face by a Bird." Was your reaction different? Sure, "hit in the face by a bird" is odd enough, but add a blond romance-novel cover model to the mix and you have late-night talk-show gold.

> It's easier to hate the models than to admit we're jealous.

It all happened in 1999. The Italian-born Fabio Lanzoni had been hired to promote the opening of Apollo's Chariot, a new roller coaster at the Busch Gardens theme park in Virginia. The PR team had been planning the moment for almost a year. The sun was shining, and the weather was ideal. It seemed as though nothing could go wrong.

Workers rolled out a red carpet, and Fabio, dressed as the Greek god of the sun, marched up to the coaster. Dressed in black leather pants and a velvet cape, he was to "drive" the chariot down the tracks past a group of reporters who were probably cursing their editors for giving them such a fluff assignment.

"I want to welcome all of you to my Apollo's Chariot," he said. "Let's have some fun." But on the first drop, as the car hit its top speed of 73 mph, a bird crashed into the model's nose and seemed to explode on impact. Blood flowed down Fabio's chin and splattered onto the pure white tunics of the "goddesses" seated beside him.

The stunned model was rushed to Williamsburg Community Hospital, where he was treated and released. "Worldwide, this has been nothing but a joke in the media," Busch Gardens spokesperson Cindy Sarko said. "He's not taking it as a joke. We're not taking it as a joke." Unfortunately for Fabio, Cindy was in the minority.

∎∎

Quick trivia question: What was the highest-selling album to be permanently deleted from a record label's catalog? Answer: *Girl You Know It's True* by Milli Vanilli. I had considered putting the most famous musical frauds of the twentieth century in the "Just Deserts" chapter. Clearly, they brought their misfortunes on themselves, but upon further reflection, I believe what gave people such a sense of *Schadenfreude* when their musical hoax was exposed was their washboard abs, spandex trousers, and such quotes as, "Musically, we are more talented than Bob Dylan. Musically, we are more talented than Paul McCartney. Mick Jagger, his lines are not clear. He don't know how he should produce a sound. I'm the new modern rock 'n' roll. I'm the new Elvis." That quote was from the more outspoken Milli, Rob Pilatus, one of the two front men of the band. (The other was Fabrice "Fab" Morvan.)

Milli Vanilli's radio-friendly pop sold seven million copies, but it was their "exotically sexy" look, as the *New York Times* put it, that got them heavy rotation on MTV. Looking at their model-handsome faces, teenage girls completely overlooked the fact that the guys had German accents when they spoke and urban American accents when they sang. Right from the start the Millis were criticized for their arrogance and were called a triumph of image over substance.

Pilatus told *Ebony* magazine that such criticism was "depressing and sad. Maybe some are afraid a bit because we have crossover. Other people get jealous." Their hit single, "Girl You Know It's True," won the European singers a "Best New Artist" Grammy. Pilatus and Morvan were secretly hoping they would not win, Pilatus later confessed on VH1's *Behind the Music*, because it might shine a light on the fact that they hadn't sung a note of the music on their hit album.

Rumors were already flying that the boys might not be the most musically ept. A *Washington Post* review of a Milli Vanilli concert called it a "triumph of technology and imagemaking over talent and originality . . . while not everything they sang sounded entirely canned, there were moments when the only voices in the hall that didn't appear to be lip-synched or electronically enhanced came from the squealing, mostly teenage crowd."

During a "live" performance a few months later, a recording of that very song began to skip and repeated the line "Girl you know it's . . ." over and over again. This may have been the last straw. Frank Farian, the German rock producer who had put the look and sound of Milli Vanilli together in a lab, told all. The guys with the faces on MTV took the brunt of the outrage and the jokes. Milli Vanilli's five Top Five singles—including three Number Ones—were hastily dropped from radio playlists and are rarely heard on oldies stations today. The album was deleted from Arista's catalog. A class-action suit in the United States allowed the consumers of the album to apply for a rebate.

The question is, why did people return the records? This leads us to another trivia question: Who were Charles Shaw, John Davis, and Brad Howe? Answer: The guys who really sang on Milli Vanilli's records. My point here is that the discs did not record themselves. There actually was music on them. The hits sounded exactly the same as they had before the public knew Rob and Fab did not sing on them. This must mean that people returned their records simply because the real singers were not good-looking enough. (And we call the faux lead singers of Milli Vanilli shallow.)

The dancer/models Rob Pilatus and Fab Morvan slinked off in disgrace. Pilatus never recovered. Addiction, a suicide attempt, and stints in rehab followed. Eight years after his fall from grace, Pilatus died alone in a hotel room from a deadly combination of alcohol and prescription pills. Fab Morvan, who it turns out has a decent voice, has quietly rebuilt his musical career by playing small clubs in the Los Angeles area, and "Milli Vanilli" continues to be a lip-synching punch line.

Poor *Little* Rich Girls

Now, for many years I have been searching on Craigslist trying to find an opening for a job as "heiress." The pay is good, and from what I have been able to observe by watching Paris Hilton, the job consists entirely of wearing expensive clothes, partying till dawn with rock stars and actresses, and being photographed a lot. As long as there is sufficient on-the-job training, I'm sure I could pick it up fairly quickly.

Yet as much as I look, there never seems to be an opening. These jobs are rather hard to come by, and there are many of us with more traditional jobs—say cleaning bed pans at a hospital or giving out change in a toll booth—who wouldn't mind a shot at one. But the only way an heiress job is going to open up is if someone gets knocked down. Hooray for Paris Hilton!

Appearing in court in a designer double-layered pinstripe suit and Jackie O sunglasses, she gave hope to millions as she faced a jail sentence for violating probation and driving on a suspended license after a drunk-driving arrest. (Prospective employers: if I were given this position, I would avoid such embarrassments by hiring a chauffeur.) Paris blamed her misfortune on bad legal advice from a publicist. She was told that she was allowed to drive to and from work on a suspended license. Given the nature of her work, she naturally assumed that she could continue to drive to restaurants, bars, clubs, and designer boutiques. Still, that doesn't really explain why she was driving seventy mph in a thirty-five zone.

> The only way an heiress job is going to open up is if someone gets **knocked down.**

After being sentenced to forty-five days in the slammer, Paris was quoted as saying, "I feel that I was treated unfairly and that the sentence is both cruel and unwarranted. I don't deserve this." Her publicist described the sentence as "ruthless." Such quotes got her a lot of sympathy, as there is nothing people enjoy more when getting back from a long day at work than hearing heiresses complain that they're being picked on. Tabloid and mainstream press alike reveled in the details of Paris's accommodations in the pokey. Her cell would measure 2.5 meters by 3.5 meters, and she would share it with another inmate whose name is more likely to be something like "Detroit Motel 6."

The 24-hour news networks chased the car that sped Paris off to jail in the exact same way that they *don't* chase the cars of people driving to Congress to make decisions that actually affect your life. All the while the seasoned journalists apologized for "having to" cover this news, as though they had absolutely nothing to do with the decision. Their cameras just happened to be drawn by gravity toward heiresses.

"Paris Hilton got forty-five days in jail," quipped late-night talk-show host Jay Leno. "A lot of people were upset by this; they were hoping she would get the death penalty." If she does, I would just like to reiterate that I'm available to start this position immediately, and I'm willing to relocate to Beverly Hills if required.

■■

Now if there is one thing America loves more than watching heiresses on parade, it is watching misfortune befall them. In case you're over the age of seventeen, I'll tell you about a program they have over on MTV. *My Super Sweet Sixteen* follows spoiled rich kids to their over-the-top birthday parties. In episode 38 we meet Ariel Milby, a cheerleader whose father calls her his "princess." As Daddy's little girl poses in a pink debutante gown, she says, "People at my school consider me the stuck-up, snobby, rich kid, but they're just jealous of me." Later she adds, "I'm used to getting what I want."

We follow Ariel as Daddy takes her shopping for Gucci and Coach and rents her a helicopter so she will have a grand entrance to her fantasy-themed birthday ball, which will be "so exclusive" she's only going to invite about 150 people. The key, she explains, is being able to exclude people who aren't cool enough. She revels in telling the uninvited to their faces that they won't be coming to the event of the season.

Next Ariel goes shopping for designer duds for her dog—who thankfully did make the cut. Ariel's tent is decked out with ice sculptures, and the guests are brought to it in horse-drawn carriages. The whole thing briefly looks like it will fall apart when no one is there to watch the debutante land in her helicopter, causing the birthday girl to fight back tears, but one cell-phone call to Mom fixes everything. The guests are herded outside to watch her pull up in a special Cinderella carriage, and of course the evening concludes with a fireworks display and Daddy's giving his princess her special gift, a shiny new BMW with a bow on top.

> The key is being able to **exclude** people who aren't cool enough.

Where did the money come from to pay for all this showy celebrating? Oil! As Ariel put it, "I love oil! Oil means shoes and cars and purses!"

Here's the thing—it was not the oil so much that brought Ariel's daddy, Gary Milby, his fortune. It was more the fraud. Gary Milby was being sued by about sixty investors who claimed he defrauded them out of at least $4.5 million. That's a lot of Versace. After he was sued, Milby made himself scarce. That is, until he decided to splash out on his daughter and appear on television doing it. The investors alleged that Milby sold securities at $18,000 each, promising at least a 49 percent return in the first year, despite the fact that regulatory agencies in five states ordered him to stop advertising and selling the securities. The state of Texas had also barred him from owning oil wells for seven years because of safety violations.

The Arizona Corporation Commission had ordered Milby to pay a $1 million penalty, but he never showed up for a hearing and never paid it. Things had kind of settled there until the commissioners were "outraged" to see the oil man's conspicuous display of wealth. Their zeal to pursue the case was renewed. (You can find more stories of the pitfalls in the quest for a little TV fame in the chapter "Publicity Problems.")

Fashion Victims

When your clothing is showy, there's a fair chance that it can make a show out of you in the most unintended ways. The expression "fashion victim" has been known to take on a very literal meaning.

My personal favorite example comes from the world of ballet, which features costumes that already make people nervous—women in tutus and men in tights! For fans, though, performances of ballet are graceful, expressive, and passionate. Using only their bodies, dancers convey a range of emotions from comedy to pathos. The most moving and anticipated moment of any ballet for the true connoisseur is the pas de deux—the love duet. And a true master of the pas de deux was British choreographer Sir Kenneth MacMillan. But on October 19, 1978, the audience found itself in stitches as a tragic pas de deux was unraveled along with the ballerina's skirt.

The performance was Kenneth MacMillan's *Mayerling*, which is based on the true story of the suicide pact between the unstable, drug-taking Prince Rudolf, heir to the Austro-Hungarian Empire, and his teenage mistress Mary Vetsera. It is popular for its impassioned erotic duets. As one critic wrote, "MacMillan, who has few equals as a creator of pas de deux, built *Mayerling* around seven brilliant examples of his technique."

Of course, the ballet features dancers emoting like silent movie stars, but all the best ballets do that, and the effect is usually elevating, not humorous. When something goes wrong, however, those overwrought, passionate gazes evoke nothing but mirth. In the final pas de deux, just as the lovely Lynn Seymour was about to dance out the dramatic climax, she tore her skirt. Her partner, David Wall, tried valiantly to ameliorate the wardrobe malfunction. With a quick bit of improvised choreography, he tried to rip off a stray piece of gauze that was trailing along the ground. This only caused the dress to unravel into strips of gauze. The more the pair danced their passionate pas de deux, the more they got wrapped in pieces of skirt. Soon they looked like a pair of zombies or, in the words of author Stephen Pile, "a sack of old rags possessed by the devil."

A *Sunday Telegraph* critic was there to witness it all. "It was the first time I have watched Mayerling's suicide through a haze of tears," he wrote, "but what with trying to maintain a decent, sympathetic silence, and desperately struggling to control a rising hysteria, the ballet's marvels were for once quite lost on me."

■■

Another victim of costuming was Timothy Baker, who escaped from prison in Waco, Texas, where he'd been housed by the state after committing armed robbery. He tried to hide at nearby Baylor University. The only thing keeping him from blending into the student population was his bright orange prison jumpsuit. He went from building to building looking for a new outfit when he happened upon the Fine Arts Center.

He thought he'd hit the jackpot when he discovered the costume wardrobe in the theater department. He shed his prison-issue orange and grabbed the first thing in his size from the rack. Then he dashed out. Unfortunately, he had chosen a nineteenth-century bright green wool costume complete with rubber galoshes, which was not as inconspicuous as he might have hoped. The police officer who arrested him said he looked like "a leprechaun."

■■

But who knows. Leprechaun may be just the thing next season. In their quest for originality, fashion designers are often literally setting their models up for a fall and providing us with unintentional comedy. A dual fashion trend in 2006 for monster high-heeled shoes that required the balance of a circus performer and minitrapeze dresses led to more than their fair share of runway stumbles. As runway reporter Michael Qunianilla put it, "Many a model at the recent collections looked as if she was balanced on supersized wheels . . . or stacked atop a ladder . . . or ready to take her tootsies on a roller-coaster ride."

Designer Vivienne Westwood wrote in her autobiography, "Fashion to me is like walking a tightrope, where you risk falling off into the ridiculous, but if you can stay on that tightrope you can have a triumph." The problem is that it's the model who actually has to do the walking.

Kamila W. stumbled, not once but twice, in a spring '07 Vivienne Westwood runway show. Teetering out on her cruel shoes, trying to perform that flat-footed, cross-ankled supermodel strut, while carrying a giant gardener's watering can—full of water!—she tripped once, then got up and wobbled a few more steps before falling again. She became a star not of the catwalk but of the blooper reel and YouTube.

It wasn't the first time a model had risked her life to strut for Westwood. Supermodel Naomi Campbell took to the runway in 1993 decked out in a tartan kilt and gigantic ten-inch crocodile shoes. She also landed on her pride. *Schadenfreude* lovers found this tumble especially gratifying because Naomi Campbell has the reputation of being the supermodel from hell, chasing off more personal assistants than the fictional reporter Murphy Brown. British tabloids sometimes refer to her as "Nutta."

> She became a star not of the catwalk but of the **blooper reel.**

Even actress Penny Marshall has suffered runway embarrassment. She was hosting a fashion show for Kmart's Sesame Street line of clothing when she lost her step, and gravity did the rest. Trying to avoid falling off the runway, she grabbed Big Bird's right wing. Next thing you know she was on the floor with the detached wing in her hand and a room full of preschoolers staring bug-eyed at the one-winged bird. The actress and film director tried to reassure the children that she hadn't caused permanent injury to the giant Muppet. "Don't worry. It'll grow back," she said.

■■

This tale is a special triple shot of *Schadenfreude*. It involves a clothing mishap, differences in status, and a little electronic revenge—that backfires. Many wage slaves felt empathy for Jenny Amner, a fifty-six-year-old secretary, when their e-mail inboxes flashed her scathing forwarded memo. Jenny worked for the "world's fifth-biggest law firm," Baker & McKenzie, in London. One day she was sitting at the canteen beside a thirty-six-year-old associate, Richard Phillips.

On this particular day she found herself the victim of one of those ketchup packets that just doesn't want to open. She poked and prodded and tore at it until it finally blasted open with a geyser of tomato redness, which landed with unfortunate accuracy on the khakis of the lawyer with the $100,000-plus salary.

Little did either one know at the time that they were to about become Internet celebrities. The next day Phillips fired off a quick e-mail with the subject line "ketchup trousers." It read, "Hi Jenny, I went to a dry cleaners at lunch and they said it would cost £4 to remove the ketchup stains. If you cd let me have the cash today, that wd be much appreciated."

Amner was a little slow to respond, so Mr. Phillips followed with a Post-it reminder on her desk. What he didn't know was that she was away at her mother's funeral, which may explain her reaction when she returned to find the note on her desk. She sent her reply and cc'ed it to everyone in the office. She wrote: "I must apologise again for accidentally getting a few splashes of ketchup on your trousers. Obviously your financial need as a senior associate is greater than mine as a mere secretary. Having already spoken to and shown your e-mail [to the staff] . . . , They kindly offered to do a collection to raise the £4. I however declined their kind offer but should you feel the urgent need for the £4 it will be on my desk this afternoon. Jenny."

After a few of the 250 staff members on the distribution list cc'ed their friends, it wasn't long before just about everyone in Britain with an e-mail account was laughing at the lawyer's tightwaddery. Devastated by the humiliation, Phillips resigned from Baker & McKenzie, saying rather unconvincingly that he'd been planning to leave "long before" ketchupgate. Jenny Amner seems to have gotten the last word, but revenge is not always sweet. She was also given leave from work after she got the cold shoulder by employees, who felt Phillips had been unfairly victimized by the whole thing.

■ ■

But these incidents were harmful only to the victim's vanity. Fashion disasters have sometimes been fatal. A famous case was that of the outspoken aristocrat, the first marchioness of Salisbury, who lived from 1750 to 1853. She perished in a fire at her home in Hatfield, England, which began at the top of her head.

Lady Salisbury had always lived a spectacular life. She stunned polite society with extravagance and gambling. She was not a fan of church and held card parties on Sunday mornings and concerts in the evenings instead. Sometimes church had to be canceled when the rector's presence at her lady's affair was required. On one of the rare occasions when she did attend church, she heard the story of Adam and Eve. She learned that Adam had blamed Eve for his transgression in eating the fruit of the tree of knowledge, and she decided that Adam was "a shabby fellow indeed!"

> Her **stunning updo** made contact with the chandelier.

She loved hunting, and even when she got to be eighty and could hardly see, she refused to give up the sport. She would sit in the saddle, and a groom would lead her around. She refused to be demure and dress her age. The octogenarian wore the fashions of her youth, with her hair piled high and decorated with feathers. One evening, after an enjoyable day at the hunt, she rose from the table, and her stunning updo made contact with the chandelier and started a fire that consumed her and her mansion. It was a fitting end to a dramatic and dazzling life.

Arrogance: Bedroom Boasting

Overconfidence in the bedroom is an absolute recipe for *Schadenfreude*. Princeton graduate Peter Chung knows firsthand what bedroom-boasting backlash feels like. In 2001 the twenty-four-year-old was sent to Seoul, South Korea, for a cushy job with the Carlyle Group, a private equity firm whose senior consultants included the former Conservative British prime minister John Major and former U.S. president George H. W. Bush. Things were looking pretty rosy for the guy on May 15, and he decided to send a message to his friends to brag about his exciting new life.

He crowed about bankers catering to his every whim, offering him lavish dinners and nights on the town. He lived in luxury accommodations, a two-thousand-square-foot, three-bedroom apartment with one room reserved entirely for sex, which was the greatest perk of all. The centerpiece was a queen-size bed where he entertained his "harem of chickies." He reported that he was getting closer to his goal of "[expletive deleted]ing every hot chick in Korea over the next two years."

He asked his friends to send him boxes of condoms. "I brought about 40," he wrote, "but I think I'll run out of them by Saturday."

"I know I was a stud in NYC," he wrote, "but I pretty much get about, on average, 5–8 phone numbers a night and at least 3 hot chicks that say they want to go home with me every night I go out."

His e-mail boasts were so over the top that some of Peter's colleagues couldn't resist forwarding it to a few of their friends. Predictably, *they* e-mailed a few friends and so on and so on. By the end of the day, thousands of people were reading about Peter's exploits. It became such an Internet legend that the *New York Times* wrote a story about it. This was not the type of publicity the Carlyle Group was looking for when they hired the young man, and they gave Chung the choice of resigning or being fired.

■■

History repeated itself in 2006, when Robert Imlah, an investment banker with JPMorgan in London, found his e-mail boasts whizzing about the Internet and printed up in the papers. In the exchange one friend dubbed Imlah "Immi, the pimp daddy." The message, which revolved around whether he used a condom in an encounter with a woman with "huge nails" was forwarded worldwide along with the warning, "Men are vile."

"Banging Lauren tonight as well," he bragged. "Prob won't bag up there!! It's all about the numbers, not the figures as a great philosopher once said!!!" *(For more embarrassing e-mail gaffes, see the "Embarrassing Moments" chapter.)*

Arrogance: Things *Not* to Say to the Police

Everyone can relate to the sinking feeling of seeing the lights of a police car flashing in the rearview mirror. But it's hard to feel sorry for Roger DePina, who was pulled over by Boston police in early 2007. He refused to stop, then tried to get away by racing onto a freeway ramp, where he was finally pulled over. When the officer asked him for his license and registration, he said, "You have no . . . right to pull us over. Regular police can't stop us on the highway. I know my rights; I'm in Harvard Law School!"

For the record, this is not on the list of "best things to say to avoid getting a ticket." The officer went on to prove that he, in fact, did have the right to pull him over, and DePina had the right to remain silent.

■■

While we're on the subject of things not to say to the police, I'd be remiss if I did not mention Adam Curtis Hunter of Cookeville, Tennessee, whose car skidded off the road in late 2006 and crashed into a house. When police arrived on the scene, they noticed that scattered among the wreckage of the car were large bags of marijuana and various drug paraphernalia.

The observant officers told Hunter that they were going to arrest him for driving under the influence of drugs. Hunter protested. He wasn't stoned. He was just a drug dealer. "I don't smoke it," he said. "I only sell it."

The officers went over this with him one more time to be sure they'd heard him correctly. Yes, he insisted, he was not a user. He only sold the stuff. The officers managed to suppress their snickers as they explained to him that driving under the influence was a misdemeanor and that selling drugs was a felony. Note to criminals: You have the right to remain silent. Use it.

Arrogance: Artistic Pretensions

Artistic pretensions make a lot of people squirm. That's why people seem to take delight in comedic scenes where a beat poet or a mime is knocked down or humiliated. With modern art, there is always the sneaking suspicion that they're just putting us all on and the people who claim to "get it" are actually just pretending to be a little superior.

If you hold this point of view, then you'll be pleased to hear about a 1944 hoax that two young poets pulled on an Australian literary journal called *Angry Penguins*. They managed to make fools of the literary establishment and uptight censors in one fell swoop.[2]

The poets suspected that the editors of the literary journal didn't know a real poem from gibberish. They strung together words and phrases at random and sent them in as "the complete poetic works of Ern Malley, who recently died in obscurity at the tragically early age of 25." The editors published the "works" in a special edition of *Angry Penguins*.

> Editors of the literary journal didn't know a **real poem** from gibberish.

The hoaxers were about to reveal their scam when the police got involved. They confiscated the special edition and arrested the editor for publishing indecent material. The prosecution contended that there was a "suggestion of indecency" in a reference in one of the poems to a man carrying a torch. "I have found that persons who go around parks at night do so for immoral purposes," the detective said. He also pointed out that the word "incestuous" appeared in one of the gibberish verses.

The judge agreed that the poems were indecent and convicted the journal's editor. It was only then that the hoaxers stepped forward to reveal the true nature of Ern Malley's work. It all goes to show that people see exactly what they're looking for.

---

2 The expression "one fell swoop" first appeared in Shakespeare's *Macbeth*. It is a reference to a falcon zooming down to catch its prey. The "fell" in question has nothing to do with falling. It's an antiquated word that meant something evil. It's related to the word "felon."

Aristocratic Arrogance

No one with blue blood was safe during the French Revolution. Being dead was not even enough to spare a royal. The magnificent royal tombs of Saint-Denis were smashed to bits, and the coffins were opened and the bones sold as souvenirs. Anything that harkened to the past was suspect. One member of the Paris Commune called for the killing of all rare animals in the museum of natural history; another wanted to burn the national library.

In this contentious time lived Marie-Jean-Antoine-Nicolas de Caritat, the Marquis de Condorcet. He was a philosopher, mathematician, and political scientist who advocated equal rights, public education, and a liberal economy. But more important than any of that for our story was that he was born and raised an aristocrat.

The politics and alliances of the French Revolutionary period are a bit complex. For the sake of brevity, we'll just say that the marquis had published something that offended a faction that subsequently came to power, branded him a traitor, and put out an order for his arrest. He disguised himself as a peasant and went into hiding. After wandering hungry and exhausted for days, he arrived in the village of Clamart and strode into an inn full of real peasants. Although his clothes were indistinguishable from theirs, the marquis had a lot to learn about how the other half lived. Unfortunately, he would have little time to learn it.

In a loud voice he called for an omelet. When the waiter asked him how many eggs he wanted in the omelet, he said, "a dozen." This was a rather extraordinary demand from a working man, and it gave him away. He was arrested and marched off to prison. The next morning, March 24, 1794, he was found dead.

Premature Celebrations

The moral of this story is hold your celebrating until the finish line is crossed. Fred Holland was participating in the Arthur Smith King Mackerel Tournament in 1986. It was one of the largest fishing contests in the world with one of the biggest prizes—$60,000 for the biggest kingfish caught.

Holland pulled in what he thought was a sure winner, a fifty pounder. As he pulled his boat up to the dock by the weigh station, he saw a crowd of photographers, and his pride got the better of him. As he was lifting the fish over his head for the cameras, it slipped from his hands and fell into the Intercoastal Waterway. Holland was sure the dead fish would float to the surface, but there was no sign of it. The dejected fisherman wandered up and down the dock and even hired two scuba divers to look for his prize. No luck. Somehow his dead fish had swum away. Holland lost the big $60,000 catch, but he did get the booby prize—the $500 Goody's Headache Powder Award, which was given to the angler with the worst luck in the tournament.

■■

Vyacheslav Ivanov, a Soviet sculler in the 1956 Olympics, might have been awarded the headache powder award if it had been invented back then. The eighteen-year-old was not expected to make an impressive showing in the single-sculls event on Lake Wendouree in Melbourne, Australia. But he stunned everyone by making a sensational spurt with two hundred meters to go to beat the two favorites.

Ivanov never imagined he would go home with the gold medal— and he didn't. When the officials handed him his medal at a ceremony on the dock, he just couldn't contain his emotion. He jumped up and down with pure joy. Unfortunately, he didn't have a strong grip on his cherished prize. It slipped through his fingers and fell between two slats of the dock. Ivanov's joy quickly turned to despair. He moaned something that would probably be heartwrenching if you understood Russian. Ivanov was not about to wait for a new medal to be minted; he jumped into the water and tried to fish his prize out of the muck, but it was no use. After repeated dives, the drenched and depressed Olympian stood dejected on the dock sans medal. It was never found.

John Cook, a member of the U.S. eight-man rowing team, couldn't help but express some *Schadenfreude* at seeing his Cold War rival embarrassed. "I know Ivanov wasn't happy," he said. "But it was a big ha-ha for us. . . . We kept joking about how that dumb Russian beats Mackenzie and Kelly and then goes and drops his medal in the lake."

It was not the first time a trophy was lost due to excessive celebration. In 1906 the Montreal Wanderers hockey team misplaced the Stanley Cup. Their lapse was arguably less dignified than that of the Russian. They couldn't keep track of the trophy because they celebrated with a bit too much booze.

Tipsy from their party, they decided to go to Jimmy Rice's photo studio to capture the moment. They held up the cup and posed for the camera and then patted each other on the back some more and headed off to a nearby bar to continue the party. The cup was left behind.

No one noticed its absence until the next hockey season began. The players wanted to gaze at their prize, and it was nowhere to be found. A long conversation followed that included such phrases as "Did you take the cup from the photo studio?" "I thought *you* took the cup. . . ." Finally, someone called Jimmy Rice, but he hadn't seen the cup since he took the photo that night. On a hunch, Rice called the cleaning lady and asked if she had any idea what happened to it. When he described the cup, she knew exactly where it was—in her house.

A few hours after the team left the studio, she came in to clean up and spotted this attractive silver cup sitting in a corner on a chair. People left odds and ends behind all the time. This one seemed too nice to just throw away, so she took it home, filled it with potting soil, and planted geraniums in it. It had been gracing her windowsill ever since. When she learned its true identity, she repotted the flowers and returned the trophy.

A more recent example was that of Diane Williams, a thirty-four-year-old employee of the Royal Institution of Chartered Surveyors in London. She was so excited when she closed an important business deal that she jumped on the banister to slide down the office stairs. She missed, fell twelve feet, broke a tooth, and was knocked unconscious.

As if that weren't bad enough, her bosses thought her behavior was unprofessional, and she was immediately fired. Anyone behaving that way would have to be "extremely drunk or crazy," her boss said.

She appealed to an industrial tribunal but lost. "They don't know how to enjoy themselves," she complained.

■■

A corollary to the "hold your celebrating" rule is to keep your celebrating to a respectable level if what you're celebrating is less than legal. You can hardly blame Davesh Borse, an Indian carpenter, for wanting to fete his newfound fortune. He'd just come into more than a million dollars by pulling off a huge jewelry-store heist.

What better way to enjoy this good fortune than with an evening at the local bar listening to the Bollywood hit song "Hum Ko Deewana Kar Gaye" (He Made Me Crazy) by Himesh Reshammiya. Reshammiya's music does make some people crazy. His detractors say his music is too repetitive and that he sings through his nose. But Borse couldn't get enough. Now that he was rich, he figured he could have whatever music he wanted. He showered the Mumbai pub owner with 1,000-rupee notes to get him to play the song over and over again.

In case that wasn't annoying enough to the other patrons, he came back the next day and did the same thing. By the third night the others in the bar were ready to kill someone if they had to hear that damned crazy-making song again. They started to ask one another where this carpenter got enough money to make their lives an auditory hell. One of the curious patrons was a police informer who alerted authorities. Borse was arrested.

■■

By far the award for the best story of premature celebration goes to World War I flying ace Rene Fonck. When a wealthy businessman, Raymond Orteig, offered a $25,000 reward to the first person to fly from New York to Paris in 1924, Fonck was certain he was the man for the task. So certain was he that he started thinking of himself as the first transatlantic pilot before he even boarded his plane.

He commissioned a special three-engine plane from aviation pioneer Igor Sikorsky, at a cost of $105,000. It was specially modified to carry extra fuel. It had a built-in bed for its crew of four and two massive state-of-the-art radios. But this was not enough for an aircraft that was to assume such a monumental role in history. Fonck hired an interior decorator to line the inside of the cabin with Spanish leather and mahogany panels to give it the look of an opulent drawing room.

The modifications put the craft ten thousand pounds beyond its engineered maximum of twenty-eight thousand pounds, and Sikorsky begged Fonck to have it stress tested, but Fonck was too busy. There was a lot to do before his historic flight. There were gifts to accept and provisions to pack. Each member of the crew brought sentimental tokens from friends. They loaded on their celebratory feast—a fancy full-course meal packed in vacuum containers, which they planned to eat in Paris. (For some reason they seem to have felt there would be a shortage of gourmet food in the French capital.) They even had a bouquet of orchids for the French president's wife.

Well prepared for the celebrations, Fonck finally attempted to take off from New York's Roosevelt Field. Unfortunately, the weight of the accoutrements was far more than the plane could carry. Its gear literally bent under the strain. As Fonck tried to get the craft up to eighty miles an hour to get off the ground, pieces of the plane tumbled off. The rear landing wheel buckled and fell off. The heavy craft finally tore through the fence at the end of the runway and tumbled into a gully, where it burst into flames.

Referring to this episode, Neil Steinberg, the author of the book *Complete and Utter Failure*, coined the expression "the Fonck Factor" to describe anyone who fails by focusing on the least important elements of a situation.

The crash was documented in newsreels, one of which was seen by a young airmail pilot, Charles Lindbergh. This is what inspired him to take his own shot at the Orteig prize. As Fonck went back to the drawing board to create another airplane worthy of the attempt, Lindbergh readied a minimalist single-engine plane and beat the heir apparent across the Atlantic and into the record books.

Do as I Say, Not as I Do

When people hold themselves up as examples or pillars of society, they're practically begging to be knocked down. There are few kinds of *Schadenfreude* more satisfying than the kind that levels someone who was lecturing us, especially if it exposes some serious hypocrisy in the process.

Moral Leadership *in the* Ministry

Sex is one of those things we love to do, but we don't want anyone to know it. Whether between a legally married man and woman or any scandalous combination of consenting adults, our sexuality is something we have to keep hidden. Who is most likely to tell us that? Religious leaders. Thus a moralizing minister's downfall is guaranteed to give us more than a little pang of *Schadenfreude*.

Ministers are people, too. They have the same secret, embarrassing desires as the rest of us. In fact, according to Stephen Arterburn, a Christian author who has written on the subject of the struggle for sexual purity among Christian men, studies show that as many as 28 to 30 percent of pastors look at pornography on a regular basis. Arterburn, the coauthor of *Every Man's Battle*, wrote about one unnamed minister who turned on his PowerPoint screen to highlight notes during a Sunday sermon. He apparently didn't quite have the hang of the laptop technology. Instead of the scripture he expected, an explicit image from his pornography collection was projected. And it was one of the most vivid, explicit, and disgusting pictures you're likely to see. One can only imagine what hymn the choir sang after that sermon.

And when Liam Cosgrave, a sixty-eight-year-old Catholic priest, suffered a fatal heart attack while watching porno films in the Incognito Club, a gay sauna club in downtown Dublin, Ireland, he was fortunate in that there happened to be two other priests at the club at the time who were capable of administering the last rites.

■■

Most Christian faiths at least allow sex within marriage for their ministers. The Roman Catholic Church is the most glaring exception. Prior to 1139, Roman Catholic priests had wives and children. All that changed when a decision of the Second Lantern Council forbid priests from marrying and annulled all existing marriages. Some of the reasons for the new rule were theological. The decision also came, in part, to keep priest's children from inheriting valuable church property. At the time, common law prevented illegitimate children from inheriting property. If priests couldn't marry, there would be no question of church lands going to sons and not congregations.

> The fourth time she went into the confession booth armed with a knife.

Not all priests interpreted this ruling to mean that they couldn't have sex. For many years priests lived with female partners and children in ways that were different from marriage in name only. Especially in country parishes, these priests and their "not wives" were looked upon as pillars of the community.

It took a while for the celibacy rule to really take hold, and some medieval monks behaved in rather unsaintly ways behind closed doors. The situation was so bad that a Franciscan monk Salimbene di Adamo, in 1221, sent a letter warning his fifteen-year-old niece of the dangers of the confessional booth. He told the story of one woman who went to confess that she'd been raped by a stranger while working in the fields. (There is no evidence that the rapist himself felt compelled to confess.) The woman must have told the story rather vividly because the priest was so turned on by the tale that he took her behind the altar and did the same thing to the poor woman.

The poor woman now had two shameful secrets to confess, and she had not yet received absolution, so she went to another confession booth, and the same thing happened again. A third priest did the same. The fourth time she went into the confession booth armed with a knife. She received absolution.

∎∎

Another penitent woman was a bit more proactive in fending off priestly advances, according to di Adamo. When her confessor made a pass at her, she pretended to be interested but said she didn't want to make love in the church. She invited him to her house the next day.

The next day she sent him a "love token" of a pie and some wine. As it happened, Pope Alexander IV was visiting the town, and the philandering friar thought he could impress him by passing the gift along. The pope was impressed but not in the way the priest had hoped. You see, the pie hadn't been a "love token" at all but a token of revenge. It contained not only delicious fruits and berries but the contents of her chamber pot. When the pope learned the history of the disgusting dessert, the priest got his just deserts and was defrocked.

∎∎

Dr. Peter Kinnell, author of *The Complete Illustrated Encyclopedia of Erotic Failure*, recounts the tale of a fifteenth-century monk who was caught taking his vows a bit less than seriously. The monk was rather smitten with one of his sisters in Christ. One night he snuck into the nun's bedroom on a mission to deflower her.

As our hero was a man of God, he didn't want to do anything that would injure the object of his affection, so he came up with a device that he thought would make the experience less painful. It involved a wooden board with a hole in the middle through which the monk could perform the act. Why this was supposed to help is a bit hazy, but what we do know is what happened next.

As the monk's, let's say, excitement grew he found himself stuck in the board. Try as she might, the sister couldn't free her lover. So she ran for a bucket of water. The clattering woke the other nuns, and the monk jumped out the window, naked and attached to a board, and hobbled back to the monastery. A doctor had to be called to attend to what a historian of the time called his "brother Priapus." There was no medicine available for his pride.

The Irish folk-rock band the Saw Doctors had a hit with a ballad that reveled in the downfall of a randy bishop. The chorus went like this:

> *Oh mighty, mighty Lord Almighty!*
> *Off with the collar and off with the nightie!*
> *Jesus, Mary, and Holy St. Joseph*
> *The beads are rattling now. . . .*

The clergyman who inspired this ditty was Bishop Eamonn Casey of Galway. The man who was chosen to act as master of ceremonies when Pope John Paul II visited Ireland in 1979 was forced to flee to South America in a 1992 sex scandal. Dubliners enjoyed his humiliation so much that they had T-shirts printed that said, "Wear a condom, just in Casey."

Casey was a complicated and very human bishop. A tireless campaigner for the homeless who founded a shelter organization in England, he was also known for his love of wine and fast cars. By the time the public learned he had broken his vow of celibacy, he'd already been convicted of drunk driving and issued a mea culpa. Somehow the episode seemed only to increase his popularity.

He was once quoted as saying that "any clergyman with more than four figures in the bank has lost the faith." Yet he was often seen speeding to his charity work in a Mercedes or BMW. Like all good Catholics, he opposed contraception. He held fast to that tenet of the faith even as he broke his vow of celibacy. The results were predictable.

It began when Casey met an American divorcée named Annie Murphy. It was love at first sight; three weeks after her arrival in Ireland, she and the bishop were having a torrid affair that Murphy described as "the most magical thing I had encountered in my life. I was on gossamer wings." Casey "knew" his lover in an eighteenth-century hunting lodge that was a summer residence for bishops, and she brought forth a son, Peter, in 1974. The pregnancy caused a crisis that ended the relationship. The bishop had sent Murphy to a convent, where the nuns pressured her to give the baby up for adoption, but she refused. She returned to America to live the life of a single mother.

For the next seventeen years, Casey managed to keep the whole business a secret while he paid between $170 and $260 a month in child support. In 1990, through her lawyer, Murphy negotiated a "final settlement" of $125,000. Casey was able to pay it right away by borrowing from diocesan funds.

This wasn't enough for Peter, who more than anything wanted his father to acknowledge him. So Murphy sold her story to the *Irish Times* and shortly thereafter rushed out a book, *Forbidden Fruit: The True Story of My Love for the Bishop of Galway*. The book was so vivid and tawdry that it didn't gain its author much sympathy in Ireland. It did, however, bring down one of the country's most prominent bishops.

Moral Leadership *in the* Television Era

One of the first evangelists to preach on TV was Billy James Hargis, and he can also claim the dubious honor of creating the first "televangelist scandal." Hargis was called to the ministry in the late 1940s, and even though he dropped out of Ozark Bible College, he became the pastor of the First Christian Church in Sapulpa, Oklahoma. His style was described by *The Economist* as "shouting, flailing and sweating with an energy alarming in a man of his girth."

At the height of the Red Scare, he struck a chord, with passionate sermons that linked the devil and Communism. His "Crusade for Christian Morality" hosted "anti-Communist" telethons and put out a weekly report on Red plots and other vast left-wing conspiracies. His books included *Communism, The Total Lie, The Real Extremists— The Far Left*, and *Is the School House the Proper Place to Teach Raw Sex?* In his heyday, he made daily broadcasts on 500 radio stations and 250 TV channels.

He set up a number of schools to teach "anti-communism, anti-socialism, anti-welfare state, anti-Russia, anti-China, a literal interpretation of the Bible and states' rights." The schools included the National Anti-Communist Youth University, the Christian Crusade Anti-Communist Youth University, and the American Christian College.

In the 1960s he spoke out against the immoral music of the Beatles and crusaded against illicit homosexual relations. But things got weird in 1974. After he performed a wedding for two American Christian College students, the bride tearfully confessed that she had slept with the reverend. She was taken aback when the groom confessed that he had, too. Questioned by *Time* magazine, Hargis admitted to having sexual relations with the young coed and with four male students. The trysts happened in the minister's office, at his farm in the Ozarks, and during tours with the college choir "The All-American Kids." One of the students said that Hargis convinced him to engage in homosexual acts by citing the Old Testament friendship between David and Jonathan, and afterwards he promised to "blacklist the youths for life" if they told anyone.

Hargis knew exactly who was to blame for his public embarrassment. Himself? You know better than that. It was the "godless, left-wing pagan press" that did him in. "I had told myself there were no new levels to which the left-wing, Eastern press could stoop," he told an Oklahoma reporter. "But I was wrong, because this time a national magazine outdid itself in its ability to put such a pile of pure trash on the page."

■■

The left-wing media conspiracy was at it again in 1995. This time, however, it was purely an accident. A reporter from the *Charlotte Observer* went to a Hooters restaurant to get opinions on an Equal Employment Opportunity Commission order that the chain had to hire men and not just busty women to wait tables. One of the regulars who spoke out against the decision was James Posey.

"The whole concept of Hooters would be undermined if they had to hire male waiters," he said. "The girls are basically what Hooters is about." Not much of a story there, until you add the fact that the man speaking out in favor of an all-girl, scantily clad waitstaff was the *Reverend* James Posey, the head of the eleven-hundred-member Woodlawn Baptist Church. The church defines its mission as "to exalt Christ through worship, evangelism and training believers for dedicated service."

Shortly after the Hooters story ran on the front page, Posey resigned, saying he was frustrated over the lack of growth at Woodlawn although "the timing [of the article] did fall into play," he admitted.

∎ ∎

A similar story is that of Robert Fraser, a forty-six-year-old teacher at Oakmead College of Technology in Bournemouth, England. He taught religion to give students "a moral lead."

His twenty-year teaching career came to a rather abrupt end when it was learned that he had a night job as a male stripper. He performed primarily at bachelorette parties, coming in costume as a lumberjack, a doctor, or James Bond before getting his kit off. Fraser was unapologetic about his career choice. "Nowhere in the Bible does it say striptease is a sin," he said. It's hard to argue with that—although he did admit, "Having said that, my wife was pretty upset when she found out."

> "Nowhere in the Bible does it say **striptease** is a sin."

∎ ∎

In the late 1990s John Paulk was the poster boy for the "ex-gay" movement. He and his wife, Anne, an "ex-lesbian," were on the television talk-show and lecture circuit, explaining how they were "cured" of homosexuality by God's grace.

Before his conversion, John was a very "out" homosexual, marching in gay-pride parades and performing as a drag queen named Cindi. He claims he had around three hundred male sex partners. Then he discovered Exodus, a group that promotes healing gays through prayer. That's where he met Anne. The couple were married in 1992, and they had two sons. "There are people who are unhappy being gay," John said. "There are just enough of these people that our message needs to be heard."

Articulate true believers, they were the perfect success story for Exodus. John was promoted to chairman of the organization, and he and Anne were interviewed by just about every newspaper and magazine, even appearing on the cover of *Newsweek*. They wrote a book, *Love Won Out*, published by the conservative Christian organization Focus on the Family.

Perhaps you have already predicted the punch line. In October of 2000 John lost his job as chairman after he was spotted in a Washington, D.C., gay bar. He said he'd only stopped there to use the bathroom, but observers say he stayed for forty minutes and bought a man drinks. Thus ended his tenure as spokesman for Exodus.

■■

No examination of this topic would be complete without the Super Bowl of televangelist scandals: the Jim Bakker trial of the late 1980s. There is nothing people enjoy more than a real-life soap opera, and this one had everything. The main characters had a cartoonish quality to begin with: Bakker's wife Tammy Faye wore unintentionally comical makeup, and both spoke with soft voices and permanent smiles. There were allegations of sexual impropriety, enough showy wealth to make Robin Leach (the host of *Lifestyles of the Rich and Famous*) blush, and behind-the-scenes machinations by rival television ministers. Editorial cartoonists drew images of a family huddled in front of the TV while an announcer says, "Before we do the religious news, we urge all children to leave the room." Ted Haggard's scandalette doesn't hold a candle to the Bakkers. (See the chapter "Excuses, Excuses.")

The mid-'80s was a great time to be a television minister. The money flowed, and viewers in need of miracles were unquestioning in their belief. In 1987 Oral Roberts went on television and announced that God had told him if he didn't raise $8 million the Lord would "call him home." Oral got the money, and his life was spared.

In early 1987 things looked pretty good for Jim Bakker. He had published a book in 1980 entitled *Survival: Unite to Live*, which discussed the importance of fidelity in marriage and the evils of greed. The book, dedicated to his wife Tammy, featured a glowing introduction by none other than Oral Roberts. Jim Bakker wrote that too many people had made gold their god. "Our dividend is not dollars, it's souls. We are placing souls into the bank of Heaven, and that's where our dollars and cents are. That's where our profit lies—in souls. Souls, souls, souls."

But there were dollars, dollars, dollars pouring into the PTL (Praise the Lord) ministry that Bakker founded. Jim and Tammy Faye made $1.9 million in salary and bonuses in 1986 from their nonprofit empire, earned a dollar at a time from faithful viewers whose contributions totaled about $1 million every two days. They owned six luxury mansions, forty-seven bank accounts, two Rolls-Royces, four Mercedes-Benzes and, most famously, gold-plated bathroom fixtures and an air-conditioned doghouse. They would sometimes spend $100,000 for a private jet to fly clothing to California. When they stayed in hotels, they ordered $100 worth of cinnamon buns—which they didn't eat—to make it smell nice. Life was good.

It all came crashing down when it was revealed that secretary Jessica Hahn had a tryst with the minister and that he'd paid $265,000 to buy her silence. She said the preacher made her feel "like a piece of hamburger somebody threw out in the street." Hahn presented herself as a devoted charismatic Christian who began her career cleaning church toilets. She said, "I just want this whole thing to blow over and for my family to be left alone."

How did the story come out? Rival evangelist Jimmy Swaggart, whose ministry focused on a battle of good and evil between God and the devil, had blown the whistle to church leaders. Two years earlier Swaggart had gotten another minister, Marvin Gorman, defrocked by accusing him of adultery. Bakker and his supporters were convinced Swaggart was trying to get a monopoly on church ministries by outing his competitors. Whether or not this is true, in his zeal to rout out the devil in others, Swaggart forgot that whole expression about people in glass houses.

Bakker admitted he'd had sex with that woman but pointed a finger at colleagues who he said set him up. He also blamed the victim, Jessica Hahn, who he claimed knew "all the tricks of the trade." Jessica Hahn curiously chose to plead her case to the public by appearing topless in *Playboy*. In the article accompanying her ten-page photo spread, Hahn declared, "I am not a bimbo." She was reportedly paid $1 million. After that she took up temporary residence in the *Playboy* mansion, where she was recovering from a series of cosmetic-surgery procedures.

> When they stayed in hotels, they ordered $100 worth of **cinnamon buns** to make it smell nice.

There were other rumors as well. Bakker was said to have had numerous affairs with both men and women, to have had sex with prostitutes and even to have condoned wife-swapping parties. The preacher strenuously denied these charges. But it was too much for the ministry to bear, and Bakker was ousted. The Reverend Jerry Falwell was called in to try to save the PTL empire, including South Carolina's Heritage USA theme park. On the way out, the Bakkers made a severance request including $300,000 a year for life for Jim and $100,000 a year for life for Tammy.

Jim Bakker appeared on *Nightline* to blast Falwell and Jimmy Swaggart, who he claimed had plotted to take the ministry from him. "It would have been kinder for these men to assassinate us than to do what they've done," he said. The show drew the largest audience in *Nightline*'s then seven-year history.

Meanwhile, Marvin Gorman (Remember him? He's the other one Jimmy Swaggart got fired.) had hired a private detective to follow Swaggart and photograph him as he battled his demons in a motel with a prostitute. The detective reportedly flattened the tires of Swaggart's Lincoln so he could confront him with the information. With tears streaming down his face, Jimmy Swaggart went before his congregation and the TV cameras and confessed that he had sinned. He asked for forgiveness and temporarily stepped down from his ministry.

The stress of being at the center of the drama got to be a bit much for Jim Bakker. Before the fourth day of his trial, he was found lying in the corner of his lawyer's office with his head under a couch, hiding and reportedly hallucinating. He was briefly committed, but was found to be capable of standing trial, and everything resumed.

People who don't know much about the case tend to remember Jessica Hahn and think that Bakker's downfall was mostly about sex. (It always is, isn't it?) But Bakker was sentenced to forty-five years in federal prison for financial crimes. He was found guilty of raising $158 million by promising lifetime, three-day-a-year lodging packages for $1,000 to his viewers, among them elderly devotees on fixed incomes, for a nonexistent hotel. Then he diverted $3.7 million in salary and bonuses to support his lavish lifestyle.

Following the verdict, he and Tammy Faye divorced. Some of the charges were later reversed, and he was released after only five years behind bars, and—most amazingly—after his release he returned to preaching with his new wife, Lori Graham Bakker. In the early 2000s the Bakkers finally ended up where they seemed destined to be all along—as characters on reality TV. Jim and Tammy Faye's tattooed, punk son became a preacher in his own right, but his church has a real alternative edge. Described as "a church for people who have given up on church," it hands out stickers that say, "As Christians we're sorry for being self-righteous judgmental bastards." His ministry was the focus of the Sundance Channel documentary, *One Punk Under God*.

Moral Leadership *in the* Political Arena

Politicians feel they're on fairly safe ground when they promise to protect the nation's children. Who is against kids? Yet it often seems the candidates who crow the loudest about "family values" have the least to crow about at home.

A 1996 press conference with Louisiana governor Mike Foster left some constituents wondering if all that talk about the importance of family was mere pandering. Foster stands on the traditional "family values" side of all the issues. He opposes sexual education in schools because he believes it should be taught at home, is pro-life, and "absolutely" favors prayer in schools.

But when asked the name of his new grandchild, he stuttered, "You know, I've been real busy." He rolled his eyes heavenward trying in vain to remember. "You know, it's not as exciting as the first one," he said. The governor's press office had to call reporters later to tell them: it's Michelle Elizabeth. She was named after the governor's mother.

■■

Righteous politicians who promise to legislate morality have been around as long as there has been electoral politics. And scandals involving such leaders have been around just as long. Representative William Campbell Breckinridge of Kentucky, elected as a Democrat in 1885, was a moral crusader who often lectured on the evils of sex. "Chastity is the fountain, the cornerstone of human society," he said. He once urged an audience of teenage girls to avoid "useless handshaking, promiscuous kissing, needless touching and all exposures."

But in the case of one teenage girl, Breckinridge determined touching was needed. He first met seventeen-year-old Madeline Pollard in 1884. She was a shy student who had asked the congressman for advice on how to handle her tuition debt; the married politician suggested they meet in private to discuss it. Shortly thereafter she moved to the Sayre Institute in Lexington so she could be closer to Breckinridge, and he started paying her tuition. That was one problem solved. But then there were other problems. Pollard became pregnant . . . three times. She gave two of the children up for adoption "because he asked me," Pollard said. "He said that if I kept them it would be traced to him, and they would be known as his children." One of the infants died shortly after it was born.

The affair came to light in 1894 when Pollard sued Breckinridge for breach of promise. It was a sensation, and the trial was savored by gossip lovers across the nation. The congressman tried to convince the court that he had no idea Pollard had three children by him. Yes, they had sex, and yes, he paid her bills and recommended her for a government job, but he knew nothing about the children.

This tactic didn't seem to play. So his attorneys tried to paint Pollard as a woman of loose morals who had seduced him in all his innocence. The jury wasn't buying that either. They came back in less than two hours with an award in Pollard's favor of $15,000. The scandal had damaged Breckinridge, but he was not yet ready to throw in the towel. He tried confessing and begging for forgiveness. "I have sinned, and I repent in sackcloth and ashes," he said. "I was entangled by weakness, by passion, by sin, in coils which it was almost impossible to break." His eloquent mea culpa was too late for many voters. He lost the election but only by 255 votes.

■■

That a politician is gay is not in and of itself a moral failing. But why do so many secretly gay politicians insist on taking strong stands against gay rights? It's enough to make you hum a bar of Alanis Morissette's "Ironic" (and subsequently to ponder what is supposed to be ironic about rain on your wedding day . . .).

Spokane mayor Jim West was a tough-talking conservative strong on family values. He opposed abortion, once wrote a bill outlawing sex between people under the age of 18, and, most significantly, opposed domestic-partner benefits for same-sex couples and cosponsored a bill to bar gay men and lesbians from working at schools and daycare centers. The appropriate place for a gay man to work, it seems, was as West's intern.

West's long political career ended when he was accused of offering a City Hall internship to an Internet acquaintance he thought was an eighteen-year-old man he met on Gay.com. It all came to light when he chatted flirtatiously with "motorbrock34" and finally agreed to meet him. But motorbrock34 was not a boy; he was an investigator hired by the *Spokesman-Review* newspaper. The paper printed transcripts of the chats, in which it claimed West offered to make "motorbrock" his intern.

"I don't know why I go there [to Gay.com]," he told a reporter. "I wouldn't characterize me as gay." But the scandal and allegations of pedophilia with Boy Scouts, which he continued to deny, forced the "family values" candidate out of office.

∎∎

Under Matthew J. Glavin's tenure as president of the gadfly organization the Southeastern Legal Foundation beginning in 1994, the group grew from 5,000 politically conservative donors to about 130,000. The organization fought to prevent the granting of medical and other benefits to same-sex partners of employees and supported the decision by the Boy Scouts of America to bar gays from leadership positions.

In 1999, the group led the charge to disbar Bill Clinton for misconduct when the president gave misleading answers under oath regarding his relationship with intern Monica Lewinsky in the Paula Jones sexual harassment case.[3] "The president must serve as a moral figure whose conduct sets an example for others," said a foundation

---

3 My reasons for not rehashing the Clinton/Lewinsky matter itself in this section are not partisan. Clinton was not a candidate who ran on a platform of "family values." Had he tried to push legislation making adultery punishable by death before being caught with his pants down, he would be included. But he didn't. Bad behavior in itself falls into the category of gossip rather than *Schadenfreude*, unless you're predisposed to dislike the perpetrator.

statement. Glavin personally added, "We intend to make sure that Bill Clinton is held professionally accountable for his misdeeds, which have brought immeasurable disgrace to the presidency, to our system of constitutional government and to public respect for our system of justice."

A year later Glavin was being quoted in the press again. "Guilty," he said. He'd been caught literally with his pants down at the Chattahoochee River National Recreation Area. An undercover officer said Glavin masturbated in his presence and fondled the officer's groin. Glavin was charged with public indecency and forced to resign as president "to protect my family and the foundation." Given his zeal for accountability, we can only assume he was pleased at the result.

■■

Another Clinton foe with a special case of do-as-I-say-not-as-I-do-itis was Rep. Bob Barr of Georgia. He was one of many politicians targeted by *Hustler* publisher Larry Flynt. Flynt made it his mission to expose hypocrisy among the people calling for the president's impeachment. When a showboating pornographer squares off against a conservative politician, you know you're going to have a good show.

> When a showboating **pornographer** squares off against a conservative **politician,** you know you're going to have a good show.

The *Washington Post* called Republican Bob Barr "the meanest anti-Clinton pit bull in the House." The *Atlanta Constitution* called him "an attack dog for impeachment." Barr began his career as a partner in a small Cobb County law practice. He had a skill for bringing media attention to his office. His highest-profile case was the prosecution of former U.S. Rep. Pat Swindall, a fellow Republican, for lying to a federal grand jury in connection with a drug case.

The moral of that case, said Barr, was that ". . . whoever you are, you have to abide by the same standard everyone else does." It is a sentiment he would repeat many times as the loudest voice calling for President Clinton's impeachment, for which Barr had been campaigning even before the nation heard the name Monica Lewinsky. Besides introducing a resolution for impeachment, he wrote a law-review article on the history of impeachment and why Clinton qualified and wrote a glowing foreword to R. Emmett Tyrell's *The Impeachment of William Jefferson Clinton*.

Barr represented a district that had previously been helmed by the head of the John Birch Society. Its constituents voted for Pat Buchanan in 1996. Barr was the perfect candidate for such a district, espousing such causes as making abortion illegal with no exceptions. He was once quoted as saying that if his wife or stepdaughter wanted an abortion he would "do absolutely everything in my power to stop it."

Barr drafted the Defense of Marriage Act, which banned gay marriage. Barr believes marriage is so important that he married three times himself. He illustrated the threat to marriage by gays with (literally) fiery rhetoric: "The flames of hedonism, the flames of narcissism, the flames of self-centered morality are licking at the very foundation of society." He even gave a speech to the Council of Conservative Citizens, a group that believes interracial marriage results in white genocide, although he denied that he knew about its white-supremacist agenda when he agreed to address them.

After all of his agitating to impeach Clinton, Barr was stunned to find that in spite of all the evidence that the Commander in Chief had broken his marriage vows with an enthusiastic intern, polls showed most Americans liked the guy even more than they had before. "If the poll results are true and Americans really don't want their leaders to be held personally accountable, then we are in pretty sad shape as a country," he said.

This is when Larry Flynt entered the picture. Flynt placed an ad in the *Washington Post* offering up to $1 million to anyone who could show proof of an affair with a high-ranking Republican. His first victim was Rep. Bob Livingston, who was slated to be Speaker of the House. He learned that Flynt was going to out him for his adulterous affairs, so he made a preemptive strike, announcing that he was sorry and was seeking spiritual counseling.

"His activity with women is pretty kinky," Flynt was quoted as saying. "I'm a little upset that he himself scooped me on this thing because we had it in the bag. But maybe it's better it happened this way because I was just trying to expose the hypocrisy."

After that Flynt set his sights on Barr. Although Flynt would like to have proven that Barr's sexual relationship with Jerry Dubbin, the wife he married in 1986, began before he divorced wife number two the same year, he never found a smoking gun. Ex-wife Gail never found it either.

Adultery, although rarely prosecuted, is a misdemeanor in Georgia. The transcript from the divorce proceedings showed that Barr refused to answer such questions as, "Have you been faithful to her sexually during the marriage?" and "Have you ever lived with Jerry Dubbin?" Thus, assuming he would have answered affirmatively, he managed to avoid the Clinton-esque charge of perjury.

The rancorous divorce dug up more juicy dirt. Gail signed an affidavit for Flynt stating that Barr paid for her to have an abortion in 1983, drove her to the clinic, picked her up, and never opposed her decision. Barr never specifically denied his former wife's claims. Instead, he issued this nondenial denial: "I have never suggested, urged, forced or encouraged anyone to have an abortion."

It was not Barr's personality to get out in front of the story. He is a fighter. He filed suit against Flynt, Clinton, and Democratic political consultant James Carville for "participating in a common scheme and unlawful on-going conspiracy to attempt to intimidate, impede and/or retaliate against" him.

And here is why, out of all of Flynt's outed Clinton foes, I chose to focus on Barr. Flynt sent out a press release to highlight the dichotomy when, three months after he filed his $30 million suit claiming a "loss of reputation and emotional distress," Barr was on the floor championing a bill that would cap damage awards for "pain and suffering" at $250,000. Oops.

What is more, the lawsuit allowed the media to quote Flynt's original allegations; for example, a section of the *Flynt Report* that called Barr "a twice-divorced family values cheerleader . . . who condoned an abortion, committed adultery and failed to tell the truth under oath." After the second round of bad press for the congressman, the suit was dismissed. A three-judge panel found that Flynt didn't publish offensive information he knew to be false and also ruled Barr failed to file his suit within the statue of limitations.

■■

Marvin Couch, a Republican representative from the state of Florida, was a self-appointed member of "the God Squad," a group of elected officials who pray regularly and vote for things like school prayer and against abortion, gay rights, and teaching evolution in science class. He campaigned in 1992 as a champion of conservative values with statements such as, "A lot of people are frustrated with the system and afraid of the moral decay of the country. A lot of the people have families, and they want people who believe in moral values." These stances earned him a "100 percent rating" by the Florida Christian Coalition. He was one of fifteen lawmakers who signed a letter threatening to boycott the Walt Disney Company for making health insurance available to partners of gay employees, which, they said, mocked "the sanctity of marriage."

One thing he would not do to defend marriage, however, was to refrain from cavorting with prostitutes behind his wife's back. On February 22, 1992, the appropriately named Couch became yet another moral crusader caught with his pants down. Police interrupted him in the act in the back of his pickup truck. Not only was he exposed as a hypocrite, he was shown to be a miser as well. The prostitute claimed that Couch offered her $30 for oral sex, then talked her down to $22.

Mrs. Couch, the mother of the legislator's six children, vowed to stand by him, but the constituents weren't as forgiving. This member of the God Squad was forced to resign.

Self-Help Gurus *and* Authors

Ellen Fein, along with her coauthor Sherrie Schneider, wrote *The Rules: Time-Tested Secrets for Capturing the Heart of Mr. Right*. Women, the intended audience for the book, were split fairly evenly into two camps. One group thought its advice was genius; they snapped up two million copies. The other group thought the "how to trap a man" ode to game playing set the feminist cause back decades.

Fein and Schneider became overnight stars by advocating playing hard to get: Never initiate contact with a man, and always end dates and phone calls first. Don't call him, and rarely return his calls, and always make him pay on the date. Never go out of the house without makeup. Once you've trapped the one you want, you should treat your husband as a client or customer you want to keep happy.

Regina Barreca, author of *Perfect Husbands (& Other Fairy Tales)*, criticized *The Rules*, saying, "They came of age in the heart of the women's movement. These babes have no excuse." Fein responded by saying that Barreca's divorce undermined her credibility. On an appearance on the Oprah Winfrey show, Fein promised that by following *The Rules*, women could avoid a messy divorce. "Instead, you will have one of those made-in-heaven marriages. A Rules marriage is forever."

Lonely hearts ate this stuff up. Rules support groups sprang up across the globe. The sequel, *More Rules to Live and Love By*, sold 350,000 copies. In 2001 the third book in the series, *The Rules for Marriage: Time-Tested Secrets for Making Your Marriage Work*, was about to hit the stands. It featured a cover blurb that read, "Ellen and Sherrie, two long-time married women themselves, know that just because you've married the man of your dreams doesn't mean your work has ended: good marriages don't happen by accident."

And then Fein filed for divorce. As if that weren't enough cause for *Schadenfreude*, the woman who told millions how to have healthy relationships rather bizarrely blamed her divorce on her dentist. Dr. Larry Rosenthal is known as the "dentist to the stars." He's cleaned the teeth of Donald Trump, Bruce Springsteen, Catherine Zeta-Jones and Joan Rivers. (Celebrity plaque!)

In the late '80s, Fein filed a complaint for what she claimed was botched dental work that gave her "gigantic teeth."

"My marriage disintegrated—of course there were other issues—but all the complications that came from the procedure were the things that led to divorce," she was quoted as saying. The complaint she filed with the New York State Office of Professional Discipline was resolved in 1998, according to the good doctor. But in 2007 Rosenthal filed a $5 million lawsuit against the author for various forms of slander, including the creation of a Web site, "lyingdentist.com," that included such statements as "Larry W. Rosenthal is a Big Fat Liar." The suit alleges that Fein barged into his office in February 2005 and "began to scream at him in front of an office filled with patients, accusing him of, among other things, ruining her life and her marriage."

■■

You can hardly go wrong selling a book that promises to make people thinner, sexier, or richer. In the early 1980s Albert Lowry went from a career as a butcher in Thunder Bay, Ontario, to a multi-million-dollar career on the book-and-lecture circuit selling the dream of easy wealth.

A gregarious self-promoter, he moved to California and hit on the idea of selling real estate advice in 1969. He started advertising that he had a PhD in business administration, although the *Seattle Post-Intelligencer* reported, "it could not be determined when or where he might have received it."

In his get-rich-quick best seller *How You Can Become Financially Independent by Investing in Real Estate*, he advocated buying property from desperate sellers with no money down and then fixing them up to sell again. His book hit the best seller list in 1980, and by the spring of 1981, Lowry was on the cover of *Money* magazine. But then inflation died down and real estate prices fell. The seminar business started to trail off. Then Lowry lost millions in a real estate development in Lake Tahoe. He filed bankruptcy in 1987, listing as assets a checking account with $11.68 and three small parcels of land.

> You can hardly go wrong selling a book that promises to make people **thinner, sexier,** or **richer.**

Ironic Author Arrests

I have to admit that when writing a book about pleasure in others' misfortunes, I have a vague fear that I'll be involved in a terrible accident involving a kitchen appliance and the newspaper report will jump on the fabulous irony of finding *Schadenfreude* in the misfortune of the *Schadenfreude* author. So it is with some caution that I pass along the following:

Maybe he was short on material for his next sequel. In 2002 James Welles, the author of *The Story of Stupidity* and *Understanding Stupidity*, was arrested for soliciting sex from a person he thought was a fifteen-year-old girl. (The "girl" was actually a forty-year-old police detective.) He corresponded with the "girl" for three weeks over the

Internet, then arranged to meet her at a Denny's restaurant, saying, "You just have to remember—bottom line, I'll be committing a crime." He was arrested when he showed up for his date.

In an even more relevant case, the author Stephen Winkworth, who reveled in mishaps in the world of sports in his book *Famous Sporting Fiascos*, once stopped by unannounced at the home of cricket announcer John Arlott, hoping to get a few gems for his next edition. Mr. Arlott was not in the mood to talk because he was working on the obituary of a friend, but Winkworth persisted anyway. He gave an example of the type of story he was looking for: "Like if a dog ran onto the pitch and bit the wicket-keeper," he said.

Arlott, not a fan of *Schadenfreude*, glared at the author and said, "Is that funny?" Winkworth finally got the hint that great anecdotes would not be forthcoming, and he excused himself. As he was walking away, a mutt ran over and bit the author on the leg. Let's just say, I've been warned.

Medical Men *and* Health Advocates

If, like many Americans, you love your Big Macs and hate those holier-than-thou people who try to sell you a Bowflex on late-night TV while you're watching reruns and eating a pint of Cherry Garcia, you will find a special joy in this section.

Of course, no one lives forever, and the fact that a health guru is mortal doesn't, in itself, negate the person's work. Sometimes, however, a certain irony manages to creep in to produce *Schadenfreude*. This is especially true if the health theory is a little suspect to begin with.

In 1889 Dr. Horace Emmett triumphantly announced in a lecture to the Biology Society of Magdalene College, Cambridge, that he had discovered the secret of eternal youth. He did it by grinding up the testicles of red squirrels and then injecting himself with them. He said that the magic elixir made him thirty years younger and that he was able to "visit" his wife every day. The discovery was all the rage—but for a very short time. Two months later Dr. Emmett's wife left him for a younger man. Shortly thereafter he died of a cerebral hemorrhage.

■ ■

Another health guru to suffer an ironic death was James Fixx, who popularized jogging in the late 1970s with his best-selling *The Complete Book of Running*. He died of a heart attack while jogging in 1984. At the time of his death, *The Complete Book of Running* had sold more than a million copies and had been translated into fifteen languages. The book received the Road Runners Club of America Award for the best writing on the subject of running. He followed up with *Jim Fixx's Second Book of Running* in 1980.

The former magazine editor started his fitness regime and quit smoking after he pulled a muscle playing tennis. When he began running, he shuffled along in combat boots that he'd worn during combat in Korea. Eventually his technique improved, and he decided to spread the word.

The irony of the most high-profile jogging advocate's falling from a heart attack while jogging was not lost on anyone. In the end, however, his death was not so much a refutation of his jogging passion but a cautionary tale about regular doctor's visits. In spite of his wife's urging, Fixx didn't get medical checkups. If he had, he might have learned before it was too late that he had serious heart disease that blocked two major arteries.

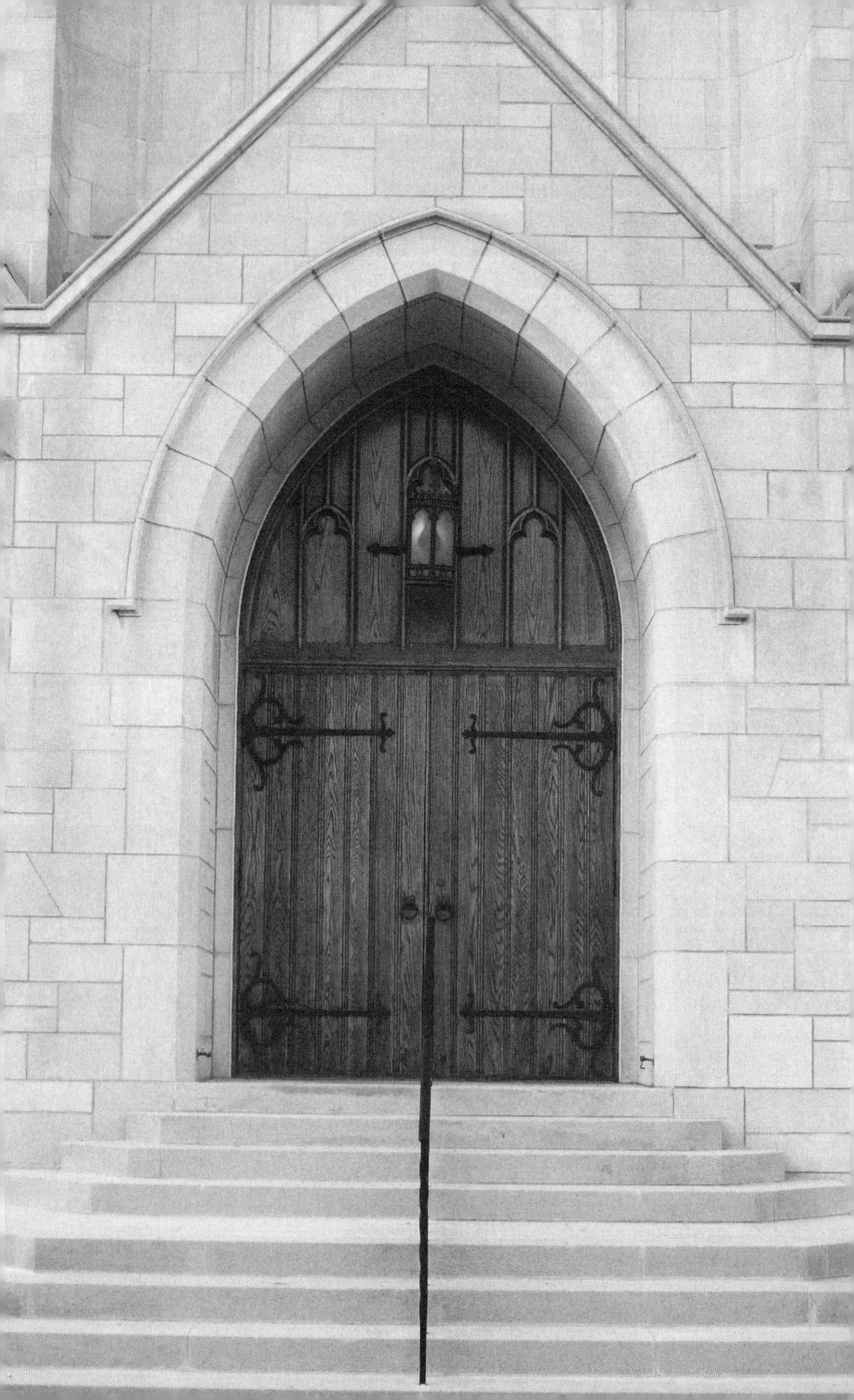

III.

Excuses, Excuses

Nobody likes to be caught doing something wrong. Often what turns a simple misdeed into an opportunity for *Schadenfreude* is the creative excuse a bad guy tries to give in his defense. Even situations that would otherwise be horrible and creepy can be transformed into humor with a really pathetic excuse. Here are a few from the "Nice try" file.

Anything *but* Gay

The Reverend John Church did nothing wrong, and yet the strangest things kept happening to him. In 1808 the twenty-five-year-old was appointed rector at Banbury in Oxfordshire, England. Rumors started to fly almost immediately that the young reverend was involved in unnatural relationships with some of the men in his parish. A hairdresser, a porter, and a grocer were all whispered to be his special friends. The whispers became screams when word got out that he had stayed at a friend's home and seduced the man's son and then his butler.

Church explained that it had all been a misunderstanding. "If there was anything of which you speak, it must have been when I was asleep and supposing I was in bed with my wife." Somehow, the parishioners were not convinced by this, and Church was forced to leave the village. He emerged in London preaching at the Obelisk Chapel in Vere Street, a homosexual brothel attached to the Swan Hotel. In his new position he officiated transvestite weddings and performed funerals for men who had been excommunicated from the church. Eventually the Swan was raided, and its proprietor, James Cooke, was charged with "detestable practices."

The juicy scandal was reported in the pamphlet *The Phoenix of Sodom*, which featured a prominent picture of Rev. Church on the front cover. One young man who recognized the good reverend was William Clarke, whose son had accused Church of sodomy. Clarke arrived at the Obelisk Chapel with not one but two pistols. Fortunately for Church, the man's heart was racing so fast that he passed out before he could fire a shot.

In 1813 Church opened a bigger and better Obelisk Chapel. Over the next few years it was business as usual, until in 1817 he was arrested for an unwanted advance on an apprentice potter. The young man testified that he had been awakened one night by "someone laying hold of me very tight." When he asked who was there, the reverend replied, "Don't you know me, Adam? It is your mistress." Church was sentenced to two years in prison for "intending to commit that most detestable and sodomitical crime (among Christians not to be named) called buggery."

That was fine with Church because it gave him time to write a book, *The Child of Providence*, in which he compares himself to martyred Biblical characters and his accusers to Philistines and Pharisees. It was all due to sleepwalking and misunderstandings.

■■

As excuses go, "Yes, I bought drugs from the male prostitute, but I didn't sleep with him," has to rank up there in the top-ten least convincing. But Rev. Ted Haggard, president of the National Association of Evangelicals, thought he'd at least give it a shot.

When a male escort, Mike Jones, accused the head of the 14,000-member New Life Church of paying for sex and drugs, Haggard explained that he had bought methamphetamines and a massage, but there was no sex. Oh, and he threw the drugs away. "I bought it," he said. "But I never used it."

It was worth a shot. After all, Rev. Haggard had a lot to lose. He was the charismatic engine that drove the huge New Life Church. As the head of one of the most powerful churches in the country, Haggard had an Oval Office chat with President Bush. His face was splashed across the cover of *Christianity Today*. "This is evangelicalism's finest hour," he told the magazine shortly after he was elected head of the National Association of Evangelicals in 2003.

With his wife, Gayle, and his five children, he seemed to be the shining example of the squeaky-clean minister. Mr. and Mrs. Haggard even wrote a book together on marriage: *From This Day Forward: Making Your Vows Last a Lifetime*. It advocated an old-fashioned husband-and-wife dynamic in which the wife takes on her husband's "likeness and calling. She loves spending time with him, pleasing him, being in his presence.... Sex between a husband and wife is a singularly divine act," the Haggards wrote. "Nothing compares to it in terms of intimacy or significance. Animals mate randomly, and, well, so do some humans, to their own ruin." Indeed.

> "Animals mate randomly, and, well, so do some humans, to their own ruin."
> **Indeed.**

Along with other Evangelical values, Haggard was a champion of a constitutional amendment banning gay marriage. Asked what he thought of gay-pride parades, he told the *New Republic* in 1996, "I don't understand it. It would be like having Murderer's Pride Day."

Seven years later he met Mike Jones, a bodybuilding male escort from Denver, Colorado. Haggard identified himself as "Art" and paid $200 each session for kissing and oral sex. The arrangement went on for another three years. Then one day Jones was watching a History Channel program about the Antichrist, as male escorts are wont to do, and he was shocked to see that one of the talking heads was none other than "Art." It wasn't long before Jones was shopping the story to the Denver media.

On October 29, 2006, Haggard gave his last sermon. "Heavenly Father, give us grace and mercy," he said. "Help us this next week and a half as we go into national elections, and Lord, we pray for our country. Father, we pray lies would be exposed and deception exposed."

Be careful what you pray for. On November 1, Mike Jones gave an interview to a Denver radio station. That's when all brimstone broke loose. Haggard at first denied having heard of Jones, but Jones had anticipated such a thing and had a recording of the preacher's voice. Next, he denied having sex with the man, but he eventually had to confess to his sins. He was forced to step down from the ministry he had created and moved to Phoenix to escape from the glare of the spotlight as Mike Jones sat down to write his inevitable book.

What, *That* Murder Victim?

Richard Rossi, the minister of the First Love Church in Mars, Pennsylvania, didn't do anything wrong, either. True, his wife was found beaten unconscious in November 1994 and left beside the road to die. When she came out of a three-day coma with severe head injuries, she did accuse her husband. But Rossi explained that it wasn't him at all. A man who looked just like him had jumped into her car and attacked her. It happens all the time.

Rev. Rossi, a graduate of Jerry Falwell's Liberty University, was popular for bringing a rock 'n' roll style of preaching to the charismatic Christian congregation, and for mixing sermons about unconditional love with fire and brimstone sermons on going to war against demons. He explained that a satanic cult in the area, or maybe even the devil himself, was responsible. The explanation was good enough for his wife, who dropped all the charges. The justice system was less forgiving. Rev. Rossi eventually pleaded no contest to a charge of second-degree aggravated assault. The case resulted in a hung jury after he had served 108 days of a four- to eight-month sentence in the Butler County Jail. Shortly after his release the happy couple held a Thanksgiving dinner for the members of their congregation.

Flimsy excuses are not the sole province of sex offenders and humiliated clergy. In 2000 a substitute teacher got himself in hot water when he told students at J. Henry Higgins Middle School in Peabody, Massachusetts, that "Hitler is cool." Historical consensus is generally against the teacher on this point. Many of the seventh-grade students were offended, and they reported the incident to the principal. The story was later covered by the *Jewish Advocate*.

When school officials asked the teacher to explain, he said that all he was saying was that Hitler is dead, and therefore his body is cold. As plausible as that sounded, the teacher was banned from ever teaching in the city's schools again.

■ ■

Denny Usui, a twenty-eight-year-old from Honolulu, Hawaii, had a few things to learn about his "right to remain silent," but he'll surely have a long time to think about it. He greeted police who came to his apartment in response to a 911 call. They asked to see his grandmother, who lived there. He told them she wasn't home. The police didn't believe his story and insisted that they needed to speak to her. Usui changed his story. "Oh," he said, "I think she's dead. She's in the shower."

The officers found her neatly covered by a blanket but dead. Usui then told them, "I don't want to say anything else until I speak to my attorney because this is a felony and I never committed murder before."

He Said, She Said

Warren Frendell and Gail Bergman, a couple who shared a home in Fairbanks, Alaska, were in agreement on one thing. Warren was taken to the hospital with knife wounds to the posterior. He told police that he was lounging around the house in his birthday suit when he and his girlfriend started to argue. He got up to go into the kitchen and get something to eat, and she stabbed him in the buttocks.

Bergman had a different account of the events. She said that he showed up at the door with two knives already sticking out of his backside. A police investigator pointed out that the knives in question appeared to be from her kitchen. "I've been asking him where those knives have been for the past three weeks," Bergman said.

The Vast Left *and* Right Wing Conspiracy

Believe it or not, even politicians have been known to have problems telling the truth. Washington state senator Joe Zarelli had collected $12,000 in unemployment benefits for 2001–2002 and neglected to mention that he was also getting a $32,000 salary as a state senator. When this was pointed out to him by a friendly reporter at *The*

Columbian newspaper, he replied that he had "no clue" that he was supposed to report his salary. He also suggested that it was the fault of the state bureaucracy for not catching him and then claimed he was a victim and that the only reason the Employment Security Agency was going after him was that he was a Republican.

∎∎

Democrats get into the act as well. New York City mayor David Dinkins was accused of failing to pay income taxes from 1969 to 1972. He explained, "I haven't committed a crime. What I did was fail to comply with the law." He went on to say that paying taxes "was one of the things I was always going to take care of, but sometimes I did not have all of the funds available or I did not have all the documents or other materials I needed." This explanation failed to garner much sympathy from the public or the IRS. He was eventually required to pay the back taxes plus penalties and interest.

∎∎

And finally, in 1984 Connecticut representative Robert Sorensen was running for reelection. When challenged on his opposition to opening legislative sessions with the Pledge of Allegiance, he huffily replied, "My patriotism should not be questioned by anyone because . . . when my country called me into service, I fought in Vietnam."

There was only one problem: he'd never been to Vietnam. When an investigative reporter helpfully reminded him of this fact, he said, "We all felt the pain of Vietnam, so in a sense I was there." Veterans who'd been there in the sense of actually marching through the jungle with rifles had a different take on the issue.

Consciousness *of* Guilt *or* Fouled-Up Cover-Ups

Sometimes perpetrators of errors go beyond making up an excuse and actively try to cover it up. We all learned in kindergarten that when you make a mistake you're much better off fessing up than trying to cover up. If you make up a story, you're bound to end up with egg—or at least mustard—on your face. Watching a cover-up unravel can provide great mirth.

In 1968 Gates Brown was suited up for the Detroit Tigers in a home game against the Cleveland Indians, but he wasn't scheduled in the regular lineup; he would be a pinch hitter in the game if he was needed. So in the sixth inning, with Cleveland leading 2–1, Gates decided to sneak out of the dugout and grab himself a snack.

He picked up a couple of hot dogs with the works and sat down in what he thought would be an unobtrusive corner to enjoy his meal. But as soon as he'd taken the first bite he heard Manager Mayo Smith call, "Gates, get your bat and hit." In a panic, Gates turned away from the manager, looking for a place to hide his contraband. The only place he could come up with in a pinch was inside his jersey. As he headed to the plate, Gates hoped he would be struck out so no one would see the hot dogs flopping around inside his shirt as he ran. No such luck. Not only did he get a hit, he smacked it into second for a double that required him to slide into second base head first. When he stood up, he was slathered in a mixture of ketchup, mustard, crumbs, and sand.

> Watching a cover-up unravel can provide great **mirth.**

"The fielders took one look at me, turned their backs, and damned near busted a gut laughing at me," he told the authors of *The Baseball Hall of Shame*. "My teammates in the dugout went crazy. That had to be my most embarrassing moment in baseball." He was fined $100 for his antics, but the worst part? "I was still pissed off because I messed up my hot dogs and couldn't eat them," he said.

■■

When a woman from Acton, Massachusetts, called the police to complain that someone had stolen her bathroom, they understandably thought she was a crackpot, but it was their job, so they headed to her house anyway. When they arrived, they were shocked to discover that the woman had been telling the truth. Her bathroom was gone. The toilet, sink, and bathtub and even the walls had been torn out. There was almost no evidence that the bathroom had ever been there. The mystery was solved when neighbors told the police that they'd seen an

Image Tile van parked outside the house. Image Tile had sent its workers to renovate the wrong house. Once they realized their mistake, they left, apparently hoping that no one would notice. No such luck.

Soviet Secrets

Vladimir Zenchenkov was a government accounting clerk in the Soviet Union of 1947. Zenchenkov went out for a few drinks after work and then realized he'd misplaced four hundred of his boss's ration cards. In postwar Russia, ration cards were like gold, and Zenchenkov was sure the penalty would be severe. His wife came up with a plan to save his neck: the next day he hid in the house, and she told his coworkers that he had run off with another woman. He spent the next twenty-two years in hiding. He didn't leave the house again until his wife died in 1969. With no link to the outside world, he decided the time had come to turn himself in to the police. It was only then that he learned that the ration cards hadn't been lost at all. They had been in his desk drawer all along.

■■

In his book *Translating History*, Russian interpreter Igor Korchilov (who interpreted for Mikhail Gorbachev, among others) recounts the following "lost in translation" story:

An interpreter at a major international conference got some notice when he heard the Soviet delegate solemnly say in Russian in his speech, "*V ogorode buzina, a v Kieve dyad'ka*" (an elderberry grows in the garden and my uncle lives in Kiev). This Russian saying means that something is incompatible with something else and is akin to the American idiom about mixing apples and oranges. But the interpreter in question didn't know the word *buzina* (elderberry) and hadn't the foggiest notion what the idiom meant, and besides, the speaker was already on his next sentence. With no time to think or to look it up in the dictionary and with no one to ask, the interpreter gambled. The delegates whose earphones were tuned to the English interpretation channel heard, "Something is rotten in the kingdom of Denmark."

The interpreter was quite pleased with what he thought was a serendipitous translation until the delegate of Denmark grabbed the floor to protest the Soviet delegate's "unwarranted slur on Denmark" and to lecture him on the virtues of democracy in his country, which, he said, was "a paragon compared to the inhuman, totalitarian system in the country which the Soviet delegate represented. . . . We do not deserve this kind of treatment," concluded the Danish delegate.

The Soviet delegate sat dumbfounded. He had never mentioned Denmark. So he interrupted the Danish delegate to express his resentment at what he called "a provocation." When it became clear that it was all the interpreter's error, he nearly lost his job.

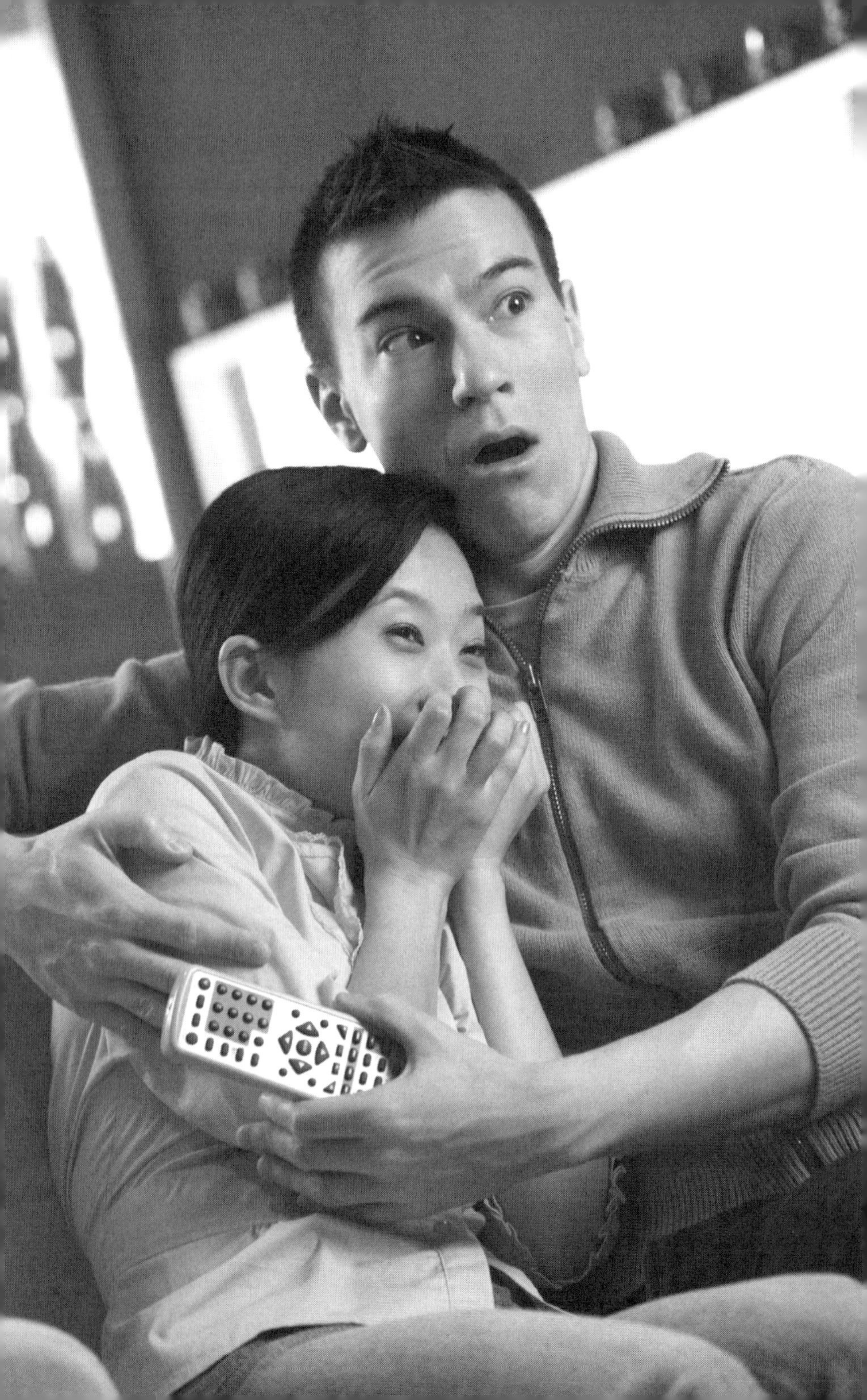

IV.

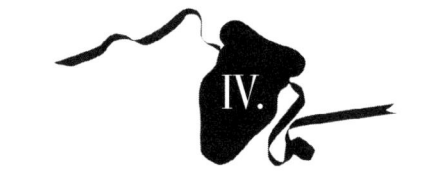

The Secret World of Children's Television

Children's entertainers may not be trying to hold themselves up as moral examples, but parents certainly expect them to be. Nothing will get Mom and Dad to hustle little Jimmy and Sue out of the room faster than discovering a shiny happy kid's icon caught in a very adult situation. Even when they don't set a bad example for the kiddies, scandals and controversies involving folks in clown makeup and big shoes will always produce a great deal of gawking, *Schadenfreude* style. No one ever liked that kid in class who offered to stay after to clean the erasers. You may not have been able to slap him across his goody-two-shoes face, but you can revel in a public version's disgrace.

Paul Reubens never set out to be a star of children's television. He simply stumbled onto a childlike, nerdy character that became a career in itself. After training as a serious actor, he got his start as part of a boy-girl act on *The Gong Show*. He graduated to the LA–based improv troupe the Groundlings, where he created many characters, including Pee-wee Herman in 1978. The prototype Pee-wee was a fumbling stand-up comic who couldn't tell a joke. Pee-wee evolved into Reuben's most popular character and soon into his only character. The act also evolved from one designed to please adults—innuendos included—to one that was clean enough for the whole family.

In the movie *Pee-wee's Big Adventure*, directed by Tim Burton, the overgrown child character did a funny dance to "Tequila" by the

Champs that was imitated by young people everywhere. By 1986 Pee Wee was starring in his own Saturday morning show for kids, *Pee-wee's Playhouse*. It was hailed as innovative and took home a bunch of Emmy awards.

The pace of producing a regular children's show seems to have taken its toll on Reuben's social life. "When you work twelve hours a day, you literally have no life," he said in an interview with *Newsday* in 1989. "I'm up at five in the morning and on the set by seven. By the time I get home at eight, take a shower, and eat dinner, it's already past my bedtime. It's built into this schedule that I can't get enough sleep. One is forced to be disciplined."

The publicity-shy actor took his responsibility as a children's entertainer seriously, and he hid some of his adult mannerisms from the kiddies. For example, Reubens kept tight security on the Pee-wee set because, he told the *San Francisco Chronicle*, "I didn't want some kid to walk on and see me smoking."

And then there was his appreciation of adult entertainment. In 1991, after the Saturday morning show was canceled, Reubens decided to let the discipline slip. He was visiting his parents in Sarasota, Florida, and decided to nip out to the South Trail Cinema, which was screening *Nancy Nurse* starring Sandra Scream. Unbeknownst to Reubens, the Sarasota Police Department had apparently rid the city of all its murderers, drug dealers, and thieves and had lots of time on its hands. They had not one but three undercover officers staking out the theater to watch for telltale hand motions among the viewers.

Pee-wee's creator was one of three men nabbed and charged with "exposure," although the report gave no indication that Reubens wanted anyone to see what he was allegedly doing alone in the dark. When word got out that Pee-wee had been caught playing with his . . . well, let's just say the name of the character worked out quite well for the sex jokes that inevitably followed. The Sarasota police received more than a hundred calls from the media the next day. CBS canceled reruns of *Pee-wee's Playhouse*. Disney

> When word got out that Pee-wee had been caught playing with his . . . well, let's just say the name of the character worked out quite well for the **sex jokes** that inevitably followed.

MGM studios stopped showing a video with Pee-wee on its theme-park tour.

It was death to Pee-wee. Reubens made one more appearance in the Pee-wee suit, during the 1991 MTV awards. "Heard any good jokes lately?" he asked. Then the costume went into the closet.

∎ ∎

Now we'll hoist our flag and sail across the ocean, where there is trouble on the set of the children's show *Blue Peter*. Frankly, to people on this side of the ocean, the title already sounds a bit suspect, but it refers to the blue and white flags hoisted by ships as they are about to sail. (Ask your British friends how they reacted when they first heard the title of the family film *Free Willy*.)

Blue Peter, aimed at the five- to eleven-year-old set, was described by a reporter for the *Independent* as "the last bastion of innocent childhood; a safe environment where our little sweethearts are protected from the nasty aspects of modern life." So it's not the best place to be employed if you also have an appetite for the white stuff. That's how twenty-two-year-old host Richard Bacon lost his £60,000-a-year job.

People who enjoy hard drinking and cocaine in their off hours don't always choose their friends wisely, and so it was with Bacon. One of his drinking buddies thought the story of a children's TV host in a compromising position would make great tabloid material. The lurid tale of one twelve-hour binge, with highlights like snorting cocaine off a toilet tank, caused an instant sensation. The news broke just as the program was about to be honored with a television achievement award. Bacon was instantly uninvited and sent packing. The *Blue Peter* show scheduled to air that day was pulled.

It wasn't the first time a *Blue Peter* host had created controversy. In 1980 it was revealed that presenter Peter Duncan had once appeared in a porn film. Five years later video footage emerged of presenter Michael Sundin showing him dancing with a male stripper at a London nightclub. In 1987 a small controversy erupted when the public learned presenter Janet Ellis was an unwed mother. But Bacon had the dubious honor of being the first person fired from the show.

The *News of the World* was clearly enjoying the *Schadenfreude* when it broke the Bacon story: "*Blue Peter* goody-goody is a cocaine-snorting sneak." Gotta love the subtlety of the Brits.

Bad behavior among adults hired to entertain kids is not a new phenomenon. One of the most outrageous examples of kiddie entertainment gone wrong took place at the opening of the Disney classic *Pinocchio* in 1940.

After scoring a huge hit with children under age twelve with *Snow White and the Seven Dwarfs* in 1937, not to mention the success MGM had with *The Wizard of Oz* and its delightful munchkins, Hollywood execs concluded that there was nothing kids loved more than little people.

Disney planned a huge opening for the *Pinocchio* premiere. Filmgoers would march in under a grand marquee. Since it was going to be impossible for the stars of the film to march in, being cartoons and all, they needed something else to hold the attention of the throngs. So they hired eleven little people to prance around up on the roof in Pinocchio suits. What could go wrong?

> Hollywood execs concluded that there was nothing kids loved more than little people.

Because *Pinocchio* was a family movie, the premiere took place during daylight hours. It began in the late morning and ran into the early afternoon. After a couple of hours leaping and turning cartwheels on top of the marquee, some of the eleven dwarves got a bit winded, and they begged the organizers to send up some lunch.

Someone thought it might be a nice gesture to send up some beer along with the food. The team of Pinocchios downed a few pints. By afternoon they were in great spirits, belching and swearing and laughing lasciviously. One of them had a flash of inspiration and decided to strip naked. Pretty soon the *Pinocchio* marquee was complete with its own miniature burlesque show. The drunken, naked children's characters were clearly out of control, so Disney called the police. By the time the cops arrived, the little men were sitting down enjoying a lively game of craps.

The police swarmed up ladders as the children and parents looked on. The Pinocchios were not ready to give up so easily. Without clothes to grab onto, the naked characters slipped free fairly easily. The police climbed down the ladder, talked it over, then returned with pillowcases. They finally trapped the little boozers in the pillowcases and lugged them, kicking and squirming, down the ladder one at a time.

■ ■

Even Santa Claus has had his share of troubles. In 1994 Graham Webb, an actor hired to portray the jolly old elf at a Southampton, England, department store, got so drunk on red wine that he teetered over and crashed through a shop window.

He had been guzzling red wine from a box all day to "put color in my cheeks and give me a bit of courage." By his own account, he'd downed about a box and a half of vino when he careened through the display window in front of a line of anxious kiddies.

Only the padded suit protected him from injury. Believe it or not, Webb didn't lose his job. His boss advised him to drink less.

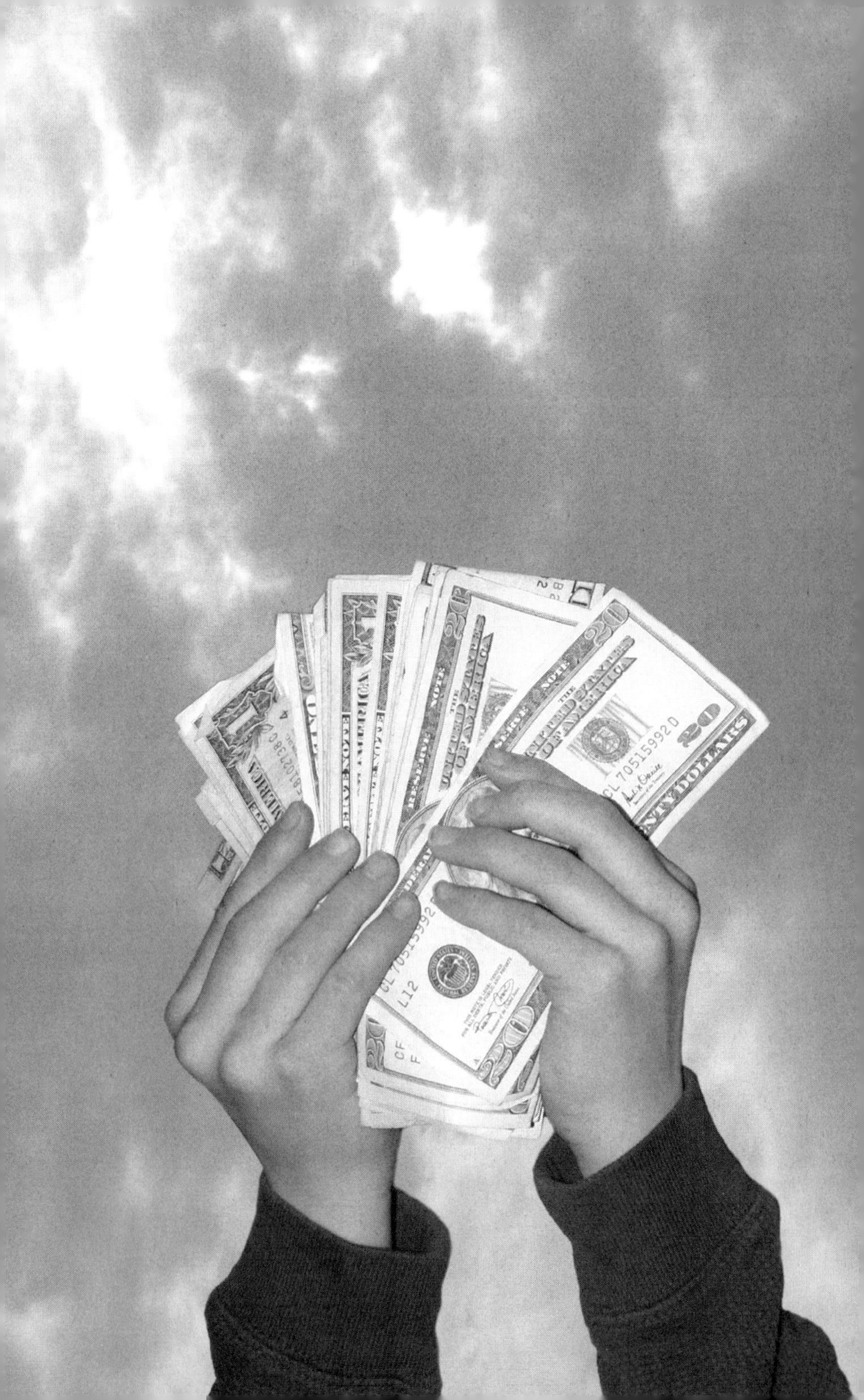
CL 70515992 D

V. Just Deserts

The expression "just deserts" has nothing to do with the dessert that comes at the end of a meal. It's derived from the French "deservir" meaning that something is "merited by service"; that is to say, deserved. But the connection to "dessert" is fitting because we tend to find these kinds of stories sweet.

"Greed *Is* Good"

To explore what makes a story of someone's merited downfall *Schadenfreude* and not simply cause and effect, we'll begin with the tale of Horatio Bottomley. Bottomley could have been remembered as a great man, a captain of industry, an influential newspaperman, a member of Parliament, but he simply couldn't resist pulling cons. In fact, *History Today* magazine labeled him "probably the greatest swindler and con artist of this century." ("This" being the 20th.)

He was a contradictory figure, four times bankrupted and twice elected to Parliament. His greatest claim to fame was launching the weekly newspaper *John Bull*. The masthead sported an overweight man dressed in a Union Jack vest posing with a bulldog wearing a Union Jack vest at his side. The jingoistic newspaper became almost a recruiting pamphlet during World War I.

With fake lotteries, real estate fraud, and other scams, he bilked the public out of an estimated million pounds, and that was when a million pounds was a lot of money. He once bragged, "I hold the unique distinction of having gone through every court in the country—except the Divorce Court." His luck ran out in 1922, when he was sentenced to seven years in jail for taking money from poor people and selling them cooperative shares in nonexistent Victory Bonds.

But this is merely the justice system working as it should. It is earthly justice. *Schadenfreude* requires something more, the intervention of a divine hand. To paraphrase John Lennon, instant karma has to get 'em.

For the *Schadenfreude* episode in Bottomley's career as a swindler, we turn to an account in Stephen Pile's *(Incomplete) Book of Failures*. The episode happened just before the First World War. Bottomley came up with what he believed would be a foolproof way of winning a fortune.

He bought all six horses entered in a race at Blankenberghe in Belgium. He hired six English jockeys and gave them strict instructions as to the exact order in which they were to cross the finish line. If the jockeys worked cooperatively, Bottomley's outcome was guaranteed. Just to be sure, he placed wagers on all the horses.

Things were going according to plan until about halfway through the race. At this point a thick sea mist blew over the course, blanketing it in impenetrable fog. The jockeys couldn't see the track, much less each other. The judges couldn't see the horses, and no one was sure who had crossed the line first. Bottomley lost a fortune.

■ ■

If you feel green with envy when you think of the people who control the green, you may find pleasure in realizing how precarious their status can be. Fortune and misfortune go together like the two sides of a coin. Bad business abounds. Even our language attests to a long and storied history of business flops. Take the word "broker" as in "a Wall Street broker." According to Sereno Pratt's book *The Work of Wall Street*: "The word broker is old. The early English form was *broceur*. By some it is believed to be derived from the Saxon word *broc*, which meant, misfortune and the first brokers indeed appear to have been men who had failed in business as principals and been compelled to pick up a precarious living as agents." Too much greed, too many gambles, bad luck, and out-and-out stupidity have all been known to lead to financial ruin.

> Fortune and **misfortune** go together like the two sides of a coin.

In the iconic 1980s film *Wall Street*, Gordon Gekko, the character played by Michael Douglas, uttered the immortal words, "Greed is good!" He had apparently never heard of Herbert and Bunker Hunt. Their attempt to corner the world's silver market turned their gold into lead.

The Hunt boys were the sons of a wealthy Texas oil man, H. L. Hunt, who was quite the character in his own right. H. L. had three families—three wives, fifteen children, all living in separate homes at one time. In 1970 Herbert and Bunker realized that silver was selling at a historic low price of $1.50 an ounce. Figuring that inflation was climbing and knowing that silver was used in manufacturing, they saw a tremendous opportunity. They started buying up all the silver they could get their hands on. By 1973 they had acquired 55 million ounces of the shiny stuff, worth about $160 million.

They should have left well enough alone, but the Hunts thought they could do better. They wanted to amass at least 200 million ounces and world control of the metal. With the help of Arab investors, they bought 130 million more ounces of silver and had contracts for another 90 million.

At first the plan seemed to work. As the Hunts snapped up the silver, the price soared. By the beginning of 1980 it was selling at $50 an ounce. The silver in their coffers was valued at about $4.5 billion. The soaring price of silver came to the attention of the U.S. government. In order to stabilize the market, they rushed to institute a limit to futures buying in silver. The remedy had its effect, and silver prices began to fall. By March 1980 the price was $21 an ounce. With silver worth less than half of its previous price, the Hunts could not cover their margin calls and the loans they'd taken to buy the silver in the first place. They found themselves in crushing debt. The market itself was in danger of collapsing, so the Federal Reserve chairman approved a $1.1 billion loan to bail them out. By 1986 they were still forced to declare bankruptcy.

■■

Seeing the greedy toppled by their own ways is particularly gratifying. That is why people love the story of Lord Elgin and how he lost his marbles. Before some Greek statues ruined his life, Elgin had everything: a great job—he had been appointed British ambassador to Constantinople in 1799, lots of money, and a beautiful bride (who was also rich).

Elgin had an appreciation for Greek antiquities. Many of the ancient ruins look the way they do today not because of the ravages of time but because people had hacked away at them, taken pieces, and ground them up for mortar much as modern folks might salvage fixtures in an old house. He didn't think these treasures should be left in the hands of the Greeks.

He got permission to copy the famous sculptures of the Parthenon in Greece, but he wanted to take things one step beyond. He hired crews to hack the ancient sculptures off their pedestals so he could take them back to Scotland. He thought they'd look good in his palace. "I should wish to collect as much marble as possible," he wrote to Giovanni Battista Lusieri, an Italian painter. "I have other places in my house which need it, and besides, one can easily multiply ornaments of beautiful marble without overdoing it."

There was one thing he failed to consider, however. Shipping all that marble back to England was going to cost a pretty penny. This is not even figuring the costs of bribing Ottoman officials to facilitate the shipment. He put in a bill to the British government, but they only covered about half of the price—about 3 million pounds in today's money.

Bad luck trailed him from then on. The Napoleonic wars kept him away from his wife—some say he was forced to flee to escape debtors' prison. In any case, while he was away, his wife ran off with his best friend, and if that was not bad enough, he acquired a wasting disease that made his nose fall off. Elgin died penniless in 1841. The marbles reside at the British Museum.

■■

John Overs made a fortune from his Thames ferryboat, so he was in a position to treat his staff generously. But being in a position to do so and actually doing so are entirely different matters. Overs, as an 1889 newspaper put it, "bought stale and musty bread . . . he never bought meat unless it was tainted, so that it would go farther and even when his dog refused it, he ate it himself." But Overs got his comeuppance, as his own stinginess led to his downfall.

One day Overs came up with an idea to keep his servants from eating so much blasted food. He would pretend to be dead, and they would follow custom and fast until his funeral. The first part of his plan worked brilliantly—the staff was convinced Overs was dead. The only flaw in the plan was that instead of descending into a somber silence, they started celebrating in "Ding-Dong, the Witch Is Dead" style. They threw open the doors to the pantry. This was too much for Overs. The "corpse" jumped up, and a startled staff member clubbed him to death with an oar because he thought it was a ghost. (That was his story, anyway, and no one seems to have questioned it.) After his death, the church refused to give him a Christian burial for the sins of usury and plain meanness.

> The "corpse" jumped up, and a startled staff member clubbed him to **death** with an oar because he thought it was a ghost.

■■

P. T. Barnum never uttered the words that have been most often attributed to him, "There's a sucker born every minute," but that doesn't lessen his position as show business's master hoaxer. All the people who bought tickets to Barnum's sideshow attraction with a sign pointing "This Way to the Egress" only to learn that "Egress" was another word for "Exit" were filled with joy when the flamboyant promoter became the victim of a scam himself.

In 1851 Barnum was forty-one years old and looking for a "profitable philanthropy," something that would transform his image as a huckster into that of a social benefactor, while at the same time bringing in a comfortable income. He came up with a plan to create the community of East Bridgeport. It would have stores, factories, and housing for hundreds of workers.

With the help of a wealthy investor, William H. Noble, he started buying up land along the Pequonnock River in Connecticut. After securing 224 acres, they parceled and sold lots, built bridges and a large park, and offered incentives to attract industry. They became acquainted with Chauncey Jerome, a representative of the Jerome Clock Company.

Jerome promised Barnum that he would move his factory, with its seven hundred to one thousand employees, if Barnum would lend his name as security for a $110,000 loan. Barnum was shown an official report of the directors of the company, exhibiting a capital of $400,000 with a surplus of $187,000. They were in need of money, Jerome said, to tide over a slow season. As proof of his wealth, Jerome produced documents showing that he had built a church in New Haven, at a cost of $40,000, and proposed to present it to a congregation; he had given a clock to a church in Bridgeport.

Barnum thought that having a huge manufacturing company like Jerome's in his beloved new town could be the key to success, so he jumped at the opportunity. He agreed to lend up to $50,000 and would back promissory notes for a maximum total of $60,000, as long as the maximum of $110,000 wasn't exceeded.

Over the next few months Barnum endorsed checks for $3,000, $5,000, and $10,000 to the company and left the dates blank to ease transactions. "My confidence in the company became so established that I did not ask to see the notes that had been taken up," Barnum said, "but furnished new accommodation paper as it was called for."

> "My agent who made these startling discoveries came back to me with the **refreshing intelligence** that I was a ruined man!"

When banks began to refuse his notes, Barnum became alarmed and sent a man to investigate. It turned out that, rather than cancel the earlier notes, Jerome had dated them as much as two years in the future while taking new paper from Barnum. Barnum had endorsed the clock company to the extent of more than a half million dollars. Said Barnum, "My agent who made these startling discoveries came back to me with the refreshing intelligence that I was a ruined man!"

"Barnum and the Jerome Clock Bubble" was the *Schadenfreude* story of the day. Barnum was forced to liquidate his assets to pay off most of his debts.

■ ■

Here is one to warm the cockles of every beaten-down and bullied corporate employee. Neal Patterson, the founder and CEO of Cerner Corporation, had a management style that would charitably be called "assertive." In early 2001 Cerner had more than three thousand employees worldwide. It also had one of NASDAQ's best-performing stocks, and Patterson wanted to keep it that way.

On the morning of March 13, 2001, the CEO was heading into his office and expected to see the troops hard at work. But he found many parking spots still unoccupied. Did those slackers think they could put in a mere forty hours a week? He went to his computer and fired off an angry e-mail to about four hundred company managers.

"We are getting less than 40 hours of work from a large number of our [Kansas City] EMPLOYEES," he wrote. "The parking lot is sparsely used at 8AM, likewise at 5PM. As managers—you either do not know what your EMPLOYEES are doing: or you do not CARE. You have created expectations on the work effort which allowed this to happen inside Cerner, creating a very unhealthy environment. In either case, you have a problem and you will fix it or I will replace you. . . . NEVER in my career have I allowed a team which worked for me to think they had a 40-hour job. I have allowed YOU to create a culture which is permitting this. NO LONGER."

He threatened to install time clocks, discontinue an employee stock-discount program and cut staff by 5 percent if things did not change. "Hell will freeze over before this CEO implements ANOTHER EMPLOYEE benefit in this Culture . . . what you are doing with this company makes me sick."

He finished up his tirade with an ultimatum: "The pizza man should show up at 7:30 p.m. to feed the starving teams working late. The lot should be half-full on Saturday mornings. . . . You have two weeks. Tick, tock."

An anonymous, but clearly disgruntled, EMPLOYEE posted the memo on an online message board on Yahoo! When investors read the memo and its frenzied tone, they started to worry that Cerner might be in big trouble. Maybe Patterson was in a panic because Cerner was going to miss its target for first-quarter earnings. In just a few days, the company's stock price had tumbled by $10, the company's market cap had fallen by $270 million, and Patterson had taken a personal hit of $28 million.

■ ■

Anyone who has said no one ever went broke underestimating the taste of the American public has never met Judith Regan. To be fair, most of the time underestimating the taste of the American public seemed to have worked fairly well for the person the *San Francisco Chronicle* called "the fearless, foul-mouthed former publisher of Regan Books," an imprint of HarperCollins.

Regan Books had published works of such literary merit as Jenna Jameson's *How to Make Love Like a Porn Star*, a book about convicted wife killer Scott Peterson, and anything sure to spark controversy. Ralph Nader, Peggy Noonan, Trent Lott, and Michael Moore's books were all Judith Regan's babies.

With O. J. Simpson's hypothetical tell-all, *If I Did It*, she seemed to have landed a surefire gold mine. She reportedly paid between $2 million and $3.5 million for the book, in which Simpson took time off from searching for the real killer to write a "fictional" account of how he would have killed his ex-wife; that is, if he were the guilty party. The story couldn't harm The Juice, who was protected against double jeopardy.

It has been tough for the former football star since the whole messy murder trial. He hadn't even made a dent in the $33.5 million judgment that the families of the victims had won against him in civil court. Living in Florida where laws protect his house from creditors, he has been forced to get by on nothing but a $300,000-a-year NFL pension.

Helping O. J. out by reading his confession turned out to be just a step too far for American sensibilities. *Newsweek* announced the pending release of the book this way: "To those who worried our violent, sex-obsessed, celebrity-crazed culture had at last reached the very farthest depths of depravity, O. J. Simpson and Judith Regan come bearing news: we had so much farther to fall."

In a brief turnaround of the normal world order, Geraldo Rivera went on TV to denounce the sensationalism of book publishing. Cable news shows spent segment after segment trotting out the O. J. Simpson murder-trial characters and voicing outrage over the book launch, and we all experienced a rosy sense of moral superiority before going back to watching people eat bugs on *Fear Factor* and searching the Internet for the unauthorized excerpts that appeared almost immediately. (Admit it, you're a little curious about what Simpson wrote, aren't you?)

Regan tried, unsuccessfully, to paint herself as a victim of abuse who wanted to publish Simpson's half confession to help victims of violence. The logic goes that hearing what hypothetically happened would create closure and give comfort. "I made the decision to publish this book, and to sit face to face with the killer," Regan said, "because I wanted him, and the men who broke my heart and your hearts, to tell the truth, to confess their sins, to do penance and to amend their lives. Amen."

The Oprah Winfrey moment did little to gain public sympathy. The amens scattered throughout were a bit over the top. A simple "I may have miscalculated" might have produced less *Schadenfreude*. If the public took glee in her misfortune, the publishing world was downright giddy. It wasn't just the lowbrow best sellers that bothered the literary types ("We're only publishing this celebrity confession to fund our true love, feminist free verse") but the fact that Regan was known to be, shall we say, tough to work with. She reportedly burned through employees at an impressive rate, about eighty during one year, including eighteen personal assistants.

As grassroots petitions circulated and one bookstore after another announced they would not carry the title, News Corporation chairman and CEO Rupert Murdoch, Regan Books's parent, was forced to announce that the company had canceled publication of the book as well as the corresponding Fox broadcast network special. Murdoch said, "I and senior management agree with the American public that this was an ill-considered project. We are sorry for any pain this has caused the families of Ron Goldman and Nicole Brown-Simpson."

The whole sordid story came to an end in December 2006, only a few weeks after the Simpson book was to have been published. Regan was abruptly fired, ostensibly over alleged anti-Semitic comments, after she ranted that a "Jewish cabal" was "conspiring" to smear her in the media and ruin her career.

"Judith Regan's employment with HarperCollins has been terminated effective immediately," HarperCollins CEO Jane Friedman said in a statement. Fortunately, with Regan's firing all sensationalism in publishing was put to an end forever.

Some Petard Hoisting

Sometimes, however, you have to sympathize with The Man, as when an employee is gleefully stealing trade secrets right under the boss's nose. In 1998 Caryn Camp was an unhappy thirty-eight-year-old chemist at IDEXX Laboratories in Maine, one of the world's leading producers of equipment for diagnosing veterinary ailments. Like many a disgruntled office worker, she spent her supposedly productive hours searching the want ads on the Internet. One day she came across a position at one of IDEXX's competitors, Wyoming DNA Vaccine.

She fired off her résumé and got a reply from the company's chief scientific officer, Stephen Martin. The pair started corresponding and hit it off well. Eventually Stephen started asking Caryn for confidential IDEXX information: ". . . absorb as much information physically and intellectually as you can. I never had a spy before. We are going to be in the veterinary business big time."

Caryn wanted to show him she could be resourceful. And resourceful she was. She sent customer lists, laboratory files, manufacturing documents and even told her competitor about acquisition rumors. The more she sent, the more she seemed to enjoy it. At one point she wrote, "Aren't I awful? I'm liking this spy business way too much." In July Caryn planned to fly to California to meet Stephen face to face for the first time. She mailed him her pièce de résistance—two boxes containing seven binders full of top-secret data such as research and development information.

She wrote Stephen an e-mail describing what he would be getting. "There's some really cool stuff coming through," she wrote. "You'll feel like a kid on Christmas day!"

Unfortunately for Caryn, she made a bit of a mistake. When she went into her e-mail program's address book, she accidentally chose the address of John Lawrence, IDEXX's global marketing director, instead of Stephen's. When Lawrence read her e-mail, he behaved more like the Grinch—he notified the authorities. Caryn got to leave her job, all right. She was fired and was sentenced to three years' probation after she agreed to testify against her accomplice. Stephen became only the second person in U.S. history brought to trial under the U.S. Economic Espionage Act of 1996. He served a year in prison.

∎∎

If you've ever had your purse snatched, you will enjoy the story of the petty thief who grabbed a suitcase at the Reading railway station in London in 1994. He was hoping that the bag would contain some valuables, maybe a camera, some traveler's checks, or at least some decent clothes. When he got outside the station and looked inside he found something quite different—wires, a detonator, and explosives. "It's a bomb! It's a bomb!" he shouted.

"I think he'll think twice about nicking bags that aren't his again," one witness observed.

The story is particularly gratifying because a petty thief and a would-be terrorist were both thwarted in one go. The Scotland Yard antiterrorist squad were called in and disposed of the explosives.

Granny's Revenge

Another would-be thief whose misfortune will bring you joy is James Sharp of Lewisville, Arkansas. The twenty-one-year-old, who was under investigation by the Arkansas State Police for burglary and rape, broke into the home of ninety-year-old Illa Hooper. He'd picked the wrong granny to rob.

Illa, whose friends call her "Miss Ike," was awakened by a light in her bedroom. She soon recognized that it was a flashlight. The nonagenarian grabbed the cane from beside her bed and started whacking the intruder. Hooper was a lot stronger than she looked.

> He'd picked the wrong **granny** to rob.

She took power walks almost every day. After stunning the robber with her cane, she escaped and called the police. Sharp was arrested. We can only imagine the reaction when he answered the question, "What are you in for?"

■■

Another item from the "Go, Granny, Go" file: In 1991 Kenneth D. Huggins, who was then twenty-four, was already bleeding from cuts he sustained trying to enter a home through a broken window when he encountered his worst nightmare, eighty-five-year-old Addie Davis. She heard the intruder and went to investigate, carrying a deadly weapon, a six-pack of Sprite. She smashed him repeatedly over the head. Allegedly, the burglar begged the octogenarian to just kill him because his cuts were so painful.

"He was cut worse than any human I've ever seen," said the arresting officer. Even so, he was lucky. "If I'd known he would've been lying there when I came in, I would've got my gun and shot him," Davis was quoted as saying.

■■

In yet another case of the revenge of the senior set, sixty-eight-year-old Earnest Coleman was sitting in his car outside an Omaha, Nebraska, grocery. Next thing you know, a teenager is waving a gun at him asking for his money. Coleman grabbed the kid's gun with one hand and punched him in the face with the other. The teen's accomplice thought the old man would be easy to take down. He ran up to the passenger-side window and punched the driver. Coleman then grabbed the second kid, pulled him through the window and gave him a good pummeling. The two teens finally managed to get away, but Coleman got to keep his money and the attacker's gun. Seniors 3, criminals 0.

Other Avengers

Another criminal got more than he bargained for when he tried to hold up a Christian bookstore. ("Give me all your money and two of those Ten Commandments posters. 'Thou shalt not. . . .' Oh, never mind, just the money will do.") Tim Davis was working alone when an unnamed robber barged into the Salt and Pepper Christian store in Murfreesboro, Tennessee. He handed over a note demanding money and claiming that he had a gun hidden under a folded newspaper.

Something didn't look quite right to the eagle-eyed Christian. The newspaper just didn't seem thick enough to be concealing a weapon. So instead of handing over the cash, he reached down and grabbed a pair of scissors from under the counter. When that didn't inspire the would-be thief to produce his gun, Davis became even more confident that he was unarmed. The robber turned and ran, but Davis chased after him, brandishing his scissors. He cornered the robber until the police arrived.

Davis later told *USA Today*, "The only thing I did wrong was run with a pair of scissors."

■ ■

From the Reuters news service comes the story of a would-be mugger in Berlin, Germany, who tried to rob a taxi driver and ended up having his own wallet snatched. The twenty-year-old German grabbed the driver's wallet, but the victim fought back. The cabbie not only got his own wallet back, but he grabbed the thief's as well. The driver then locked himself inside his taxi and called the police. They arrived on the scene and found the mugger waiting for them on the curb.

"He wanted his wallet back," a police spokesman explained.

■ ■

An elevator got its revenge against two young Norwegian vandals in May 2007. (Great rock band name, that: "Norwegian Vandals.") The young men, who were unnamed in news reports, decided to smash up an elevator at the Lillestroem Train Station north of Oslo. They made the rather unwise decision to do this from the inside. They kicked the doors so hard that they jammed, and the elevator stopped and sealed the bad guys inside. Not only that, the lift was programmed to send an alarm to security guards if it became trapped between floors.

Guards arrived and tried to lower the elevator, but this only jammed the doors more. So they called the police and fire department. And just in case being detained by the elevator you're vandalizing is not evidence enough, the young men had failed to notice that there was a security camera, which caught the whole attack on tape.

Tumbling Toms

Raul Zarate Diaz got his comeuppance by falling down. Diaz was the warden at a Tapachula, Mexico, jail. The facility, near the border with Guatemala, allowed conjugal visits. As far as Diaz was concerned, this—the free porno—was one of the perks of the job. One afternoon as a Nicaraguan prisoner was enjoying such a visit with his wife, the warden was gazing down through a skylight with a pair of binoculars. This time, he lost his balance and crashed through the roof. Diaz was killed when he met with the cement floor. The prisoner who had been providing the unintentional show tried to start a riot, but it was squelched by security.

■■

In a similar case with an even more fitting conclusion, police in Tennessee, Illinois, were called to rescue a man who was trapped waist deep in a cesspit outside a toilet at a local roadhouse. The man was unconscious and almost dead; his body temperature had fallen to 91°F. When he regained his senses, he told police that he'd been beaten and mugged. But authorities became suspicious when they found his wallet, checkbook, and credit cards lying in a neat pile in the men's restroom.

Forced to fess up, the man explained that he had actually been standing on top of the roof of the ladies' room watching them do their business through a "glory hole." He slipped and fell into the pit. He had taken his wallet out of his pocket because he didn't like to have any identification on him when he went peeping.

Losers *in* Lust

You can't buy love—unless you're really, really rich. But even in that case, you tend to buy nothing but heartache. Nowhere is this better illustrated than in the story of real estate tycoon Edward West Browning. Of course, in this case it helps that the middle-aged Browning was particularly interested in falling in love with a teenage girl.

After his wife left him for a dentist in 1924 ("A dentist of all people! How can any sensible woman fall in love with a dentist?" he said.), he went looking for a new girl among the cute little flappers at high schools. His creative approach was to place the following ad in the *New York Herald Tribune*:

"Adoption—Pretty refined girl, about fourteen years old, wanted by aristocratic family of large wealth and highest standing; will be brought up as own child among beautiful surroundings, with every desirable luxury, opportunity, education, travel, kindness, care, love. Address with particulars and photograph."

How could that go wrong? Well, first of all, a few fuddy-duddies questioned "Daddy Browning's" motives. He explained that his daughter Dorothy wanted a sister. Before the ink was even dry, there was a steady stream of young women at Browning's door. Mothers showed up at the office offering up their daughters. Browning interviewed more than twelve thousand gold diggers—I mean, potential adoptees—in two weeks, as the news cameras clicked away.

Daddy Browning finally made his selection, and she was perfect: Mary Spaas, a sixteen-year-old from Astoria with the perfect backstory. A teary-eyed Browning told the press that she had been living on the street and didn't have a penny to her name. She had walked dozens of miles to apply to be adopted. The *New York Times* described the girl as "small for her age" and "rather shy."

As Browning shuttled his choice around in a Rolls-Royce and took her on a shopping spree for expensive new duds, one enterprising reporter headed to Astoria for a feature on the girl's humble roots. It turns out that one or two things about her story weren't quite accurate. The part about being a penniless orphan, for instance. She had actually been a movie extra at Paramount Film Studios, and she was twenty-one years old. She was also engaged to a plumber named Emil Vasalek.

When Browning confronted his new "daughter," she said, "I'm sixteen because I want to be sixteen." That was the end of one beautiful relationship. But the duped millionaire was not deterred; there were lots of young girls to choose from. His office was deluged with their letters even after the Mary Spaas fiasco. Surely, the next one would have purer motives.

At about this time, Browning came up with the idea of giving financial support to high school sororities. By paying off their debts and funding their dances, he was invited to attend as guest of honor. There the fifty-year-old could dance with the pretty girls and pinch them on the cheeks.

In 1926, at one of these soirees, an overdeveloped fifteen-year-old, Frances Belle Heenan, caught Browning's eye. Heenan was an unpopular high school dropout, but she crashed the sorority bash in order to catch a glimpse of a millionaire. Browning was immediately smitten. "You look like peaches and cream to me!" he said. "I'll call you

Peaches." He described her to the press as "five feet, seven inches tall, weight 145 pounds—with her dress on of course."

He was outraged when the Society for the Prevention of Cruelty to Children questioned his relationship with the girl. "I am not an old man seeking improper friendships with little girls," he huffed. His argument was somewhat diluted when he married the teen on April 11, 1926. The press couldn't get enough of the May-December pair, and they snapped dozens of photos of Browning gazing with complete and utter love at his child bride. They moved into the posh Kew Gardens Inn on Long Island, close to Manhattan's nightlife and, more importantly for Peaches, expensive shopping. Almost every day for six months, Peaches could be found in the shops on Fifth Avenue. Browning planned to grow, well, older, with her.

Much to his shock, on October 2, 1926, Peaches bundled herself up in her toniest furs and jewels, packed her suitcase—make that twenty suitcases—and had the servants walk them out the door. "Money isn't everything," she shouted dramatically as she whipped a dead ermine around her neck. (It's hard to make a dramatic exit with a caravan of suitcases full of jewels, furs, and shoes in tow, but she gave it her best shot.)

The poor old man was taken completely by surprise. After the painful and public divorce, Browning lost his taste for romance; he died in 1934. Peaches parlayed her scandalous fame into a vaudeville career, but she died at the age of forty-six in a freak accident when she slipped in her bathtub and fell.

■■

He's young, cocky, and rich, and he made his fortune by getting drunken college coeds to flash the camera. The arrest of Joe Francis, the creator of *Girls Gone Wild*, on charges of tax evasion produced a widespread glee. As Annette Lawless wrote in the Kansas State University newspaper, the *Collegian*, "Maybe someone should pitch in, send out a spy cam and release the first 'Prison Gone Wild' series, starring Mr. Francis. Let's give him an experience more enlightening than a floozy college student flaunting her breasts on screen."

Francis' soft-core porn empire began in 1997 when he was a production assistant on a syndicated show of home-video bloopers, *Real TV*. Much of the material was just too gory for the regular show, but

Francis never underestimated the public's desire for gawking at gruesome misfortune. So using his credit cards to finance the project, he released *Banned from Television*. If accidents sold well, he reasoned, surely people would pay even more for bare collegiate breasts and girls French kissing their roommates on spring break. The performers in the videos perform in exchange for a *Girls Gone Wild* T-shirt. Thus one of the most recognizable brand names—at least by folks who watch TV late at night—was born.

Lawsuits followed immediately. In 2000 Les Haber, another *Real TV* producer, sued Francis for breach of implied contract, claiming that *Banned from Television* had been his idea. A jury found in the plaintiff's favor in the $3.5 million suit.

Over the years more than a dozen women have sued Mr. Girls Gone Wild, claiming that they were shown on video-box covers and in television commercials without their permission. They rarely win their cases.

Girls Gone Wild grew to take in an estimated $40 million a year in sales. Francis, meanwhile, travels from party to party on a private jet and dates tabloid regulars like Paris Hilton and rock star Rod Stewart's daughter, Kimberly. When *Los Angeles Times* reporter Clare Hoffman decided to follow the millionaire pornographer for a feature, she ended up part of the story when Francis pinned her to the hood of a car and left red marks on her arm. He later tried to apologize by purring, "Baby, give me a kiss." A number of women have sued Francis for harassment and threatening behavior.

Another time he was arrested for filming underage girls. His "they said they were adults" defense did not rule the day, and he agreed to pay undisclosed damages to the emotionally distressed teens. His courtroom behavior probably did little to help his case. While being reprimanded by a judge for swearing, he replied, "If my mother was suing me for $20 million, you better believe I would use that language." He was arrested for contempt of court.

Another time, Francis showed up at a mediation session four hours late dressed in shorts, put his feet up on a table, and went wild, launching an obscenity-filled tirade. But in April 2007 he was facing up to ten years in prison for the unsexy crime of tax evasion. A federal grand jury in Reno, Nevada, alleges that Francis and his companies claimed more than $20 million in false business deductions in 2002 and 2003 and his money is in offshore bank accounts. Later bribery charges were added to the mix. While in jail he allegedly offered a guard $100 for a bottle of water. When the guard turned him down, investigators say Francis showed the guard $500. Jail inmates are not allowed to have cash. A search of his cell then turned up sixteen contraband prescription medications. Those charges could carry an additional five years.

Commenting on his tax evasion arrest, Francis told the *Los Angeles Times*: "Envy makes you a target." That's it. It's the envy.

And One *Schadenfreude* *Schadenfreude*

Now here is an interesting one—it is a bit like a Pet Milk can. It's a *Schadenfreude* story within a *Schadenfreude* story. If you enjoy seeing people get comeuppance for taking joy in others' misfortunes, this one is for you.

It began in Baltimore in early 2007 with a vandalized billboard. This is not the kind of thing that normally makes national headlines. But then this billboard featured a man so many people love to hate—Rush Limbaugh. When the man responsible for cleaning up graffiti saw someone had done an imitation of Jackson Pollock over the radio ranter's chin, he chuckled with glee.

Robert Murrow of the Department of Public Works called up the *Baltimore Sun*. "It looks like they took globs of paint and threw it on his face," he reported. "It looks great. It did my heart good." Murrow, who was described by the *Sun* as "a soft-spoken man who is usually in the limelight only when a water main breaks," saw his quote splashed onto the online version of the newspaper in less than 30 minutes. With a few cuts and pastes, the story started to spread. People who hated Limbaugh gleefully sent it to

> If you enjoy seeing people get **comeuppance** for taking joy in others' misfortunes, this one is for you.

friends. Meanwhile, Limbaugh fans, known as "dittoheads," sent it to highlight Murrow's inappropriate comments.

It was inevitable that Limbaugh himself would get wind of the story and make a joke out of it. "What's happening to the civility of our society?" he asked. The Department of Public Works was inundated with calls, and Murrow's bosses were not at all amused.

"I don't care if it's Rush Limbaugh, Michael Moore, or Britney Spears," said Kurt Kocher, a department spokesman. "You don't deface anything—period. And you don't endorse defacing anything—period." Murrow was said to have "deeply apologized."

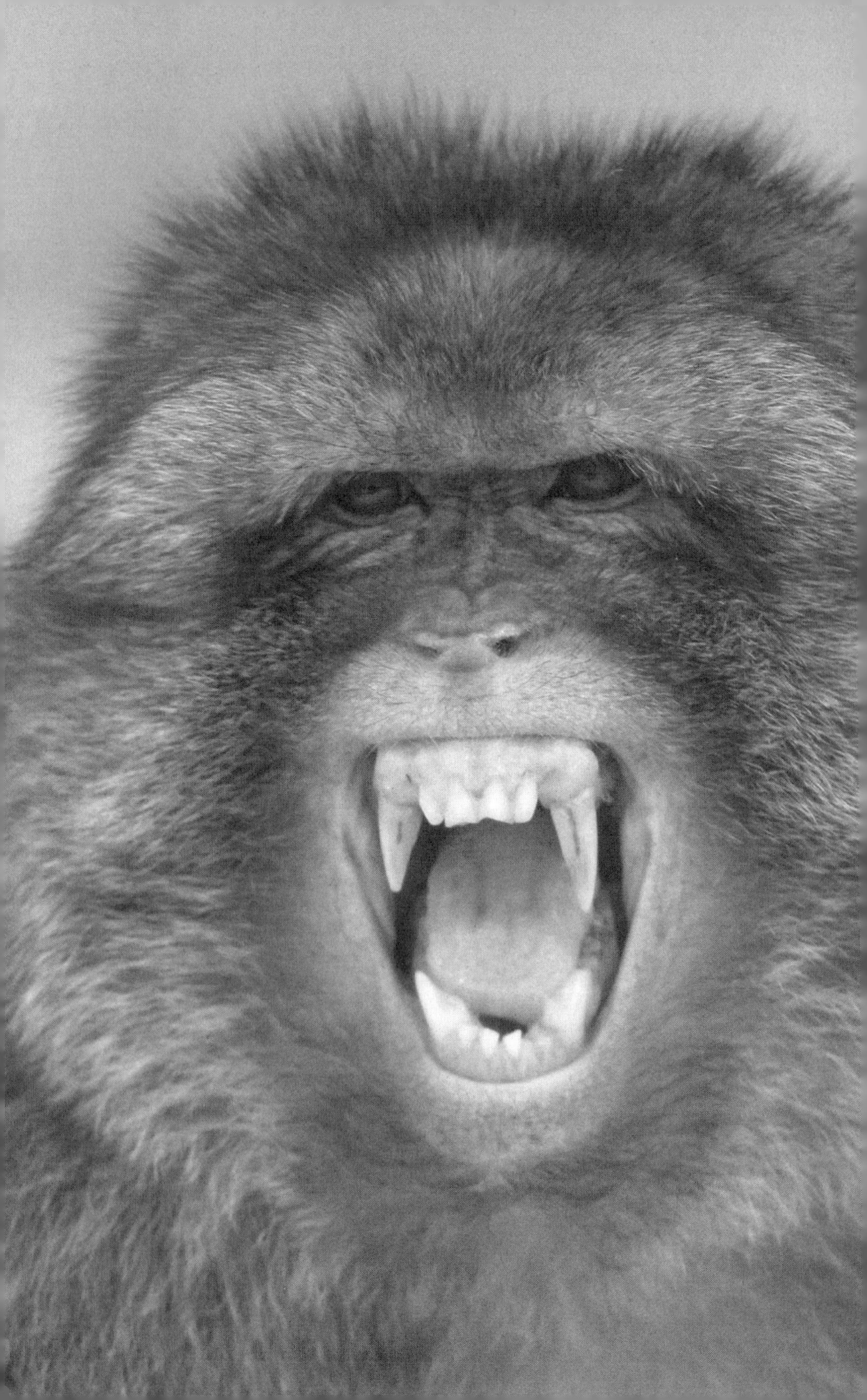

VI. Nature's Revenge

We're pretty cocky up here at our supposed station at the top of the food chain. Most of us live in cities and think of nature as something to visit in an RV. We're safe and secure in the knowledge that the plants and trees and birds and bees are much stupider than we are. Sometimes nature gets the last laugh.

Revenge *of the* Animals

This short and sweet story happened in 1949 and has oft been repeated in "did you know" features over the years. Henri Villette, 67, of Alencon, France, set out to drown a kitten. He threw the animal into the water, then lost his balance and fell in himself. The kitten swam to shore. Villette drowned. That's the essence of the "nature's revenge" brand of *Schadenfreude* in a nutshell.

■ ■

Flash forward now to 1995. A group of students trapped a gopher and brought it to the custodial staff of Fowler Elementary in Ceres, California. The three janitors could have called animal control, but they thought they had matters under control. How hard could it be to kill a rodent? They didn't know much about gophers, but they came up with a method of execution that would involve little blood, ergo less clean up.

What they lacked in pest-control experience, they made up for with knowledge of cleaning products, in this case Misty Gum Remover, an aerosol that freezes chewing gum so it can be scraped off surfaces. They reasoned that it could double as a gopher killer.

They put the critter in a bucket in the custodial closet, closed the door, and started spraying away. When one of the men was satisfied that the other two had the whole freezing-the-animal-to-death thing under control, he leaned back and lit up a cigarette.

The flame interacted with the Misty Gum Remover fumes, and—Bang!—the resulting explosion blew them all out of the closet. The three janitors were hospitalized, and sixteen others received minor injuries in the blast. The gopher survived and was later released into a field.

■ ■

In a 2001 case an unnamed woman suffered serious burns after her boyfriend tried to burn an opossum in their yard. The man told fire rescue workers he had killed the animal and then decided to burn the carcass. In the process he tripped, fell backwards, and splashed gas on his girlfriend's leg.

That's not the same story he told the 911 emergency dispatcher. When he first called, the man said that he tried to kill the marsupial by setting it on fire and that the flaming creature ran around the yard before running into his girlfriend and setting her leg alight. The woman's injuries were not life threatening, but she was treated in the burn unit.

■ ■

This next story isn't exactly a case of nature's revenge, but it does involve a duck. Mr. Peepers waddled through a crime spree that included theft, fleeing the scene, and hit and run completely unscathed. Our feathered hero came to a Seattle PETCO store with his owner (the Associated Press didn't reveal her name) and her boyfriend, Kenneth Blaine Quinlan.

As Mr. Peepers and his owner were browsing the PETCO store, Quinlan was allegedly enjoying some shoplifting at a nearby Linens 'n Things. (He needed some "things.") A security guard thought he saw

Quinlan stashing an iPod speaker system, and a scuffle ensued. The guard chased Quinlan to the PETCO store, where he got the car keys from his girlfriend.

He ran out of the store and jumped into the driver's seat. The confused girlfriend followed him, carrying the duck. When she tried to stop him from driving away in her car, she was knocked down by the open door as he backed up. Mr. Peepers fell from her arms. A PETCO employee was watching the scene, and she ran to save Mr. Peepers from the car. The car ran over the woman, inflicting serious injuries.

Quinlan's getaway ended shortly thereafter, when he smashed into another car. The duck was fine. There is no truth to the rumor that when he saw the accident he quacked out "AFLAC!"

■ ■

Almost every newspaper that reported this next story used the word "revenge" in the headline.

"Please don't say that deer was out for revenge," said taxidermist Tim Knight. Knight had stepped away from another tough day stuffing dead deer heads and was enjoying a lunch break in a fast-food joint across the street when a large whitetail buck leapt from the sidewalk and crashed through the front window of Knight's Wildlife Studio in Dublin, Georgia. He destroyed an entire showroom of hunters' trophies, including many of his stuffed and mounted cousins. The deer also broke the windshield of a 1988 Cadillac parked near the store before leading police and an animal-control officer on a mile-long chase through city streets, a park, and a residential neighborhood where it was finally tranquilized. The deer was taken to a wildlife sanctuary.

■ ■

If you live outside Asia you may never have heard of "bear milking." In a practice that has been widely condemned by animal-rights activists throughout the world, bears are kept in captivity so that they can be drained of bile, which is an ingredient in traditional Chinese medicine. It can fetch as much as $1,000 per kilo in Asian markets.

If you're squeamish, you may want to skip the description of how they get it. First off, the bears are usually kept in cages so small they can barely sit up or turn around. To milk the bile, a hollow stick is inserted into the animal's gallbladder through the abdomen and the bile runs into a basin under the cage. In the past catheters were inserted twice a day, almost never by veterinarians. The Chinese government did finally ban the catheter method. Instead farmers use a "free dripping method," which is believed to be more humane, albeit more disgusting. The farmer simply cuts a hole in the bear and leaves it open so the bile can *freely drip* out. The thing is that the cuts eventually heal and the continuous reopening of the wound often leads to infections. So you tend to end up with a mixture of bear bile and pus, not to mention a very angry bear.

So it was with some pleasure that animal lovers read that Han Shi-gen, a bile farmer, was attacked by a bear in 2005 while cleaning its cage. According to the Xinhua news agency, the bear was so enraged that rescuers couldn't get into the cage to remove what was left of Shi-gen's body for two hours.

Plants *and* Other Parts *of the* Natural World

I call this one "The Revenge of the Cactus." The Arizona desert is home to a unique giant plant, the saguaro cactus. Some are 175 to 200 years old, and they are pretty amazing. Several years ago researchers at the University of Arizona discovered that they actually bleed. A substance similar to adrenaline shoots through their systems when they're injured, and a clear fluid coagulates around the wound.

These rare plants are protected. They have to be. Every year thousands of the cacti are stolen by people who think they'll look good in their gardens at home. The saguaro is the kind of cactus that you see in Western movies and that kids shot around in the early-'80s Atari home game *Outlaw*.

Our story takes place in 1982, so maybe David Grundman was imagining himself as one of the square cowboys of *Outlaw* when he and his friend James Suchochi got the idea to shoot saguaros in the desert near Lake Pleasant. First, Grundman blasted a ten-foot saguaro so many times that it toppled. "The first one was easy," he supposedly said. Then he shot three more shouting "Timber!" as they fell.

Finally he set his sights on a twenty-seven-footer and shot it twice from ten feet away. He only had enough time to say "Tim . . ." before a prickly arm fell over and crushed him.

The Austin Lounge Lizards were filled with so much *Schadenfreude* upon hearing this tale that they wrote the song "Saguaro" about it:

> He crossed a small arroyo, the sun was in his eyes
> He was looking for the leader, he'd know him by his size
> When all at once upon a ridge the squinting gunman saw
> Twenty-seven feet of succulent challenging his draw. . . .

■■

Even the skies have been known to enact a little revenge.

In the late nineteenth and early twentieth century, there was an entire industry dedicated to producing rain. The importance of rain couldn't be overestimated when the majority of people's livelihoods were still directly or indirectly tied to farming. The rainmakers were known as "pluviculturists," and they had all kinds of theories on how the clouds could be compelled to precipitate. They were all quacks, of course, but they had many believers who paid handsome sums to alter the weather on a whim. They generally used a similar system to that described by modern-day comedian Eddie Izzard in his book *Dress to Kill*.

A street comedian used to use the clouds in his act: ". . . it kept raining on us, so you're quite aware of the weather," he wrote. "When it was cloudy, and he could see the sun was about to come out from behind a cloud, he'd say, 'And can we have the lights up, please?' and then the sun would come out. It was beautiful. Instead of trying to make things happen your way, you use what is happening. You sense it's gong to happen and then say, 'I am making this happen.' They know you haven't done it, but they like your timing."

The difference was that a century ago many people didn't know the clowns hadn't done it. Before we get to the protagonist of our tale, Charles Mallory Hatfield, let's take a quick look at the world of rainmaking that he inhabited.

Some of the earliest attempts to control the weather involved the use of cannons and church bells. The scientific explanation went like this: rain inevitably followed thunder; therefore, loud noise must cause rain. Somehow this noise-and-rain correlation led to two contradictory beliefs: one, that warfare caused rain and the other, that storms could be broken up by firing guns into them.

> Some of the earliest attempts to control the **weather** involved the use of cannons and church bells.

In the late nineteenth century the Weather Bureau and the Department of Agriculture funded various tests in which explosives were unleashed in the clouds to release their rain—money that the *Chicago Times* believed would have been "less ridiculously employed if it were devoted to the attempted manufacture of whistles out of pig's tails."

Around this time Frank Melbourne's Inter State Artificial Rain Company used a noxious, smelly concoction to make it rain. He enjoyed a great reputation for a time until people discovered that the dates he selected as ideal for "producing" rain were the same as those *predicted* for rain in a popular almanac. When critics got a look at his top-secret equipment, they discovered that it was a barometer.

The most famous pluviculturist of all, however, was Charles Hatfield. Born in Fort Scott, Kansas, in 1875, Hatfield came with his parents to San Diego in the mid-1880s. An adherent of the "foul smell" method of cloud compelling, he began experimenting with rain control by mixing various chemicals on the stove in his kitchen. By the turn of the twentieth century, he was mixing batches on a grand scale, producing a smell compared to "a Limburger cheese factory." He would mix his concoction, place it in evaporating pans on tall wooden towers, and let it be vaporized by the sun. Claiming that this system attracted clouds nineteen out of twenty times, he made a deal with the city of Los Angeles—he claimed that he could guarantee at least eighteen inches of rain between mid-December and late April in exchange for $1,000. If they didn't get the rain, he wouldn't collect a cent. Normally, he claimed, Los Angeles's rainfall "rarely exceeds eight or ten inches."

It was a good gamble. His claim that the rainfall rarely exceeded eight or ten inches was simply untrue. Historically, the city had gotten more than eighteen inches in that time period about half the time. Promising eighteen inches of rain—$1,000. Publicity for guessing correctly—priceless.

Soon people were selling "Hatfield umbrellas," and the word raining was sometimes replaced by the term "Hatfielding." Hatfield went on the lecture circuit and was paid handsomely to expound at length on how he was able to draw clouds. Now being called by the honorary title "professor," Hatfield started to believe his own press. He hoped he would be given the opportunity to rid London of its fog and to make the deserts bloom. "I should like to have the contract for watering the desert of Sahara as soon as the French Government can be made to appreciate that I can really make as much rain as my employers order," he boasted.

In late 1915 Hatfield's agent (of course he had an agent) contacted the San Diego City Council. The city had been suffering a drought. Hatfield offered to fill the Moreno Dam to "overflowing" by December 20, 1916, for the sum of $10,000. The council agreed, although a formal written document was never signed by the council. By January 1, 1916, Hatfield was hard at work setting up a tower of stinky chemicals. A few days later the rain started. Hatfield must have jumped for joy when the record rain pelted the city. It rained and rained and rained. It rained so much that on January 27 Lower Otay Dam, southeast of the city, gave way. Crops were ruined, rail connections were wiped out, streets flooded, and San Diego had an estimated death toll of fifty.

When Hatfield tried to collect his prize money, he was chased out of town by an army of farmers wielding pitchforks and other implements of destruction. That's where most accounts end, yet this was not the end of the story.

Hatfield came back and insisted that he had created the deluge and that he deserved to be paid. The council's lawyer argued that Hatfield had done nothing at all. The flood was an "act of God." Eventually city lawyers came up with a settlement that they thought was more than fair. They would agree to pay Hatfield the $10,000 if he would sign a document attesting to his responsibility for the events—which would also make him responsible for the pending claims for damages of about $3.5 million. Hatfield's urge to take credit for "his flood" was dampened. The lawsuit was never settled, and it remained on the books until 1938, when it was finally dismissed as a dead issue.

City Slickers *on* Nature Vacations

When city people are taken out of their natural environment and faced with real nature, the results are often *Schadenfreude*-worthy.

Gemini Wink, a twenty-six-year-old from Louisville, Kentucky, got lost while visiting a friend in Tampa, Florida. He waded into a swamp to take pictures of alligators. To find his way back, he marked his path with duct tape. When he was ready to head back, however, he couldn't find the marks. It was so late, he decided to camp for the night and find his way out of the swamp in daylight. But worried that the alligators would eat him, he climbed up a tree and taped himself to a branch.

Meanwhile, Wink's friend got worried when he didn't come home by dark, so he called the police. They found Wink in the tree, which was only four hundred yards from the friend's house, but he had taped himself down so enthusiastically that they had to climb up the tree and use tools to get him loose.

■■

A park ranger at Lake Mead in Nevada, Jim Burnett, recorded some of his adventures with wildlife and the public in his book *Hey Ranger!* One of his stories involves a snake, some men in a fishing boat, and things they should have learned in biology class—but didn't. Had they been watching the slide show instead of defacing their natural science textbook, they would have remembered that snakes are cold-blooded, and when they get cold they become sluggish. Given this fact of nature, Burnett recommends the following rules if you encounter what you believe is a dead snake:

1. Just leave him alone;
2. Never make assumptions about whether a snake is dead or alive based on its level of activity;
3. If it's just not in your genetic makeup to obey rules 1 and 2 or if the situation absolutely, positively, beyond a shadow of a doubt demands that you take some action concerning the snake, at least never pick it up; and
4. If for some reason beyond my comprehension you decide to break rules 1, 2, and 3, never pick up a snake by the tail, because that leaves the "business end" of the snake free to put you in a Melancholy Situation.

Needless to say, our heroes did not follow this advice. Burnett learned of this when someone came to his ranger station to report that he had found a boat drifting down the river full of fishing gear, a couple of half-consumed beverage cans, and only one occupant—a rattlesnake.

The ranger found the boat and had it towed to the bank, then started exploring farther upstream. There on a sandbar were the two fishermen, waving their arms and waiting for rescue. The snake, it seems, had somehow fallen into the river, and the cold water put it into a state of suspended animation. The boaters saw a dead rattler floating and thought its rattles might make a good souvenir. They fished it out of the water and put it in their boat. Once the hot Nevada air dried the snake off, the fishermen heard an ominous rattling sound. They looked at the snake, and the snake looked at them. Someone was going to have to get off the boat, and the snake wasn't making the move, so the two men leaped overboard. Fortunately, they were wearing their life vests, and they were eventually reunited with their boat.

Politicians *and* Nature: *Schadenfreude* Waiting to Happen

When politicians decide to head into nature for a little R&R, the oddest things happen. On April 20, 1979, President Jimmy Carter was enjoying a relaxing afternoon of fishing in his farm pond in Plains, Georgia.

> He heard a menacing hissing, and next thing you know, he saw a **crazed rabbit** paddling towards him with teeth flashing and nostrils flared.

He heard a menacing hissing, and next thing you know, he saw a crazed rabbit paddling towards him with teeth flashing and nostrils flared.

The Secret Service sat by and did nothing as the president valiantly fought the rodent off with his paddle. Surely this security hole has since been fixed and a unit of rabbit protection detail has been added to the president's entourage after this event. Fortunately for hungering newsmen and standup comedians, a White House photographer captured the battle on film.

Neither the president nor the rabbit was injured in the attack, and no one thought much about it until one day when the president himself told the story at a White House gathering. He thought it was pretty funny, as did his press secretary Jody Powell. Powell's instinct for how the story would play in the media proved to be a bit off. For some reason, he decided to leak the story to an Associated Press reporter just before the Democratic convention.

The bunny story had legs. It was so much more fun than discussing issues of substance. So for more than a week, pundits and comedians discussed every aspect of presidential bunny battles. Conservative George Will called the president timid for not having the rabbit shot. On the other end of the spectrum, tree-hugging types criticized the president for beating on an innocent bunny. Even the Rabbit Breeders Association had something to say. The story was giving rabbits a bad name. "I've never heard of an attack rabbit," a spokesman said.

Instead of being asked about his plans for the nation, everywhere he went Carter was asked about the "Banzai Bunny." Many people believe the rabbit story was the beginning of the end of the Carter presidency. Already fighting the perception that he was weak in dealing with situations like the Iran hostage crisis, the image of the commander in chief fending off Bugs Bunny with a canoe paddle did nothing to help him at the polls.

Interestingly, a few years later, then vice president George H. W. Bush was also menaced by a rabbit. A Secret Service agent (who had presumably received that updated rodent training) had to shoo a rabbit away from the veep at the Denver airport in 1981. That story failed to capture the public's imagination, but don't think George Sr. gets off completely scot-free. He had his own run-in with nature after he got a seat behind the desk in the Oval Office.

During his nineteen-day summer vacation in 1989, Bush decided to go fishing near his summer home in Kennebunkport, Maine. Being president, he had the press corps following him wherever he went, even into the water. A few minutes of video of the president doing a manly outdoor activity would certainly not play badly on the evening news, but then again. . . .

Bush failed to catch a fish on his first outing. It happens to everyone. The next day, still no fish. No fish the next day . . . or the next. Meanwhile, all the other folks on the lake were hoisting in bluefish after bluefish. The press loved it.

By the tenth day, the *Portland [Maine] Press Herald* started publishing a daily "fish watch" next to a drawing of a bluefish inside a red circle with a slash through it. The president's men did their best to spin the story. They explained that although the president himself hadn't exactly caught a fish several members of his fishing party had caught them "under the president's very careful tutelage."

> Although the president himself hadn't exactly caught a fish several members of his fishing party had caught them "under the president's **very careful tutelage.**"

By day thirteen, members of the press corps were wearing T-shirts emblazoned with the newspaper's "no fish" logo. Bush feigned outrage, saying the shirts were "a vicious assault on my ability." He marched off to his boat determined to "murder" some fish. He even brought First Lady Barbara Bush along for good luck.

If Mrs. Bush brought luck to the boat, it didn't affect her husband. Other members of the presidential fishing party kept reeling them in, and George Bush's fish count held steady at zero. By the fifteenth fishless day, Bush's grandchildren gathered at the shore to chant their support. They held up signs saying, "Grampy, You can do it!" and "A Fish A Day Keeps the Press Away."

A White House photographer, Dave Valdes, hooked *two* bluefish on a single line. The president's fish count—still zero. The story had become a national feature. On the very last day of the presidential vacation, Bush made a stop at St. Ann's Episcopal Church and prayed for divine fishing intervention. Then he put on a cap that read USS Bluefish, took a deep breath, and got back in his boat. After a short time a miracle occurred. Bush felt a tug on his line. He reeled in a two-foot, ten-pound bluefish. Reporters and the Secret Service on surrounding boats let out the kind of cheer normally reserved for things like news that a war has ended.

■ ■

It is little details that turn a tragedy into *Schadenfreude*. Try this: A couple of senior citizens go out for an afternoon of bird hunting on a Texas ranch. The hunting buddies had known each other for years. One of the men, a 65-year-old, heard a bird break from cover, and he turned quickly to shoot it with his 12-bore shotgun. It was only after he had swung around and pulled the trigger that he realized his seventy-eight-year-old friend had been standing right behind him. Some of the pellets hit him in the face, and he was rushed to a nearby hospital by ambulance.

> It is **little details** that turn a tragedy into *Schadenfreude*.

Not much *Schadenfreude* there. Oh, but did I mention the sixty-five-year-old was the vice president of the United States and that he was known for his humorless, almost grumpy countenance?

In 2006 Dick Cheney, considered the most powerful vice president in U.S. history, blasted his buddy and earned himself a spot in the *Schadenfreude* Hall of Fame. Late-night talk-show hosts broke out the champagne. "Dick Cheney Hunt Club" T-shirts and bumper stickers were quickly printed. An online gambling site started taking bets on who the veep would mistakenly shoot next. (Odds were on the president.) Elmer Fudd comparisons flew. Even conservative talk-show hosts couldn't resist a few jabs. The accidental-shooting victim, Harry Whittington, survived without any lasting damage, but the jokes will surely follow Dick Cheney for years to come.

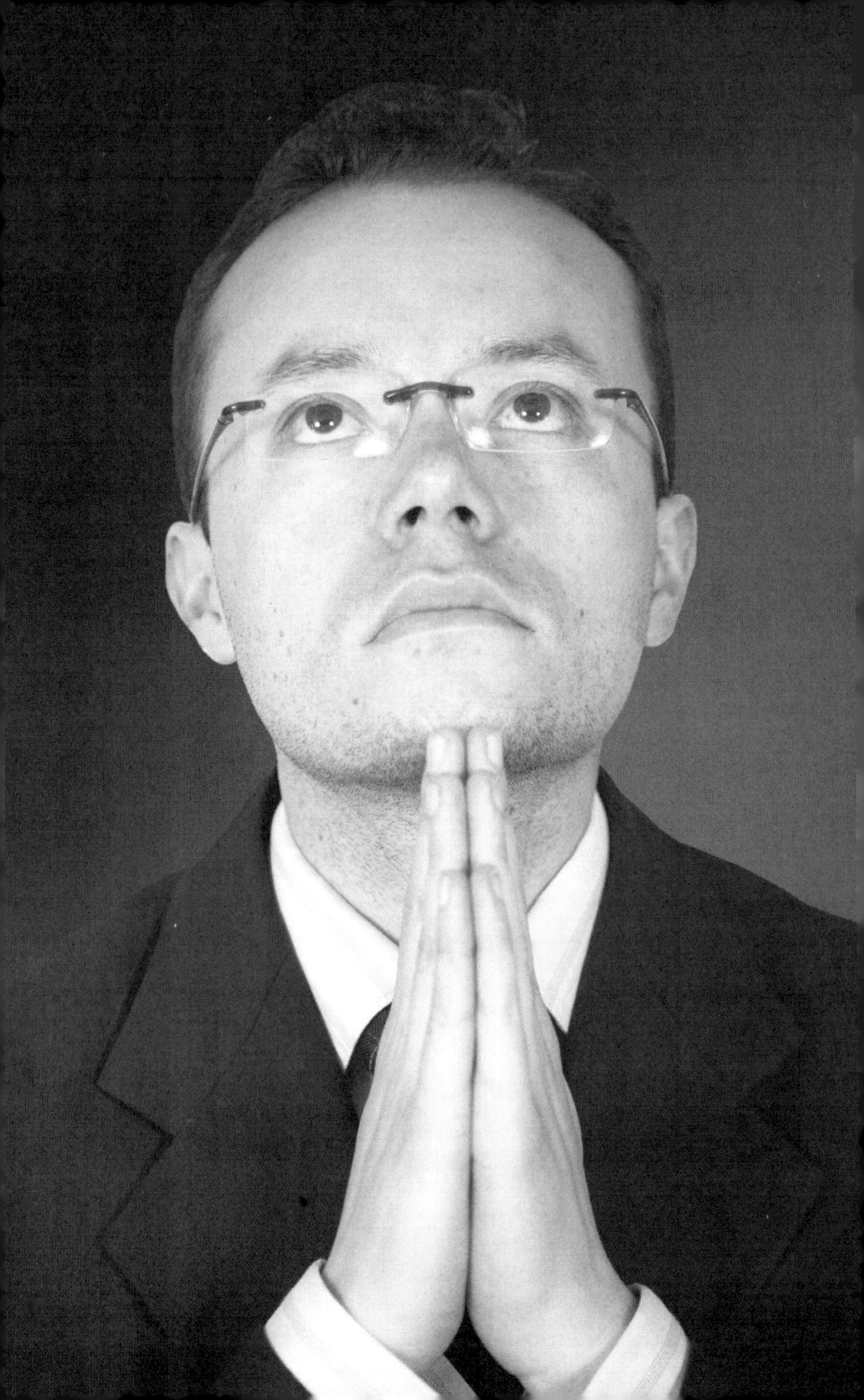

VII.
Publicity Problems

One way to court *Schadenfreude* is to go looking for attention. We can't help but enjoy attempts at publicity that end like they did for the Jacksonville, Florida, Chevrolet dealer who launched a sales campaign featuring the slogan, "Look for it: Something big is going to happen!" A few hours later the showroom ceiling collapsed on six new cars. Here are the stories of some people who went after the limelight and got burned by it.

Rev. Harold Davidson, rector of the parish of Stiffkey in Norfolk, England, was one who craved attention. He tried to make a name for himself as an actor and a stand-up comedian but didn't quite possess the talent he needed to sustain that career. His true talent was in self-promotion, and he decided to apply this trait to a career in the ministry. It was only logical, as he was descended from a long line of Protestant ministers. Yet he lacked a certain ministerial temperament. After he found the community surrounding his small Norfolk church a bit stifling for his taste, he popped off to London whenever he could.

> His **true talent** was in self-promotion, and he decided to apply this trait to a career in the ministry.

His special calling was to "save" young women. He especially liked to save pretty girls. He often enticed them to the church by pretending to confuse them with famous actresses and then promising them roles in theatrical productions. The church was not convinced that Davidson was moved only by the spirit in his dealings with women, and they held a hearing to defrock him. Davidson arrived an hour late and breaking with protocol walked to the altar ahead of the bishop instead of following him. This behavior did little to win the bishops over, and he was dismissed from his post.

After that, he was free to chase publicity full time. He spent his days protesting his innocence and preached at a circus side-show in a booth lined with his press clippings. He then decided to go on a hunger strike. He sat inside a barrel and refused to eat until the church reinstated him. Initially, the crowds were sympathetic, but after a while they started to notice he wasn't losing any weight. He was secretly nibbling from a stash of food whenever he took a potty break. The outraged authorities arrested him for attempted suicide by starvation.

In 1937 Davidson made his last attempt at headlines. He would protest his innocence from inside a lion's cage. The lion mauled him to death.

■■

By the mid-1980s, the image of the cocky former *20/20* correspondent Geraldo Rivera had taken a bit of a beating, and Rivera was determined to prove his critics wrong. The former lawyer's journalistic career began with great promise with a groundbreaking exposé of abuse at a New York State mental institution.

His penchant for showboating and putting his own feelings into a story earned him many critics, although it does seem to have paved the way for a whole breed of opinionated reporters who now dominate the airways. When ABC decided not to renew Rivera's contract, he went in search of a story that would put him on the map, and he thought he found it in the Lexington Hotel in Chicago. The hotel was known to have been a headquarters for Al Capone's mob from 1928 to 1931. In 1986 the Sunbow Foundation decided to rehabilitate the hotel for resale and discovered several sites in which it believed vaults had been constructed. Rivera got the rights to blast out the secret vaults on live television and show their contents to the world.

The Mystery of Al Capone's Vaults was one of the most hyped television shows of the season. "I think this will be watched by more people than ever watched anything I did at the network," Rivera boasted to the *Chicago Sun-Times*, adding, "I'm one of the few people who ever got a 43 share in prime time." This was true. Rivera's report on Elvis Presley in 1979 received a 43 share, although some people might attribute that more to the star power of Elvis than to Rivera.

In any case, he was right about the ratings for the highly advertised *Mystery of Al Capone's Vaults*. People gathered to watch the show at 1920s-themed Capone safecracking parties. The audience rating for WGN/Channel 9 was 57.4, with a 73 share of the audience, the second-highest rating ever recorded in Chicago, second only to the previous January's Super Bowl. Unfortunately, Rivera may have ended up wishing it hadn't been.

He introduced the two-hour broadcast by saying, "This is an adventure you and I will take together." After the buildup of the legend of Al Capone and other Chicago mob lore, the big moment had arrived. A charge was blown, and a wall fell down, revealing nothing but an empty bottle. Not knowing what else to do, the self-promoting journalist finished by singing "Chicago, Chicago, that toddlin' town."

Crime *and* Publicity Don't Mix

It would seem obvious, but if you're doing something illegal, it's best to keep it to yourself. Throughout history, however, there have been people who were so attracted to attention that they just couldn't keep their mouths shut. (You'll also find criminals who unwittingly drew attention to themselves in the midst of their crime sprees in the section on Incompetent Criminals).

Before we get to the previously anonymous publicity seekers, a cautionary note for anyone whose face is already splashed across tabloid covers. If you're already famous, people will watch what you do. You're not likely to get away with petty theft. For example, after the former child star Dana Plato tried to rob a 7-Eleven for drug money, The cashier called 911 and said, "I've just been robbed by the girl from *Diff'rent Strokes*." She'd have been fairly easy to find, even if she hadn't decided to return to the scene of the crime. Plato's death at age 34 from a drug overdose makes her story too tragic to work as a universal *Schadenfreude* tale, so let's focus instead on a Hollywood thief whose misfortune we can fairly guiltlessly enjoy: Winona Ryder.

Most shoplifting cases do not even make the papers, much less attract the paparazzi. But few shoplifting cases involve someone whose name was once tattooed on Johnny Depp's arm. And as the *London*

Independent pointed out, ". . . nobody ever went broke following the old tabloid maxim that you should always adopt an attitude of envious resentment towards the rich and famous."

Winona was arrested outside a Saks Fifth Avenue department store in Beverly Hills. She'd stashed about $5,000 worth of stolen clothing. Of course, being the Saks of Beverly Hills, this amounted to about three things. The juxtaposition of the words "Academy Award nominee" and "shoplifting" left many people scratching their heads. The *Edward Scissorhands* star commanded as much as $11 million a film. In 1996 she'd helped Giorgio Armani promote his Manhattan stores. She'd been chosen as one of *People* magazine's 50 Most Beautiful People in 1997. What on earth was she thinking?

First, she told the security guard, Colleen Rainey, that her assistant should have paid for the items. She didn't have an assistant with her that day. Next, she claimed she thought she had an account there. Then she changed her story and explained that she was only playing at shoplifting to prepare for a movie role. Television comedians soon came up with titles for this movie such as "Saks, Lies and Videotape," and "Dude, Where's the Security Camera?"

The twenty-four-hour television news networks gleefully filled the public's need to stare at celebrities gone bad, camping outside the court and airing a play-by-play of every nail-biting moment. On one occasion the flashbulbs revealed a visible panty line under her court attire and the Drudge Files, the same muckraking Internet site that first broke the Lewinsky case, blared the exaggerated headline: "Panties on Parade: Winona Goes to Court in See-Through Frock."

After all was said and done, the actress was placed on probation and fined $2,700 and was ordered to pay restitution to the store and the court. As a curious *Schadenfreude* side note, Winona Ryder went on to appear in a film based on *The Darwin Awards*, the Web site and book series that takes pleasure in stories of people who suffer stupid deaths. The film was critically panned.

Some gossip columnists have argued that the shoplifting case put an end to Winona's box office appeal, although her diminished screen presence may have more to do with the fact that *Pirates of the Caribbean* actress Keira Knightley looks just like her and is fourteen years younger.

■ ■

More interesting, however, are the folks who had never seen the glare of the spotlight before they took to crime. Take, for example, Mary Carleton, the boastful con artist. Mary became bored with her seventeenth-century life as a shoemaker's wife with two children. So she decided to take off to Dover, England. She found it easy to con rich men out of their money. First, she convinced a wealthy surgeon to marry her by omitting the detail that she was already married.

Faced with bigamy charges, she traveled to Germany and quickly found her next victim—I mean fiancé. He lavished jewels and money on her. She managed to avoid another charge of bigamy by leaving him at the altar. Back in England, in 1663, she told everyone that she was a German princess with a sad story. A number of men at the inn were so taken with her tale that they "lent" her all their money. She promised to give it back as she skipped off to the next inn.

An innkeeper named Mr. King thought the princess was charming, and he introduced her to his brother-in-law. Carleton, now well invested in her own story, was offended that a commoner would try to court her, but eventually she agreed to marry him. The wedded bliss was cut short when someone recognized her, and she was charged with bigamy again.

She managed to escape by joining a traveling theatrical troupe. She entertained the crowds with a play she wrote and starred in herself. It was called *The German Princess*, and it was a boastful account of her own exploits. In order to really drum up interest with audiences, she made no secret of the fact that it was a drama of her real life adventures.

At first it was a great success. Mary was as quick and witty on stage as she had been in conning lovers. If her admirers thought she had changed her ways, they were mistaken. Twice men who saw her on stage tried to court her, and twice she took their money and disappeared. On another stop, she asked a French weaver to bring her some silks worth £40 (nearly £6,000 in today's money). She entertained the weaver with some wine and charmed him with her stories. Then she

> In order to really drum up interest with audiences, she made no secret of the fact that it was a drama of her real life adventures.

took the silk into another room to show it to her niece. After some time the weaver became concerned. He was told that his "customer" had already left the inn with her bags in tow.

The princess now needed someone to turn the silks into a fine dress. She agreed to hire a master tailor to outfit her for a grand ball. He finished the dress and brought it to her just in time. Then, before he was paid, he stayed to enjoy the festivities. Mary refilled his wine glass so often that he had to be helped home by his wife. While that was happening, Mary, in her lovely gown, made a hasty exit. So did most of the silver tankards, cutlery, and jewelry that had been in the room.

Each time she pulled another con, Mary added it to her performance. She couldn't get enough of the crowd's laughter and applause. Inevitably, one of her victims bought a ticket to the show. He returned the next evening and brought a friend—a policeman. He sat and watched a full confession unfold on stage. Her next performance was at Old Bailey, London's central criminal court. There she was found guilty of bigamy and sentenced to be hanged.

■ ■

Not all criminals nabbed by their own publicity are caught bragging about their exploits. Sometimes the glare of the spotlight turns their lucky day into a very unlucky day, indeed.

In 1990, Amanda Guild, an avid bowler and thirty-year-old mom, was playing in a tournament at the American Lanes in Buena Vista, near Saginaw, Michigan. This week everything was rolling right. Although her league average was only 131, she ended her series with an average of 196—65 pins higher than her usual average. She was proud when she was named "Bowler of the Week." The *Saginaw News* even ran a story with her photo. Amanda's friends clipped copies of the article. So did a U.S. marshal, Steven Kurkowski. He'd been looking everywhere for Amanda, who, it turns out, wasn't just a bowling mom; she was a fugitive from justice who had fled from Tennessee to her hometown of Saginaw one step ahead of the law. She was wanted for her role in a major interstate money-laundering and drug-trafficking operation.

Now that the Feds knew where she hung out, they were able to make an arrest at the bowling center. They arrived during the fourth frame of her first game. When she showed up for her preliminary hearing the next morning, she was still wearing her bowling shirt with the "Bowler of the Week" pin attached.

■■

Politicians are notorious for seeking attention. One who should not have was Dorothy Joyner, a Republican candidate for mayor of Baltimore in 1999. Polls that year showed that crime was the issue that most concerned Baltimoreans. So when Joyner appeared on the *Newsmaker* TV program, she spoke at length about crime.

"I think that we need to retrain our police officers," she said. "Our officers need to steer clear of the abrasiveness they project. Instead of abrasiveness, what about courtesy? What about manners?"

The message had an impact on one police officer who happened to be watching. He recognized the candidate as Dorothy Joyner, wanted for burglary. He called his supervisors, who had a police car waiting for her as she left the studios of WBFF-TV in Baltimore and arrested her. Cameras captured her leaving in handcuffs. Hopefully the officers were polite about the whole thing.

■■

In 1988 Patrick Quinn became the biggest winner in the history of the *Super Password* game show hosted by Bert Convy. The show consisted of two contestants paired with celebrity guests. Contestants would try to guess the identities of people, places, and things with one-word clues. After four days on the show, the thirty-six-year-old had won $58,000.

When his episodes aired, an Alaskan viewer thought the contestant looked familiar and called the police. It turns out that Quinn was wanted for fraud across the country. He was a conman who'd stolen everything, including the name Patrick Quinn. (It was the name of his old college professor).

His real name was Kerry Dee Ketcham, and when he showed up to collect his winnings, he was arrested for insurance fraud. He went straight to jail without passing go or collecting his $58,600.

■■

On June 16, 1998, Elizabeth Ann Oliver became the first woman to broadcast the birth of her son live over the Internet. She said that she wanted to help educate other women about birth. The decision to broadcast a birth over America's Health Network Web site drew strong criticism, but that only gave the event greater publicity.

At least fifty thousand people tried to log onto the Web site, which had been set up for about ten thousand people at a time. Cameras were held at the mother's side as nurses stood strategically to block any view of the delivery itself. The picture was fuzzy, but clear stills from the event were sent to television news stations. One nightly news viewer recognized Elizabeth as a criminal wanted for passing bad checks. In fact, she was wanted on *nine* misdemeanor warrants in Orange County. She turned herself over to police and was eventually cleared of the bad-check charges because too much time had elapsed since the original charges were filed.

Never Pick a Fight *with* People Who Buy Ink *by the* Barrel

If you're going to go toe to toe with the media, you'd better be careful. If there's anything about you that wouldn't play well in the news, chances are you're not going to come out the winner.

Here is a tip: If you're running for political office and having a questionable relationship with a woman who is not your wife, don't challenge the press to follow you around. Sure, it seems like common sense, but in 1987, when Democratic presidential hopeful Gary Hart was questioned about claims he was a womanizer, this is exactly what he did. Even Democrats couldn't help but feel a little *Schadenfreude* as they watched the inevitable results.

Hart began to pique investigative reporters' curiosity during the 1984 campaign when they discovered that sometime between his early college years and his transfer from Yale Divinity School to Yale Law School, the candidate had changed his name from Hartpence to Hart. Of course, a change to a shorter name by a person seeking a public career is not all that noteworthy. There was this one other thing, though.

He'd also changed his birth date. His birth certificate showed that he had been born in 1936 and not, as he had been telling everyone, 1937. "It's whatever the records say," he said by means of clarification.

The inevitable question was, "What else isn't he telling us?" Rumors were flying around Washington of dirty laundry and marital infidelity. The famously private politician became annoyed with people questioning his veracity. "When I tell the truth, I expect my word to be taken as truth," he said. "Obviously, if I don't tell the truth and people can prove it, that's a very disastrous thing." Indeed.

Walter Mondale eventually won the Democratic Party's nomination and the opportunity to be crushed in the 1984 election by the charismatic actor Ronald Reagan. Hart went back to the Senate and waited. On April 13, 1987, he once again announced his candidacy for the presidency. "As a candidate," he promised, "I can almost guarantee that I'm going to make some mistakes." Truer words were never spoken.

> "As a candidate," he promised, "I can almost guarantee that I'm going to make some mistakes." **Truer words** were never spoken.

The old charge of philandering continued to annoy the candidate. In a May 1987 *New York Times Magazine* profile, he gave a challenge. "Follow me around. I don't care. I'm serious. If anybody wants to put a tail on me, go ahead. They'd be very bored." They did, and they weren't.

The *Miami Herald* staked out his Washington townhouse and discovered that Hart had spent most of one weekend with a blonde woman not his wife. Hart said he had "no personal relationship" with that woman, whose identity would later be revealed as actress and model Donna Rice. She explained that she was at Hart's house to pick up a book.

But there was this other little matter. Rice and her friend Lynn Armandt, Hart, and Hart's friend Bill Broadhurst had all taken an overnight cruise to Bimini on a yacht with a name—the *Monkey Business*—that was rather unfortunate if you're trying to avoid a political scandal. Hart continued to protest that the trip was absolutely innocent, but the photo of Hart with Rice on his lap and the footage that CBS released of the candidate relaxing on the *Monkey Business* with a different woman, the winner of a "Miss Hot Bod" beauty pageant, really didn't do anything to help.

As word was spreading that the *Washington Post* was about to go public with proof positive of Hart's womanizing, the candidate withdrew from the race.

■ ■

A quote that is often attributed to Abraham Lincoln is, "'Tis better to be silent and be thought a fool, than to speak and remove all doubt." This is why if someone calls you an idiot in the paper you're best to just let it go. Here are a few cautionary tales to illustrate the point.

On June 23, 1918, the *Chicago Tribune* accused Henry Ford of being an "ignorant idealist." "The man is so incapable of thought that he cannot see the ignominy of his own performance," the paper wrote. Ford sued for $1 million, and the religiously followed celebrity trial became a showcase of Ford's ignorance. The *Chicago Tribune*'s attorney asked if he knew anything about the American Revolution, to which Ford answered, "I understand there was one in 1812." When asked about the one that happened in 1776, he said, "I didn't pay much attention to such things." Asked to define the word "ballyhoo," he said it was a "blackguard, I guess." And who was Benedict Arnold? "A writer."

Ford did win the case, but it was a Pyrrhic victory. The judge awarded him only six cents in damages. Small compensation for so much self-inflicted egg on the face.

■ ■

William Scott, Republican senator from Virginia from 1972 to 1979, was apparently trained in the Ford school of media relations. When an obscure publication, the *New Times*, wrote that he was one of the dumbest men in the Senate and one of the least effective, Scott immediately held a press conference to deny his stupidity. The press conference gave the local story national attention.

Not that he needed to make an announcement to shine a light on his shortcomings. He only had to open his mouth. For example, during a Pentagon briefing in which army officials were discussing missile silos, he is reported to have said, "Wait a minute! I'm not interested in agriculture. I want the military stuff."

In 1975 he visited several Middle Eastern nations on a fact-finding mission and managed to, in the words of one State Department official, "insult almost every country—especially Israel." It may have been his question to Prime Minister Yitzhak Rabin, "What's all this Gaza stuff?" While he was on a tour of the Suez Canal, Scott reportedly told Egyptian premier Anwar El-Sadat, "I've always wanted to see the Persian Gulf." He also refused to enter a mosque because it wasn't "a Christian building."

Scott denied having made the comments but this time did not hold a press conference to issue the denial.

Spin Out of Control *and* Comical Crisis Management

Companies pay millions of dollars to advertising and PR firms, and generally speaking, they are trying to make the public think their products are good. Things sometimes go wrong when executives are allowed to open their mouths and speak on their company's behalf.

In 1991 Gerald Ratner, the head of Britain's biggest jewelry chain, was a great success story. Almost a decade before, he had taken a chain of jewelry stores that were losing money and expanded it into a chain of more than two thousand stores. He bought up rival retailers, and by 1991, despite a recession, he was making profits of $195 million. Life was good. He had a £600,000-a-year salary, lived in a £1.6 million mansion, and had his very own Sikorsky helicopter. An analyst asked Ratner what could go wrong with the company, and Ratner said he didn't know.

That was the day before he decided to reveal the secret of his success in a speech before Britain's venerable Institute of Directors. He explained how Ratners was able to keep prices low. Their products were, like the Ratners sherry decanter that sold for £4.95, "total crap." He went on to quip that a pair of the company's 99p earrings cost "about the same as a . . . prawn sandwich, and probably wouldn't last as long."

Suddenly everything came crashing down. The value of the company fell by £500 million. The press hounded him, he lost his job, he had to sell his house, and—the biggest insult of all—the group he'd built up for twenty years dropped his name from the sign and became Signet.

To this day in British business circles, the expression "doing a Ratner" is used to describe anyone who puts his foot in his mouth in a spectacular way, especially by speaking an ugly truth about the products of one's own company. Here are a few others who have pulled a Ratner:

In 2000 Anita Roddick, the Body Shop tycoon, said that most antiwrinkle creams are "a load of pap." In 2002 lottery sales dropped after Dianne Thompson, chief executive of Camelot, said anyone buying a ticket would "be lucky to win a tenner." That same year Keith Cochrane, the chief executive of Stagecoach, described his American bus passengers as "riff-raff." In 2004 Vittorio Radice of Marks and Spencer made unflattering headlines when he said fat customers drove young people from the store by "trying on size 26 elasticated-waist trousers." In 2004 Barclaycard's chief executive Matt Barrett called his bank's credit cards "too expensive" and said he'd advise his children against having one. And most disgustingly, in 2001 Lloyds Bank told its association members that the September 11 attacks were a "historical opportunity" for insurance underwriters to make money.

■■

Individuals occasionally have to manage a PR crisis. You may not be aware of this, but those chartered accountants can really party. One New Year's eve, Howard Potter, a spokesman for the Association of Chartered Certified Accountants in Cardiff, Wales, enjoyed himself so much that he couldn't even remember what had happened. His friends, on the other hand, couldn't stop talking about it. Whatever his adventures, they seem to have involved buying lots of drinks for people he discovered when he got his credit-card bill. "I could have bought a car with what I spent," he said. To rectify the situation, Potter decided to take out an ad in the newspaper to offer a "contrite, abject and public apology" to the people he "castigated, vilified, embarrassed or worse, bored."

The ad didn't have quite the effect he was looking for: he was fired. "We don't object to him having a drink," said the new spokesman for the ACCA, "but to how he drew it to public attention."

■■

Our commander in chief, George W. Bush, put his foot in his mouth during a 2006 press conference. Bush has a habit of joking with reporters and often comments on their attire. When Peter Wallsten of the *Los Angeles Times* stood to ask a question about the Valerie Plame investigation, the President quipped: "Are you going to ask that question with shades on?"

Wallsten answered: "I can take them off."

"I'm interested in the shade look, seriously," said Mr. Bush.

"All right, I'll keep it, then."

"For the viewers, there's no sun."

"I guess it depends on your perspective," Wallsten replied.

Wallsten is legally blind. He wears dark glasses because he has Stargardt's disease, a genetic disorder whose degenerative effect can be slowed by wearing sunglasses and avoiding bright light. The president later called the reporter to apologize.

■■

Crisis management is one of the greatest challenges of any PR flack. Few spokespersons have had to maintain their spin under such adverse circumstances as Mohammed Saeed al-Sahhaf, the Iraqi information minister, charged with representing Saddam Hussein's government as British and American troops were swarming into Baghdad.

A graduate of Baghdad University with a degree in English literature, al-Sahhaf had been Iraq's foreign minister for a decade before becoming the mouthpiece for the doomed regime. Despite all evidence to the contrary (for example, the sound of gunfire in the background), al-Sahhaf was resolute that allied forces had not invaded Baghdad. The more hopeless the situation, the more he clung to his Wizard of Oz stance. (Pay no attention to that tank behind the curtain!)

"The infidels are committing suicide by the hundreds on the gates of Baghdad.... Be assured, Baghdad is safe, protected."

On April 7, 2003, after U.S. troops stormed Saddam Hussein's palace, he said, "There is no presence of the American columns in the city of Baghdad at all.... We besieged them and killed most of them." He made one more appearance at his post the next day. The following day Baghdad fell.

Somehow the Americans and the British couldn't help but feel an odd affection for this man's admirable ability to ignore airports being taken and tanks rolling through the streets. The Americans dubbed him "Baghdad Bob," while his British nickname was "Comical Ali."

John Buckley, Bob Dole's spokesman during the 1996 presidential campaign, told *Slate*'s Timothy Noah that he looked at al-Sahhaf with "nothing but admiration, because when you're going down, style counts.... Why try to get credible at this late date?"

He has his own "fan" site, www.welovetheiraqiinformationminister.com, and an enterprising company even marketed a talking action figure with some of his most blustery quotes.

Problematic Protests

It's not only family values and conservative political candidates who get on their high horses. Those lefty, vegan, peacenik, whale-hugging protestors can get a little holier than thou as well. There are a lot of people who would love to see Daryl Hannah fall out of a tree. These stories are for you.

Sometimes environmental activists are accused of being alarmist and distorting facts to prove their agenda. As a spokesman for the environmental activist group Greenpeace, Steve Smith spent much of his time reacting to these kinds of claims and denying them. Then there was that one time he went out of his way to prove them correct.

> Those lefty, vegan, peacenik, whale-hugging protestors can get a little **holier than thou** as well.

When President George W. Bush was visiting Pennsylvania in 2006 to promote his nuclear energy policy, Greenpeace took a novel approach to highlighting the flaws in his plan. They let the media fill them in themselves. Specifically, a fact sheet released by Smith described nuclear reactors as a "volatile and dangerous source of energy.... In the twenty years since the Chernobyl tragedy, the world's worst nuclear accident, there have been nearly [FILL IN ALARMIST AND ARMAGEDDONIST FACTOID HERE.]"

The spokesman later explained that a colleague had been making a joke with the draft and that it should not have been released. The final version, with its references to Armageddon excised, got much less attention for Greenpeace than the original version had.

■■

An animal-rights demonstrator, dressed in a cow costume, had to call off his protest when he was pelted with cartons of milk. In October 2002 Sean Gilford of PETA (People for the Ethical Treatment of Animals), clad in bovine gear, planned to stand outside Aberdeen Grammar School in Scotland and hand out literature on the hazards of milk and the poor treatment of cows on factory farms.

He had little time to ruminate before about a hundred students carrying banners and shouting "milk for the masses" surrounded him and pelted him and an unidentified second protestor with cartons and doused them in milk. Mr. Gilford remained idealistic in the face of his reverse protest. "I'm sure they will still go home and think about our message," he said.

■■

In 2003 Jody Mason of Olympia, Washington, watched George W. Bush on television and became hopping mad. In his speech Bush warned Saddam Hussein and his sons to leave Iraq or face war. Mason could not sit there and let war happen; he needed to protest.

He wanted to make a clear and dramatic statement. His plan was to chain himself to the entrance of the local office of the U.S. Department of Energy and block access. He showed up early and padlocked himself to the building. At around 11:45 a few employees walked by. When he told them he was protesting war, they just seemed confused.

There was good reason. Mason had fettered himself to the wrong building. He was at the Grange building. The Grange is a non-profit, non-partisan group that advocates for farmers and rural residents.

Dedication *to the* Cause

Some martyrs are a little more determined than others. Boston city councilman Felix Arroyo wanted to make a strong statement against the war in Iraq. What could be more effective than a hunger strike? Of course, a hunger strike requires a lot of sacrifice. So Arroyo amended his protest. He would only allow himself liquids. Anything to bring our troops home. Then Arroyo decided he didn't want to be too fanatical about the whole hunger thing. He would limit himself to liquids during daylight hours. At night he could go ahead and eat whatever he wanted.

Thinking that perhaps he was carrying this whole protest a bit far, he decided to scale back a bit and limit his hunger strike to the second and fourth Fridays of each month. So every other Friday nothing but fluids would sustain the councilman until after dark. In the face of a great moral crisis, it's good to see someone stepping up to the table, except every other Friday at lunch. Surprisingly, he was not able to convince his fellow legislators to join him in his passionate protest.

■■

The Animal Liberation Front is a radical animal-rights organization that "carries out direct action against animal abuse in the form of rescuing animals and causing financial loss to animal exploiters, usually through the damage and destruction of property." If you own a lab rat or a tank of live lobsters watch out for these guys. If, on the other hand, you own something a little larger, say, a Siberian tiger, you may have less to worry about.

The group's illegal actions have caused widespread outrage and have occasionally backfired, as in 1998, when they tried to show their respect for the sanctity of animal life by releasing sixty-five hundred mink from a mink farm. Thousands of hungry mink went on a killing spree across the English countryside, feasting on household pets like cats, small dogs, hamsters, and guinea pigs. They ravished fisheries and farms. They made a wild-bird sanctuary "a restaurant." One liberated mink killed a beloved fourteen-year-old kestrel named Spitfire who made educational trips to local schools.

> Thousands of hungry mink went on a **killing spree** across the English countryside, feasting on household pets like cats, small dogs, hamsters, and guinea pigs.

Even more unfortunate for the wild-animal population is the fact that the mink farm was located near one of the last remaining habitats of the highly endangered water vole, which British conservation officer Ian Davidson called "the fastest-declining animal in the United Kingdom, probably declining faster than the white rhino or tiger." The starving mink were just the right size to slide down vole holes.

And the mink themselves may have been safer on their farm. Wandering through homes and pubs, they were shot and pounded on the heads with mallets. So this gives you some idea of the tactics of this group.

You might think that a group sometimes dubbed "animal terrorists" would stop at nothing to free creatures it believed were suffering abuse at a circus, but there is the whole matter of razor-sharp teeth to consider. It's not that the members of the Swiss faction of the Front didn't give it a go. They broke into the Circus Royal at night with every intention of stealing the rare white tiger and handing him to a zoo. But when they were face to face with the six-hundred-pound carnivore, the liberationists changed their minds—and stole a bunny instead.

They then posted pictures of their daring rescue online. They are seen wearing black army uniforms and balaclavas and holding the rabbit. Circus director Oliver Skreining said, "The pet rabbit was not even in the show; it belonged to our clown's six-year-old daughter."

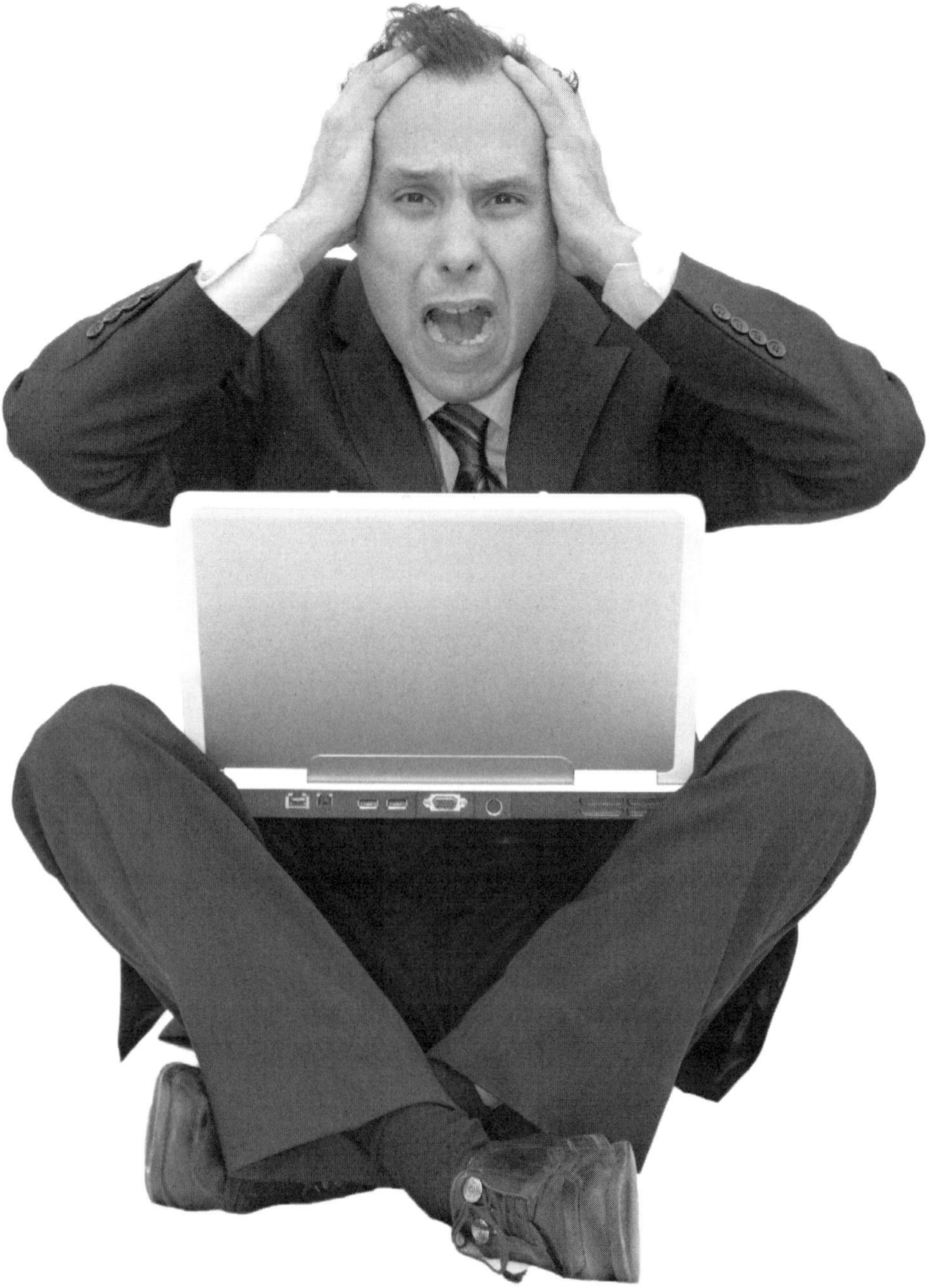

VIII.
Incompetence

Each of us wants to be a master of our chosen profession. At least we hope not to suck at it. Incompetence is a misfortune. It is certainly nothing to celebrate—unless it's someone else's. Sure, you've made some mistakes at work, had a few disastrous days. Maybe you've lost an account or destroyed a deal. But then there are the people who go above and beyond. They are so spectacularly ill-suited for their chosen fields of endeavor that their attempts become a sheer joy (for everyone else) to watch. At the center is a poor guy doing his best, and you can't help but love his bungled attempts. The person you're cheering, well, he'd probably rather be cheered for something else. As with Vinko Bogataj (see Introduction), we love them for the agony of their defeat.

The Wide World *of* Sports

Harry Heitman may be to baseball what Vinko Bogataj was to skiing: a symbol of the Agony of Defeat. It wasn't always that way. Heitman began as a local hero, the "Iron Man" of the international league team the Rochester Red Wings from 1916 to 1918. He earned his nickname by pitching and winning both games of two doubleheaders in one memorable five-day period. He was clearly heading to the big leagues and baseball stardom.

When he finally got to the majors, the story was a little different. Heitman's brief biography leads off the Bruce Nash and Allan Zullo book, *The Baseball Hall of Shame*. "Hapless Harry," as they call him, "holds a dishonor no other can claim." Heitman's major league career lasted all of a half hour.

He suited up for Brooklyn and started the second game of a doubleheader on July 27, 1918, against the St. Louis Cardinals at Ebbets

Field. Heitman became the hit man, allowing two singles and two triples and only managing one out before he was yanked without completing a single inning. After that he hung up his glove and shipped off with the navy to fight in World War I. He finished his major-league career with an official ERA of 108.00. As incredible as that stat may sound, the Society for American Baseball Research wants to tweak this number.

"Since he had no innings pitched," said Lyle Spatz, the chair of SABR's Records Committee, "because he faced four batters and all scored, his earned-run average should actually be infinity. We're going about getting that changed in future encyclopedias." An earned run average of infinity is a stunning and perhaps unbeatable achievement in failure.

But did the people who witnessed the game realize they were seeing baseball history in the making? It seems they did not. A reporter for the *Brooklyn Eagle* didn't think Heitman's showing was that bad. "The poor start made by Harry Heitman in the second game should be discounted and the 'Iron Man' of the International League" given another big league trial," he wrote. The reporter blamed his poor showing on a questionable call against Brooklyn by the umpire that "put [Heitman] in a bad way right off the reel."

Perhaps this assessment should have been part of the baseball player's obituary, which would have put his only major-league appearance into the context of his brilliant minor-league career, not to mention his service to our country. But this was not to be. A newspaper strike shut down nine New York–area papers from December 12 through the 28 in 1958, and Heitman's passing on December 15 was not noted with an obit. And so he is remembered for the dubious honor of throwing the only infinite ERA in major-league baseball history.

■■

The Harry Heitman of bullfighting was Rafael Gomez Ortega, born in 1882 and known as "El Gallo" (the rooster). His father, Fernando Gómez García, and his younger brother, José Gómez Ortega, were both famous matadors. They were known for their skill, but Rafael was known for his flamboyance. Occasionally, as if by chance, he would perform admirably in the ring. But he was loved for the particular style he brought to running away. He made a show out of everything he did in and out of the ring; he would stride into the ring, throw a flower to a beautiful woman, and then dedicate the fight to her in a poetic speech fit for Don Quixote.

"To thee alone I dedicate the life of this bull," he would intone. Then he would strike a pose and await the entrance of the noble beast. When it charged at him, he employed his signature technique, "sudden flight," which was exactly what it sounded like. It was a bit like the Monty Python line, "Maybe if we run away faster, we'll confuse it." He dropped his cape, sprinted across the ring, and dove over the barrier.

Ernest Hemingway was a fan. He wrote about the nervous matador in his books and once said that for a bull to kill El Gallo would be "in bad taste." The bullfighter was such a fan favorite that he was brought out of retirement seven times by popular demand. In his last fight in 1918, he gave his longest and most flowery speech, dedicated the bull to three different dignitaries, and then refused to kill it because it had winked at him. The crowd loved the show, but El Gallo's brother—not so much. He jumped into the ring himself to kill the animal and save the family honor. El Gallo died in 1960 at the age of 72 of a kidney infection.

■ ■

Most baseball players dream of tying a major-league batting record and receiving a standing ovation. They don't dream of achieving this in the way Ron "Rocky" Swoboda of the New York Mets did in 1969.

It all happened in front of fifty-five thousand fans who had come to watch the Mets go up against the St. Louis Cardinals at Shea Stadium. Rocky didn't start the game to cheers from the hometown crowd. In the first inning, Rocky struck out. The fans booed. They booed again in the third inning when Rocky took a called third strike and slunk back to the dugout. The boos were deafening in the fourth inning when he struck out. Leading off the seventh inning, Rocky continued his striking streak.

With no help from Rocky, the Mets were beating the Cardinals 5–1 at the bottom of the eighth inning. This is when the fans started to realize they might have a chance to witness baseball history if only Rocky could get to the plate. Only 12 men in a century of baseball had managed to strike out at five consecutive at bats in a single nine-inning game.

Rocky was the sixth batter due up. After two walks and two outs, Donn Clendenon was up to bat with Rocky Swoboda on deck. Clendenon was given an intentional walk. The crowd went wild.

"I didn't want to strike out," the batter later told the authors of *The Baseball Hall of Shame* series, "But if I didn't, the fans would have felt cheated. . . . I told myself, I owe it to the fans to strike out." The first pitch from Ron Willis was a strike, and the cheers were almost deafening. When the umpire called the next pitch a ball, the fans booed. The last thing they wanted was an anticlimactic walk. Next Rocky fouled off. He was only one bad swing away from immortality. A swing and a miss—Rocky missed it by a mile.

> He was only one bad swing away from immortality. A swing and a miss—Rocky missed it by a **mile.**

Oh, somewhere in this favored land the sun is shining bright,
The band is playing somewhere, and somewhere hearts are light,
The bleacher bums are laughing, as little children shout;
There is great joy in Metville—mighty Rocky has struck out!

The fifty-five-thousand-member crowd leaped to their feet as one and whooped and shouted with delight. The only one in the stadium who was not celebrating was Rocky Swoboda. He dropped his bat and hung his head in shame as he walked to his outfield position.

Fortunately, Rocky's performance didn't cost the Mets the game. If it had, Rocky later said, "I would have been eating my heart out. As it is, I'm only eating out one ventricle."

∎∎

Jose Nunez of the Toronto Blue Jays was perfectly competent as a pitcher. As a batter, however, it was a different story. During a spring-training game, his shortcomings were on full and embarrassing display.

Now, to be fair to Nunez, the question of batting usually didn't come up. The Toronto Blue Jays are part of the American League. In this league you're allowed to have a designated hitter who stands in for the pitcher in the lineup. When Nunez was in the minor leagues, they also played with a designated-hitter rule. The National League, however, doesn't have a designated hitter.

In March 1988 the Jays played against the Philadelphia Phillies by National League rules. Nunez would have to bat for the first time *ever* in his professional career. Turns out it's not one of his best skills, but he gave it the old college try. He walked to the batter's box with a serious expression, tapped the end of the bat on the plate, then waggled it like the other guys did. At that moment he felt a tap on his shoulder. It was the home-plate umpire, Dave Pallone. He tactfully pointed out that Nunez still had his warm-up jacket on. Nunez went back to the dugout, took off the jacket, and resumed his menacing pose.

That's when Pallone cleared his throat. Nunez was wearing the wrong batting helmet. He was a lefty and was sporting the helmet for a right-handed hitter, with the earflap leaving the wrong ear exposed to an errant ball. No problem; Nunez just turned the helmet around and wore it backwards. Now the flap was over the right ear.

Pallone wasn't having it—Nunez needed to wear the right helmet. But Nunez really didn't want to have to march back to that dugout again. He had another solution: he walked across the plate and batted right-handed. Now that hat matched.

By now Pallone was nearly doubled over with laughter. So were pitcher Kevin Gross and catcher Lance Parrish. The laughter was also audible from both dugouts. Everyone finally composed themselves and started play, but Nunez wasn't looking at the pitcher. He was craning his neck to look at the catcher. When Parrish asked what he was doing, Nunez explained, "I want to see the signs."

Parrish decided to cut the guy some slack. "Okay," he said. "What pitch do you want?"

"Give me a fast ball," Nunez said. He fouled it off. Then he turned and asked the catcher to call for a changeup. With tears streaming from his eyes, Pallone had to call time so he could stop laughing. When the giggles had finally subsided, Nunez grounded out, mercifully putting an end to his first time at bat.

■ ■

Football players are generally said to have a bad day when they fail to prevent the other team from scoring points. To actually score points for the other team is a special achievement indeed. It happened on

October 25, 1963, in a game between the Minnesota Vikings and the San Francisco 49ers.

Jim Marshall, a starting lineman for the Vikings, picked up a fumble by the 49ers and ran sixty-six yards. His teammates would have been much more impressed had he been running in the right direction. As the crowd roared, Marshall somehow failed to notice that the 49ers were giving him a wide berth and all the guys trying to tackle him were on his own team.

He scored two points for the 49ers. Still unaware that anything was wrong, Marshall threw the football into the stands in celebration. His celebration turned to confusion when San Francisco center Bruce Bosley shook his rival's hand and said, "Thanks, Jim."

In 1994 NFL Films released a video called *NFL's 100 Greatest Follies*, Marshall's wrong-way touchdown was number one. Asked how he felt about it, thirty-five years after the game, Marshall had still not quite found the humor in it.

> "Think of the **worst thing** that you've ever done," he said. "The thing you're most **ashamed** of—and it was seen by 80 million people."

"Think of the worst thing that you've ever done," he said. "The thing you're most ashamed of—and it was seen by 80 million people. Then think of people coming up and reminding you of it for the rest of your life. That gives you a sense of what I've gone through."

It was not the first time a player had gotten turned around and run toward the wrong goal. Roy Riegels, center for the University of California, had beaten Marshall to this by thirty-five years, although in his case Riegels only came close to scoring a touchdown for the other team. On January 1, 1929, California faced Georgia Tech in the Rose Bowl. When Georgia Tech's John Tomason, nicknamed Stumpy, fumbled the ball, Riegels picked it up. Someone shoved him, and he pivoted and lost his bearings. He started racing toward his own end zone.

California's star halfback Ben Lom chased after his own player but was not able to turn him around. Riegels was finally tackled by helpful Georgia Tech players at the California one-yard line.

Although he didn't score points for Georgia Tech himself, he did set the other team up for two more points, which allowed Tech to win, 8–7. From then on Roy was saddled with the nickname "Wrong Way Riegels."

∎ ∎

If you were to get into a boxing ring, chances are you could at least land one punch before being KO'ed. Not so for Carmine Milone, who achieved an all-time record by knocking himself out in nineteen seconds. The fight took place in 1943 in Bristol, England, between two American soldiers. Technician Fifth Grade Milone rushed toward his opponent, Private Louis Fetters. Milone lunged so fast that he lost his balance, beaned himself on the ring post, fell unconscious, and was counted out by a referee.

∎ ∎

Stuart Hill of Manningtree, Essex, England, was a yachting hobbyist whose enthusiasm greatly outpaced his ability. This earned him the nickname "Captain Calamity." After Hill's adventures, the Royal National Lifeboat Institution suggested that in the future amateur yachtsmen should contact them before setting sail.

    Hill, a bearded, fifty-eight-year-old Internet company director by day, was determined to circumnavigate the British Isles in June 2001, in a lovingly converted fourteen-foot rowboat called the *Maximum Exposure,* a vessel a coastguard official described as "more like a bathtub" than a yacht. Hill's plan was to raise money for charity with his two-thousand-mile voyage, but his problems began even before he hit the water: He had an allergic reaction to the resin he was using on the hull of the *Maximum Exposure,* and he had to delay his launch for a month to recover.

    When he finally hit the waves, he had only been in the water for a few minutes when he rammed another boat and had to stop for repairs. Six days later, he had to ask the coastguard for help when his mast broke and left him stranded. But he was not deterred. After resting for three weeks, he set out again. This time the winds were against him, and he managed to travel less than three miles in four days. He finally had to let a lifeboat tow him into port.

Even after temporarily giving up, Hill put the emergency services to work. He set twenty-two miles out to sea into a busy shipping lane where coastguards couldn't find him. Once he made his way back to the coast, he came in too close, and the lifeboat had to warn him that he was in danger of running aground.

In all, by August he had already logged five rescue missions by lifeboats and helicopters. A coastguard operations manager warned Hill that his ship was not seaworthy enough to survive his mission, but he couldn't dissuade Captain Calamity from taking to the seas again. Hill insisted he didn't need help and that the *Maximum Exposure* was unsinkable, a strategy that had worked very well for the crew of the *Titanic* in days gone by.

This time around, however, Hill promised the coastguards he would contact them every day, but ten days went by without one word from the captain—a hole in his hull had let in gallons of water and soaked his radio. When people onshore saw what they thought was a windsurfer in trouble, they sent out a rescue team. After a week's break to dry out, he was off again.

Finally the "glorified surfboard" capsized in twenty-foot-high seas. Hill spent an hour clinging to its hull and waiting for his friends in the coastguard. He finally spotted something overhead and fired three flares, almost bringing down his rescue helicopter. "Flares and helicopters are incompatible." said Keith Oliver of the Shetland Coastguard with wonderful British understatement.

With the boat upside down in the Atlantic, the captain's journey seemed to be over, although no one was willing to entirely rule him out. In all, Hill's adventures cost emergency services £40,000—double what he'd hoped to raise sailing around the British coast.

■■

Another hobbyist was Fumyo Kawamura, a fanatical Japanese golfer. According to a recent *Golf Journal*, so enamored is Kawamura with golf that his lifelong dream has been to travel to the home of the Masters tournament, Augusta National Golf Club. For Kawamura, merely to walk those hallowed magnolia- and dogwood-lined fairways would be a preview of heaven. And playing Augusta—in the footsteps of champions such as Ben Hogan, Jack Nicklaus, and Tiger Woods—would be nirvana itself. So Kawamura arranged for himself the trip of a lifetime. And after a long flight across a dozen time zones and then a cab ride, he arrived, golf bag over his shoulder and suitcase under his arm, at the Augusta golf club.

"All my life I dream of coming to Augusta," he told Augusta's resident golf pro. "I see it on television every year. It is very popular in Japan. I go to America to walk famous Augusta. First may I eat lunch?" It was then the golf pro delivered to Kawamura three pieces of good news and one piece of very, very bad news: Kawamura was welcome to eat lunch. He was welcome to walk the course. He was even welcome to play as a guest of the club. But unfortunately, he was at Augusta Country Club in Augusta, Maine, 1,112 miles from Augusta National Golf Club in Augusta, Georgia, the actual home of the Masters.

Not *a* Master *of* His Profession (Bad Days *at* Work)

The record for outstanding achievement in medical malpractice must go to Dr. Robert Liston, who is the only surgeon in history to ever cause three fatalities with a single operation.

Dr. Liston was known as one of the greatest doctors of his day. There was always a long waiting list for his services. Liston worked before the introduction of anesthesia, and as you can imagine, under such conditions getting the job done quickly was prized above almost all else. No surgeon of the 1840s was speedier than Robert Liston, the first professor of clinical surgery at University College Hospital in London. He would call out to students watching in the operating theater, "Time me!"

He once removed a forty-five-pound scrotal tumor in four minutes flat. He could amputate a limb in two-and-a-half minutes. To be sure he didn't waste precious seconds setting down a bloody knife and picking it up again, he sometimes held the instrument in his teeth. Working at such a pace, accidents did occasionally happen. For example, once during one of his speedy amputations, he accidentally sliced off the patient's testicles.

In another case, Liston set another time record, but the furiously flying blade also cut off the fingers of the surgical assistant, who later died of an infection. It also slashed into a colleague observing the operation, who dropped dead from shock, and then the patient died of gangrene shortly after the procedure.

■■

Anyone who goes door to door for a job (mail carriers, salespeople) risks a run-in with an overprotective family pet. In his book *Idiots at Work*, Leland Gregory reports that a salesman in Essex, England, filed a complaint after being mauled by a dog while demonstrating a vacuum at a potential buyer's home. What he failed to mention, however, was that at the time of the attack he had been demonstrating the vacuum's strength by trying to clean the dog. The case was dismissed.

■■

Perhaps Edwin Gibbons Moore was a talented CIA employee. We don't know. What we do know is that he was a rather woeful spy. Moore left "the company" in 1973 and found himself a little bit strapped for cash. So three years later he decided he could make some extra money through espionage. He packed up a set of classified documents that he'd stashed away for just such an emergency and then tossed the package over the fence of the Soviet embassy's residential complex in Washington.

The Soviet guards had not ordered any classified documents, so they were suspicious of the mysterious package. Thinking it was a bomb, they called the U.S. Secret Service to check it out. When they arrived on the scene, the Secret Service discovered the documents along with a helpful note from Gibbons promising more material in exchange for a payment of $200,000.

He must have needed the cash quickly, because he'd given the Soviets a date to make the drop the very next night. He'd also helpfully specified a location right in his neighborhood. At the appointed time, FBI agents drove by the site and dropped a package. A child happened to be playing in his yard at the time. He spotted the drop and ran over to pick up the package, but Gibbons, who had been raking his lawn, ran over and shooed the kid away. He gleefully tore the package open on the spot but was crestfallen when he discovered there was no money in it. He was even more crestfallen when he was swarmed by G-men, arrested, and sentenced to twenty-five years in prison.

George H. W. Bush, who was heading the CIA at the time, called Gibbons "the Inspector Clouseau of volunteer spying."

■ ■

No one can be expected to know the future, unless you're a professional psychic. Soviet psychic E. Frenkel felt he had found the secret of psychic-biological power. Using only the power of his mind, he had stopped bicycles, automobiles, and streetcars. He believed that "only in extraordinary conditions of a direct threat to my organism" would all his reserves be called to action. In October 1989 he devised the ultimate test of his ability. He wrote his plan on a piece of paper and put it in his briefcase, then strolled beside the train tracks near the southern city of Astrakhan. He focused all his mental energy and stepped in front of the train, prepared for it to stop in its tracks. It didn't.

> He focused all his mental energy and stepped in front of the train, prepared for it to stop in its tracks. **It didn't.**

Another failed demonstration of psychic prowess comes courtesy of a British stage hypnotist who performed under the name "Romark." On October 12, 1977, he announced he would drive a car, blindfolded, through the town of Ilford guided only by his sixth sense.

He prepared for this feat with great pomp and circumstance. He placed a coin and then a wad of bread dough over each closed eye, and then covered the whole thing with a blindfold. He then climbed into his yellow Renault and started the gas. His demonstration ended after only 20 meters when he slammed into the back of a parked police van. He later explained that "the van was parked in a place that logic told me it wouldn't be."

■ ■

Back in the days when executioners were celebrated, Richard Arnett was to hanging what William Hung was to *American Idol*. They were already having some problems with the position when Arnett was hired in 1719. His predecessor, William Marvel, could no longer do the job because he'd been hanged for stealing ten silk handkerchiefs valued at twelve shillings. So Arnett got the gig.

He made an impression right away by showing up late for his first day on the job. By the time he turned up for the hanging, the crowd was so restless that they threw him into a pond used for watering horses. The three condemned men were sent back to prison to be hanged another day, while the stunned Arnett was treated by a doctor for his minor injuries.

Perhaps he was a reluctant killer. A year later he decided to strengthen his courage for the task with a little drink. He was so inebriated that he tried to hang the Reverend John Villette, the Ordinary of Newgate and a Catholic priest who was there to administer the last rites. When the mental fog finally lifted, the platform collapsed, and the three officials fell to the ground, landing on top of the two prisoners. Arnett had forgotten to secure the bolt that held the platform together.

In 1724 he was back to his old tricks. He took so long preparing to execute a prisoner that pickpockets had made the rounds and relieved the spectators of their wallets. The mob threatened to throw Arnett into the horse pond again if he didn't get on with it.

Arnett died in August 1728 and was succeeded by John Hooper, known as "The Laughing Hangman" and a real favorite with the crowds.

Arts *and* Entertainment

Admit it, you have a notebook full of poems you wrote when your boyfriend dumped you, and you've been kidding yourself for years that they are great literature. And maybe you've never quite gotten over the shameful fact that you are not a rock star. We all love to get creative from time to time, but we can't all dance with the stars.

While we dither unproductively, achieving only moderate embarrassment, there are the gloriously incompetent performers and artists who elevate a lack of talent to dizzying new heights. They possess the magic qualities that separate a William Hung (the *American Idol* reject with a record contract) from all the other folks who were axed for singing flat. It is impossible to put your finger on exactly what this genius is. But the right spirit, a lot of luck, great confidence, and a complete lack of self-awareness seem to help. That's why we can't get enough of *Star Trek* captain William Shatner's overly dramatic narrations on his album *The Transformed Man*. Meanwhile, Brent Spiner, the actor who played Data on *Star Trek: The Next Generation*, released an album called *Ol' Yellow Eyes Is Back*. Spiner's crooning of show tunes was disappointingly competent—and only the most diehard *Trek* fans even know the album exists.

The long tradition of pitiful performers can be traced back to a few pioneers like Robert Coates, an actor who lived from 1772 to 1848. His specialty was his incomparable Shakespearean performances. Sometimes Coates would mangle the prose but insisted that, although it wasn't pronounced as Shakespeare had written it, he had "improved upon it."

At the 1810 debut of his *Romeo and Juliet*, which he performed in crimson pantaloons and a white hat with feathers and diamonds, the thespian was pelted with orange peels and chased from the stage. After that, his fame as the worst actor in England was sealed. People came to London from miles around to see the spectacle for themselves. The theater was always sold out, and people waited in long lines for seats. They came armed with "almost every conceivable throwable object." Other actors ducked and ran for the wings—poor "Miss FitzHenry," who played Juliet, shrieked and clung to the scenery, afraid to move.

But Coates stood and belted out his lines and let the rotten fruit hit him. Once, while intoning the line, "Oh, let me hence, I stand on sudden haste," he was beaned by something especially large and fell to the floor. As the stage manager waved him backstage, he crawled about looking for his diamond knee buckle. Once someone threw a live rooster at him. He battled it to the death and received a thunderous ovation. The performances were so extraordinary that a good half-dozen people laughed so hard they needed medical attention.

Robert Coates died in 1848. He was run over and killed by a carriage as he ran from a theater with a mob of angry critics in pursuit. But his legacy lived on. Others would soon rise to the challenge of breaking bold new ground in inept theatricality.

■■

The Cherry Sisters made their debut in Marion, Iowa, in 1893 and took their act all the way to Broadway, despite having no discernable talent for music, acting, or recitation. Originally there were five Cherry Sisters, but only two of them, Addie and Effie, had the stamina to stick with the show.

They were earnest young women, who wore floor-length dresses in keeping with their modesty to the very end and liked to punctuate morality tales with sweeping gestures and exaggerated pantomime. After singing off-key ballads and self-penned black minstrel numbers, one sister or the other would read a serious essay of great import. On a typical evening, one of the sisters would recite an ode to Prohibition, then make a plea for the elevation of theatrical art, to which the orchestra would respond with a chorus of "Ta-ra-ra boom de ay."

The day after their disastrous debut, they read the review in the paper and immediately sued for libel. A judge held the trial in the theater and had the sisters perform their signature act, "The Gypsy's Warning." After only a few minutes, the judge ruled in favor of the newspaper.

Here is how the Cedar Rapids *Gazette* reviewed an early Cherry Sisters performance on February 17, 1893:

> "Such unlimited gall was exhibited last night at Greene's opera house by the Cherry Sisters is past the understanding of ordinary mortals...; If some indefinable instinct of modesty could not have warned them that they were acting the part of monkeys, it does seem like the overshoes thrown at them would have conveyed the idea in a more substantial manner.... But nothing could drive them away and no combination of yells, whistles, barks and howls could subdue them."

> "I've been putting on the best talent and it hasn't gone over. I'm going to try the worst."

Oscar Hammerstein got wind of this budding talent. He said, "I've been putting on the best talent and it hasn't gone over. I'm going to try the worst." He brought the girls to Broadway, where they sold out every night. One night Effie was emoting to her utmost; with her arms spread wide, she intoned, "I'm a pore innercent maiden without no kin, and I'm a-hankerin' for a morsel o' grub." Just then she was whacked in the head with a giant squash.

After that the Cherrys erected a wire screen to protect them from flying tomatoes.

If squash and tomatoes couldn't put an end to the Cherry Sisters' act, what did? Tastes change, and the novelty wore off, but even worse, the girls actually started to improve. Once they got to be mediocre but passable performers, their career came to an end.

■■

Another notable performer from the era was Florence Foster Jenkins. She had a burning dream to be an opera singer that was completely unmatched by any singing ability. Until she was about forty years old, she did not have the means to inflict her voice on anyone but her immediate family. But when her father died in 1904, she inherited his fortune. Now a wealthy heiress, she gained a newfound ability to assault the world with her peculiar talent. Her voice could be compared to that of a member of Monty Python performing in drag, but funnier and further off key.

She didn't allow any of this to stop her from carrying herself with the dignity of a true diva. She thrilled audiences with a minimum of three costume changes per performance. She would appear as an angel with a huge pair of wings to sing "Ave Maria," then return with a flower between her teeth dressed as a senorita for her grand finale, "Cavelitos."

Her moment of glory came when, on October 25, 1944, at age seventy-five, she rented out Carnegie Hall for a concert. During the show's climax, she threw flowers into the audience to punctuate each verse. She then sent her accompanist Cosme McMoon out into the auditorium to collect them so she could do it again for the encore.

"She only thought of making other people happy," a friend of hers once said, and indeed she did. While most performers of her era are long forgotten, her headache-inducing album is still in print and can even be downloaded in MP3 format—you can put her brilliance on shuffle play along with William Hung and William Shatner.

■■

If bad Elvis is what you want, you can choose from among thousands of Elvis impersonators of dubious merit. But one in particular is a stand-out. Eilert Pilarm has been amazing international audiences by performing as The King while completely failing to either look or sound like Elvis Presley. To make things even more entertaining, his English is virtually nonexistent, so he sings with joyful abandon unconstrained by the meaning of the lyrics. His "Jailhouse Rock," says Joe Hagan in the *New York Times*, "boggles the mind with its originality." For all of these reasons, Eilert has become something of an international cult figure. On his Swedish language Web page he offers for sale no less than five CDs, including a *Greatest Hits* compilation.

Incompetence— *The* Criminal Element

Fortunately for the rest of us, criminal types tend not to be the sharpest pencils in the box. Tales of criminal stupidity provide the perfect excuse for guilt-free *Schadenfreude*, as the people suffering the misfortunes are, after all, breaking the law. We get the double joy of laughing at incompetence while seeing bad guys get their comeuppance. There are far too many wonderful examples of criminal incompetence in the world to do the topic justice, but I have chosen a few gems to stand as representative samples.

These criminal masterminds are like Philip McCutcheon of England, who was arrested for the twentieth time in 1971 when he drove his getaway car into two parked vans. The judge, Mr. Rodney Percy, gave McCutcheon some career advice.

> "I think you should give burglary up," he said. "You have a withered hand, an artificial leg and only one eye.... You are a **rotten** burglar."

"I think you should give burglary up," he said. "You have a withered hand, an artificial leg and only one eye." You have been caught in Otley, Leeds, Harrogate, Norwich, Beverley, Hull, and York. How can you hope to succeed? You are a rotten burglar. You are always being caught."

∎∎

At least he did not beat himself up, which is more than can be said for a woman who charged into a small post office inside a newsstand in West Midlands, England, brandishing a crowbar. She threatened the clerk, but the clerk refused to cooperate. There was a struggle, and the robber accidentally hit herself on the head with the crowbar and cut herself with the hook. Then her shirt got caught on something and was torn off. At that point she ran out. A spokesman said the police were looking for a distinctive person, "a female bloodstained with just her bra on...."

The post office was never in any danger, the spokesman noted. "It was closed."

■ ■

In 1978 a librarian from Swansea, England, named Ceredig Dennis decided to try his hand at blackmail. His target was a solicitor named Mr. Shoemaker. He had his girlfriend seduce Shoemaker, as he waited in the cupboard. At the compromising moment, he jumped out of the cupboard, took a Polaroid and demanded money. The only problem was that, when the film developed, it showed only a large refrigerator in the corner of the room.

■ ■

I'll just come right out and say this: putting a live lobster down your pants, for any reason, is not a good idea. You wouldn't think this is something anyone would have to say, but Winston Treadway could have used this advice when he got it in his head to steal food from his local supermarket. If you're going to all the trouble of shoplifting, he reasoned, you don't want to get ramen noodles and Spam; you want luxury items. So when he saw the tank of live lobsters, he grabbed two of them, stashed them in his underwear and sprinted for the door.

The results were predictable. One of the lobsters, apparently not enjoying the ride, clamped onto a part of the thief's anatomy that most men prefer unclawed. The police had no trouble catching up with Treadway where he was doubled over.

"When we saw him he was trying to prise the claws off," a policeman said. "He was purple as an aubergine...." They called the medics who used pliers to get the crustacean off. They confirmed that the robber had performed possibly the world's first vasectomy by lobster.

■■

In 2005 a thief nabbed a statue of a "land grandfather god" from a Taoist temple in Taipei and sent a ransom note asking for $50,000. The statue-napper, who had perhaps seen too many detective shows on TV, told the temple not to contact the police. They called the police anyway. The criminal had vastly overestimated the statue's sentimental value.

"What is he going to do, kill the god?" asked a temple spokesperson. "Hell, with $50,000 we can buy ten gods."

■■

We don't know how well this nineteen-year-old Philadelphian performed in his day job as a Kentucky Fried Chicken cashier, but he certainly lacked talent for his second job as a burglar. When choosing a store to rob, he settled upon his own KFC. He came in with a gun, and with no mask or disguise demanded all the money. The people he was robbing recognized him right away; after all, they'd worked with him for the past two years. Because he worked there, he realized that they were correct when they explained that they couldn't give him the money because the store's time-locked safe shut at 9:00 a.m. and it was now 9:15. He left without the money and managed to elude police for three days but was arrested when he showed up for work as if nothing had happened.

> When choosing a store to rob, he settled upon **his own** KFC. He came in with a gun, and with no mask or disguise demanded all the money.

■■

After an extended weekend drinking session in Wales in July 2006, nineteen year-old Stephen Brennan and twenty-year-old John Mahoney, of Dublin, missed the last passenger ferry home so they made the only logical choice. They stole a fishing trawler. The only flaw in their plan was that neither one had ever piloted a boat before. They didn't even know how to switch the cabin light on. But, they figured, how hard could it be?

After eight hours at sea, sailing in circles, they had their answer. A search-and-rescue helicopter and a coastguard lifeboat were sent out to find them. They were finally located heading in the wrong direction about twelve miles from where they started. The police dropped them off on the ferry dock and let them off with a warning.

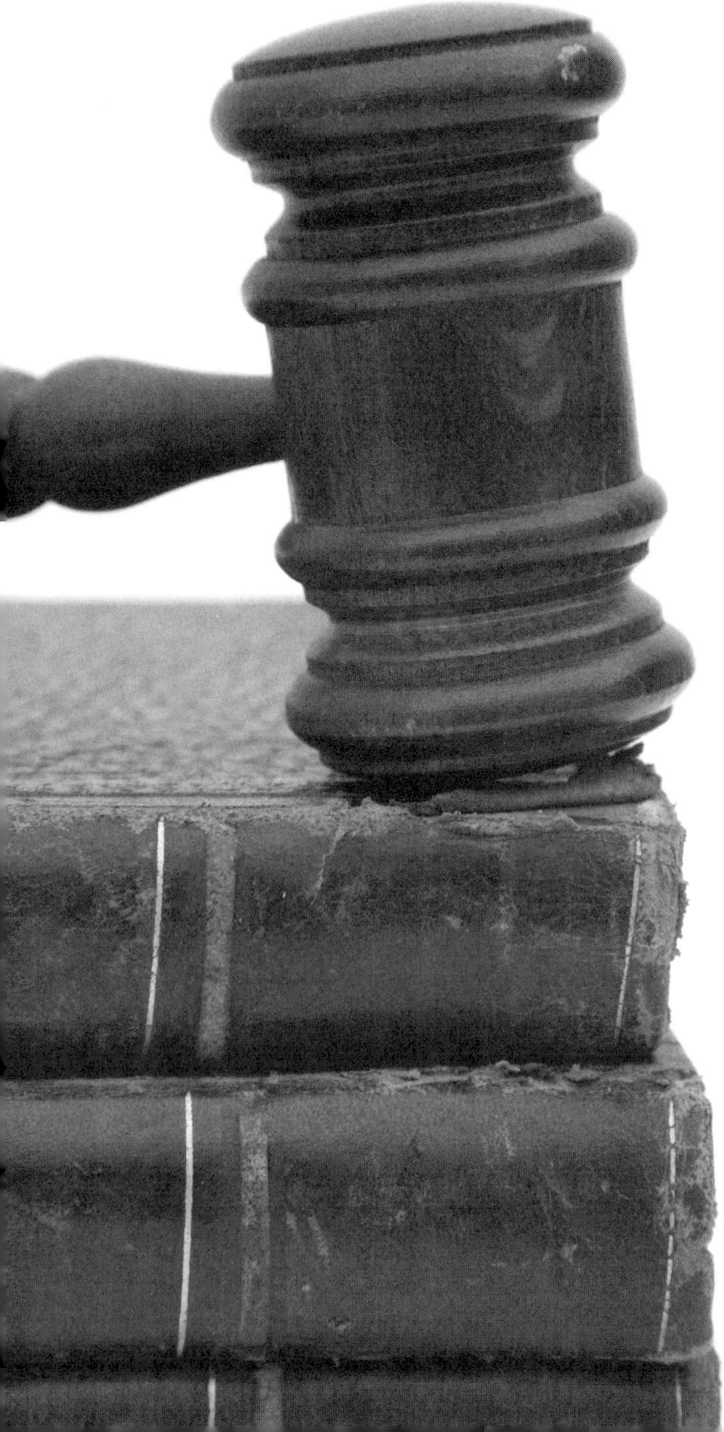

IX. Bureaucracy and Other Legal Madness

Dealing with an unyielding bureaucrat is one of life's little displeasures. When an actual human being comes up against one of these giant, inhuman systems or pencil pushers who care more for rules than people, the results make you want to tear your hair out. When you hear about them afterwards, you can't help but laugh. While you're waiting in line at the DMV, ponder these tales of bureaucratic encounters of the insane kind.

It Says *in* My Computer...

Here are two items from the "Make it stop!" file: In the early days of computer use, Joseph Begley of England saved up cigarette coupons that you could redeem for prizes. When he had two thousand of them, he mailed them in and asked for a watch. The next day he received not one but three watches. He only had two arms, and only wanted a watch on one of them, so he mailed the other two back. From then on he was inundated with free gifts. The first day there were ten packages; the next day there were eighteen. He received a golf bag, two electric blankets, a doll, three tape recorders, a cot, saucepans, record albums, and a pressure cooker.

Now nearly buried in premiums, Begley wrote to the company and asked them to please stop. The firm replied, explaining it was "a computer error" and that it had been sorted out. To make up for the difficulties they sent him ten thousand coupons. Begley used them to order some tools and a bedspread, presumably to go with the electric blankets. The computer sent him a plant stand and two stepladders.

Not that modern, high-tech computers have fixed things much. People are often a bit nervous when they get a letter from the IRS, so imagine for a moment receiving sixteen thousand letters from the IRS. Thanks to a software glitch, a San Diego dentist was the recipient of thousands of tax forms. The software the government was using misread the word "suite." It had been abbreviated as "su," but the software had only been programmed to recognize "ste." When something like this happens, the software is supposed to jump back to the previous line in the address, but the previous line contained a foreign spelling of a word, and the computer simply could not cope. Using the type of logic only computers can, it started printing out the address over and over until sixteen thousand individually addressed tax forms were sent to the good doctor—$4,064 worth of postage later, the government fixed the glitch with a software patch.

Rules *Are* Rules

Any time written rules take precedence over common sense you have a triumph of bureaucracy, whether that happens in a government office or the Wal-Mart parking lot.

In March 2002 a seventy-three-year-old woman stopped at the Wal-Mart in Geneseo, Illinois to pick up some prescriptions at the pharmacy. On the way in, she thought she'd get a newspaper to read while she waited for the prescription to be filled. She put two quarters into one of those newspaper boxes by the door. As she turned to go, the door slammed shut on the strings from her coat's hood. The woman tried to pull it lose, but she couldn't. She tried to shimmy out of the coat, but she'd had recent shoulder surgery and didn't have the flexibility. She also couldn't reach into her pocket to get more coins to open the box.

Finally, a young woman passed by and asked if everything was all right. Clearly it was not. The older woman explained her plight and the good Samaritan ran into the store to alert the employees. The friendly Wal-Mart clerk explained that the newspaper boxes didn't belong to the store and that they were not allowed to tamper with them. The customer returned to the newspaper box to convey this news to the woman who'd now been hunched over the vending machine in the cold for five minutes.

A store employee finally poked her head outside the door and said she would call the *Dispatch*—the newspaper that owned the boxes—and see if they could send someone out to open it. The woman tried to explain that all she wanted was for someone to put two quarters in the slot so it would open and she could get out.

The employee responded that Wal-Mart was "not responsible for making refunds for the machines." She then disappeared back into the store. A few minutes later the employee reemerged to say that she'd tried to reach the *Dispatch*, but she couldn't get hold of anyone. Presumably there was not an option for "If you're trying to free an old woman from a newspaper vending box, press six" in the voicemail menu.

By now, twenty minutes had gone by. The woman pleaded with the clerk to just put two quarters into the slot, and she would repay her as soon as she was able to move. The employee finally agreed. Why none of the customers walking in and out of the store had come up with this solution is another question to ponder.

Later that day, the woman's daughter went to Wal-Mart and gave the manager a $5 bill. The money, she said, was for an emergency fund to free any other unfortunates who might be trapped in one of their vending machines.

Wal-Mart's Bentonville, Arkansas, headquarters called the incident unfortunate but said that store employees were "merely following company policy by not tampering with machines."

> Presumably there was not an option for "If you're trying to free an old woman from a newspaper vending box, press six" in the voicemail menu.

■■

Another triumph of bureaucracy resulted in a slowdown of Tokyo's famous bullet train, known for reaching speeds of up to 167 mph. One day it was seen chugging along at about 13 mph. It turned out that the train had been placed on autopilot with the controls unattended for about five minutes. The Central Japan Railway driver was only following the rules, which said he had to wear his hat at all times. The rules didn't spell out that the driver was supposed to stay at the controls when the train was in motion. The driver realized he'd left his hat somewhere in the train and went looking for it. Central Japan Railway has since updated its rules to say that drivers should wait to look for missing hats and other such items until the train has reached a station.

Lethal Litigation

You know you're having a bad day when you're woken up by a process server knocking at the door. Mr. Plaintiff is telling out-and-out lies about you, but you have to defend yourself anyway, and that means paying $250 an hour out of your $12 an hour salary. How much justice can you afford?

Civil litigation may not be the subject of TV dramas like *Law & Order*, but to the person being sued, it is as much a life-or-death struggle as any high-profile murder trial. Someone is fighting to keep his business open, to preserve her professional reputation, even to maintain relationships with children and family members. There are very few cases in which the stakes and passions are not tremendously high.

Unless you have a legal degree, other people—lawyers and judges—will be in control of a process you do not fully understand. Although it is your life, your opinion will be only a small part of the lawyers' decisions—even your own lawyer's. If you haven't had the pleasure yet, don't worry. There is plenty of litigation to go around. There are 19 million new lawsuits filed each year—one for every ten adults. If it's happened to you, you'll surely enjoy a little pleasure at the expense of lawyers and the lawsuit happy.

Lengthy Litigation *and* Vexatious Litigants

If your neighbor or ex has literally made a federal case out of a misunderstanding, don't whine. It could be worse. Chances are it will at least be wrapped up in your lifetime, which is more than we can say for the royal litigants involved in the Berkeley Suit. This courtroom drama lasted more than 190 years—that's years. Fights over estates can be bitter—ask anyone who's ever known Anna Nicole Smith. But the blonde model who took her suit over her senior-citizen husband's estate all the way to the Supreme Court, only to start a new legal circus after her death, had nothing on the Berkeleys.

It all started in 1416, when Lord Berkeley's daughter Elizabeth married Richard Beauchamp, earl of Warwick. Their kids each wanted the castle, and things got very ugly. No matter how bitter your ex-business partner is, she is probably not going to come after you with a sword and an army of 150 friends, as Elizabeth's great-grandson Thomas Talbot did to answer a legal filing by his cousin William, Lord Berkeley. More than three hundred people were injured in the fray. Talbot would not be deterred, and he passed his claim on to his sisters, who passed it on to their children. It wasn't until Henry, the eleventh earl of Berkeley, obtained a decree in his favor in 1609 that the litigation and bloodshed stopped.

■■

Another grand achievement in fruitless litigation was that of Myra Davis, who spent her entire life trying to prove that she was the rightful owner of most of New Orleans. Her claim began with a man named Daniel Clark, a young Irishman who settled in New Orleans in 1784 when it was still a Spanish province. Using his political connections, he was able to amass one of the largest real estate fortunes in the area. When he died in 1819, half of New Orleans was his. The property was worth a cool $50 million (about $864 billon in today's money). Unmarried, with no children, Clark left a will that directed his fortune be held in trust for his elderly mother.

Fifteen years later Myra Davis appeared, claiming that she was Clark's illegitimate daughter and that she was the true heir to Clark's fortune. She claimed that her mother, a French Creole woman, had secretly married Clark and that the tycoon had drafted a second will which left his property to her. She couldn't produce this will, but she had a witness, who claimed that Clark had confessed as much to him.

If her story was true, it could throw New Orleans into complete chaos. Much of Clark's property had been sold and resold. Even if she were entitled to the property, getting it back would be a nightmare. Davis wasn't worried about the current owners; she was determined to have the deed to her inheritance, and she sued more than 150 people in 1866 for occupying "her" land. The next year she sued 70 more and the following year 250.

No one was sure how to carry out business. They were afraid to buy property in New Orleans lest Myra Davis sue. One buyer was so concerned that he sought a guarantee that a parcel of land he wanted to buy lay outside Davis' claim. She agreed to sign a guarantee that she would not claim the property—for a $500 fee.

Davis was soon the least popular woman in New Orleans. She couldn't appear on the streets without risking bodily injury. Once an angry real estate holder fired a gun at her. He missed, just barely, and Davis took to proudly wearing the silk bonnet with the bullet hole.

Her legal quest became the longest ever recorded in American jurisprudence. It ran for more than sixty years, going all the way to the Supreme Court twelve different times. The justices couldn't agree on whether Davis's story was fact or fiction. Was she a true heir or an imposter? Each time a court ruled against her, she would appeal to a higher court. She outlived most of the lawyers who argued against her.

The case completely took over her life. She managed to find a wealthy husband to fund her days in court. When he died in 1849, he left her $100,000, a handsome sum that she could have lived off comfortably for the rest of her days. Instead, her lawyers would live off the money while she lived in a run-down, roach-infested rooming house in the worst section of town. Although she often needed to borrow money for food, she turned down every attempt at settlement or compromise.

In 1890, sixty years after she first launched her suit, the justices of the Supreme Court heard the case for the last time. One of them,

Justice Wayne, who had been born four years after Davis filed her first case, wrote, "Those of us who have borne our part . . . will pass away, the case will live."

The court ruled that the burden of proof that Davis was not Clark's daughter fell on the defendants, and they had failed to do so. Yet they were not willing to simply hand the city of New Orleans over to her. They awarded her one large tract, involving 140 acres. They ordered the city to pay her $2 million, then the value of the property, and interest amounting to $500,000.

One can only imagine the gratification Davis must have felt after a lifetime of fighting to finally be vindicated. She died two months before the verdict was handed down. Most of the $2 million was divided up among the many lawyers.

> She died two months before the verdict was handed down. Most of the $2 million was divided up among the many lawyers.

■■

Myrna Davis may have had the longest lawsuit in American history, but a candidate for the most litigious in terms of quantity is Colonel Edward A. L. Roberts, the founder of the Roberts Torpedo Company. Before he died in 1881, he had filed an amazing sixteen thousand lawsuits to protect a single patent, a device for shooting oil wells. He had spent a quarter-million dollars, roughly equivalent to $4,926,841.57 in today's money. Even though he always won his disputes, infringement was rampant and unstoppable. Roberts's company charged exorbitant prices—$200 for one shot (about $4,000 today.) Hey, he had to pay the lawyers somehow. So oil men who wanted to avoid these fees hired people to work at night with their own nitroglycerin mixes. The men who put in torpedoes at night came to be known as "moonlighters." That's the origin of the term.

There's an interesting story from the days when men blasted oil wells with nitroglycerin. It has very little to do with patent lawsuits, but it's worth telling. As the *Oil City Times* reported in December 1869: "Rouseville furnishes the latest unpatented novelty in connection with Nitro-Glycerine."

A torpedo man had taken a small parcel of the explosive and left it by the door in a small container while he stopped into an engine house.

A wandering hog came by, rooting for something to eat and devoured the entire contents of the package. The torpedoist returned to find the pig gulping down the last bits.

> "Now everybody gives the greedy animal the widest latitude. It has full possession of the whole sidewalk whenever disposed to promenade. All the dogs in town have been placed in solitary confinement, for fear they might chase the loaded porker against a post. No one is sufficiently reckless to kick the critter, lest it should unexpectedly explode and send the town and its total belongings to everlasting smash! The matter is really becoming serious and how to dispose safely of a gormandizing swine that has imbibed two quarts of infernal glycerine is the grand conundrum of the hour. When he is killed and ground up into sausage and headcheese a new terror will be added to the long list that boarding-houses possess already."

∎∎

Albert Carter of Colorado, who was the king of litigation in the 1980s, hasn't even come close to Colonel Roberts, but he's made a good showing. Whenever Carter is offended, he heads to court. Authorities say he's filed more than 225 lawsuits. If a judge dismisses the case, Carter sues the judge and files in a different court. How can he afford it? He files without a lawyer. U.S. District Court Judge Sherman Finesilver concluded that most of the cases were "frivolous or vexatious." He ordered Carter to stop suing. Carter filed an appeal of Finesilver's action.

∎∎

Patricia McColm of San Francisco filed so many lawsuits against her neighbors that real estate agents had to warn people moving into the area about her. "We had a crack dealer with a pit bull and weapons," one neighbor said. "It was easier and less anxiety producing getting rid of him."

McColm filed dozens of lawsuits, from noisy kids playing in people's yards to a door that hit her in the foot and various auto accidents.

She went to law school so she could learn to defend herself, but she failed the bar exam twice. Of course she sued the state bar for emotional distress.

"You are the most vexatious, vexatious litigant I've ever dealt with," said the judge.

■■

You can also thank your lucky stars you've never crossed paths with Brenda Butler Bryant. You would undoubtably be named in a lawsuit, not that this would necessarily mean much. Bryant holds the award for the largest number of nonsensical lawsuits. In 1994 U.S. District Court Judge John P. Fullam ordered her to stop suing people until she either hires a lawyer or finds a doctor to certify her mental competence. Acting as her own attorney, she filed more than seven hundred handwritten suits, which contained no complete sentences and were filled with "incomprehensible rubbish." An example: "Slavemaster Service, B/S Wholesale Club, Lane Bryant, Negro Service, BBB/KKK/LLL-Linda Lovelace/AAA."

Lawsuits *That* Blow Back

Often when egos clash over something in print, no one wins but the lawyers. Such was the case when two of the great egos of the 1870s battled over a scathing arts review. Arts are, of course, always subjective.

In 1872, for example, the Royal Academy received a painting from the artist of our tale, James McNeil Whistler. The academy deemed the painting, *Arrangement in Gray and Black, No. 1: The Artist's Mother*, "worthless." It was hidden away in the cellar until a powerful member took an interest in it and insisted it be put in the gallery. The other members of the academy brought it up but hung it in a dark corner. *Whistler's Mother*, as it is more commonly called, is now one of history's most famous works of art.

Don't let the image of Whistler's rather staid and buttoned-up mother, Anna McNeil Whistler, fool you. Her son was every bit the artist—provocative, brash, and rebellious. He believed in art for art's sake, not to convey any literal story. This view was not shared by everyone in the art world.

In 1877 the British art critic John Ruskin had a different view. He believed that paintings should be valued for "the clearness and the justice of the ideas they contained and conveyed." So he took umbrage with Whistler's painting *Nocturne in Black and Gold: The Falling Rocket*. He wrote: "'I have seen, and heard, much of Cockney impudence before now; but never expected to hear a coxcomb ask two hundred guineas for flinging a pot of paint in the public's face."

The combative Whistler decided to sue for libel. John Ruskin was no weekend reviewer. He was probably the most influential art critic in his day and a celebrity in his own right. The lawsuit might be akin to Matt Damon suing Roger Ebert for giving him the thumbs down. The international press loved it and covered it as later reporters watched the Michael Jackson trial.

It was a jolly good show, with quotable bon mots and curious moments galore. The jury, made up of wealthy landowners with no particular background in art, were ostensibly asked to judge whether Whistler had been unfairly maligned, but to do so they had to decide whether art should be literal or more abstract and whether Whistler's work was worth its asking price of two hundred guineas (about five times the yearly salary of a factory worker). At one point the prosecution wheeled in Vincenzo Cateno's *Titan* to show what a *real* painting looked like.

In another of the trial's memorable moments, the prosecution asked Whistler how long it took him to "knock off" the painting in question. Whistler admitted that it took him about two days.

"Two days! The labor of two days, then, is that for which you ask two hundred guineas?"

"No," the artist replied. "I ask it for the knowledge of a lifetime."

The jury, in spite of instructions from the judge that were so garbled many people believed he was drunk, came back with a verdict. It was, in the words of the *Examiner*, a victory for Whistler but "a victory which bears a very striking resemblance to a defeat."

Whistler was awarded only a farthing in damages. He wore the farthing on his watch chain and boasted that he had won, but in reality no one but the lawyers had. Ruskin, stung by the verdict, resigned from his position as Slade Professor of Fine Arts at Oxford, and Whistler was bankrupted by the legal fees. He lost his house and furniture, moved to Venice, and toned down his provocative style to sell a series of conventional etchings.

■■

The Rev. William E. Christian and his wife Carolyn thought they'd suffered "pain and suffering" when they filed a lawsuit in 1993, but it was nothing compared to the pain they would have to endure from the backlash.

It all started when a blind man learning how to work with a seeing-eye dog in a mall in Tampa tried to navigate around the couple. He hadn't quite mastered working with the dog, and he stepped on Carolyn's foot, breaking her toe. Witnesses said she'd made no attempt to get out of the way.

Being the Christians that they are, Mrs. Christian sued the guide-dog school for $80,000 in medical bills, pain, and suffering and the reverend added his own suit for $80,000 for loss of his wife's "care, comfort and consortium."

When news of the lawsuit hit local newspapers and radio talk shows, the outrage forced the couple to retreat. The lawyer who filed the suit withdrew it and said his firm would donate $1,000 to the school.

> Being the **Christians** that they are, Mrs. Christian sued the guide-dog school for $80,000 in medical bills, pain, and suffering.

■■

And finally, what do we know about Michael Costanza of Holtsville, New York? We know that he is bald and stocky and has "bathroom quirks." We know that he was a nerd in high school who was called "Can't-Stand-Ya" by his high school gym teacher. Why do we know these embarrassing things about an otherwise anonymous real estate agent? Because Costanza sued the creators of the *Seinfeld* TV series saying that the bumbling character George Costanza was based on him. The facts I just mentioned were part of his case. Costanza went to school with Jerry Seinfeld and said his pain and suffering was worth a cool $100 million. Cocreator Larry David said he had based the character of George 100 percent on himself. The court agreed. To add insult to, well, insult, in a statement following the court decision, Larry David said, "The universe would be out of kilter if someone named Costanza won anything."

Bad Days *in* Court

Sure you have to take time off work and you're paid only $5 to listen to dull testimony about insurance fraud, but don't feel too sorry for yourself for being called to jury duty. Be glad that you're not living in nineteenth-century England. The prisons were so terrible in those days that inmates waiting for their day in court invariably caught typhus and other diseases, which they brought with them to trial. The prisoners, in turn, had a habit of infecting anyone in the courtroom. At one trial in London's Old Bailey in October 1750, forty people died of typhus, including six jurors, three lawyers, and four judges. So do your civic duty, and stop complaining.

He may not have braved typhus, but jury deliberation caused some embarrassment for the foreman at a 1998 trial in Lewes Crown Court in East Sussex, England. The month-long trial was for four men accused of planning a jewel robbery. The jury had been deliberating for four hours when Judge Simon Coltart was told the foreman had handcuffed himself. The foreman had been studying one of the finer points of the case: The gang allegedly planned to use a pair of handcuffs on a shop assistant before cracking the safe. While experimenting with the evidence, the man got his hand stuck, and there was no key to free him. The judge sent for the fire brigade, but there were a few problems. No one was permitted to enter the jury room during deliberations. What is more, the fire officer in charge that day was a relative of another one of the jurors. Lawyers and firemen debated the legal implications of the rescue and finally decided to clear the court. The twelve jurors returned to the ballot box, and the "sheepish" foreman was cut loose with bolt cutters.

"Perhaps I should have warned the jury not to experiment with the handcuffs," the judge said. After the demonstration of the effectiveness of the cuffs, the jury found the defendants guilty.

■ ■

You can also be thankful that you were born too late to be brought before Sir George Jeffreys of Wem, a justice so tough he was known as "Bloody Jeffreys." Serving in the seventeenth century as Britain's Lord Chief Justice, he passed 331 death sentences and had hundreds deported. He sentenced one Lady Alice de Lisle to be roasted alive. The church begged for clemency and managed to get her sentence reduced to a simple beheading. Jeffreys was one for a speedy trial and didn't allow niceties like a word on behalf of the defense to slow things down. It is said that he needed to race through the trials because of a painful bladder stone. He needed to urinate hourly and couldn't sit on the bench any longer than that.

■ ■

Here's one from the "I'm not a lawyer, but I play one on TV" file. You'd think that Raymond Burr, known to millions of TV viewers as the unbeatable trial lawyer Perry Mason, would have an advantage in a real court of law. You would be wrong. When Burr was sued by a creditor, he identified just a little too closely with his character and forgot that he was not actually an attorney. In 1963 Ward George Shaheen filed a suit claiming the actor had owned him $1,083 since 1949. The judge, Charles C. Stidham, said he would have dismissed the case because it was not filed in a timely fashion, but instead of answering the summons through a lawyer, Burr decided to plead his own case. Then he failed to appear on his own behalf for a court-ordered deposition. The judge ruled that Burr didn't follow proper procedure and ordered him to pay the money he owed.

Divorce Court

Even at its most amicable, divorce has never been particularly fun. But at least if you say your wife's divorce lawyer has you by the balls, you're probably using the expression metaphorically. There was a time when this was more literally true. Before the French Revolution, the only

> If you think testifying in a divorce case is painful today, imagine having to demonstrate your ability to **ejaculate** before witnesses.

legal ground for divorce was sexual impotence. The authorities wouldn't just take a partner's word for it, they checked things out for themselves. If you think testifying in a divorce case is painful today, imagine having to demonstrate your ability to ejaculate before witnesses. The midwives who were employed to test such things checked not only the existence of an erection, but its quality as well.

The divorce of Baron d'Argenton from Magdeleine de la Chastre was great entertainment for enquiring minds with no access to tabloid television or Internet porn. It was less entertaining for the baron. After four years of marriage, Magdeleine's mother went on the warpath, determined to break up the union on the grounds of impotence. The baron tried to prove that he had consummated the marriage by publicly displaying the bloodstained bed sheets from the wedding night. (Why they still had the bloodstained bedsheets is a question to ponder at another time.) The ecclesiastical court was not convinced and ordered an examination. They reported that the husband "had no visible cullions, but as if a purse without sovereigns, the which did withdraw inside his person when he turned over, in such fashion that he had nothing left him but his member, and even this being far smaller than is customary among men."

The baron argued that he did have cullions, thank you very much, they were just "hidden within." He appealed to the pope himself, but it was no use. He was ruled to be impotent. After his death on February 3, 1604, doctors examined his body and finally found his manhood. Although they were "concealed from view," they were "in all respects similar to those of other men."

■■

Which leads us to the subject of alimony. If you are paying alimony, you might consider yourself unlucky. It is estimated that only 25 percent of ex-spouses are awarded alimony. Some of those who are just can't get enough. The 1992 edition of the *Guinness Book of World Records* gives the nod for the largest divorce settlement to Soraya Khashoggi, the wife of Saudi arms dealer Adnan Khashoggi. Born in Leicester, England, to a hotel waitress, the former Sandra Daly received $950 million plus property in 1982. Bad news if you're Mr. Khashoggi, but good news for the Mrs. You'd think Soraya would be set for life, but foes of alimony and fans of *Schadenfreude* will note that in 2002 the *Evening Standard* reported that the money was all gone, and the former Mrs. Khashoggi was running a flower shop.

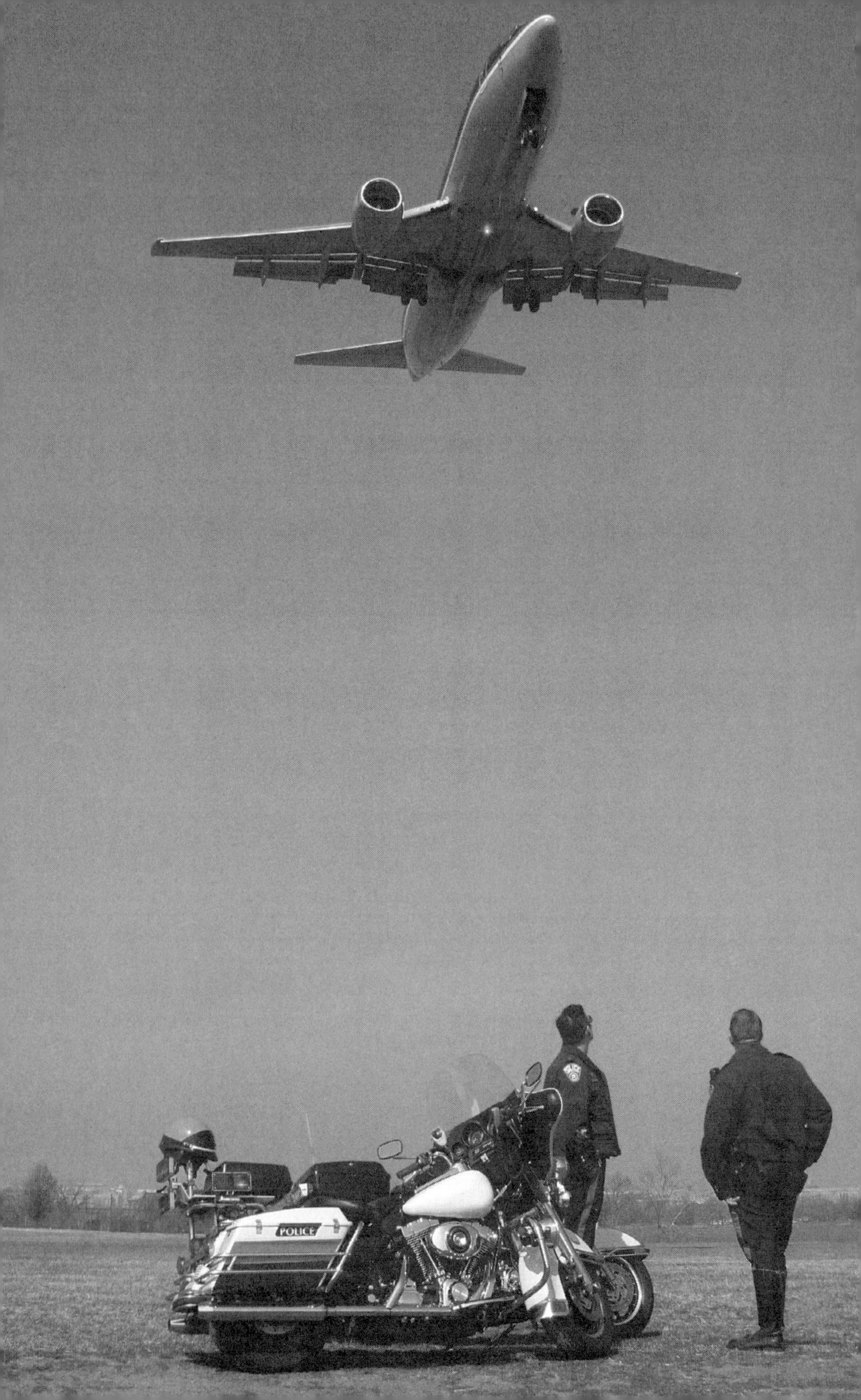
POLICE

Department of Homeland Insecurity

It's good to keep safety in mind, but when you become sufficiently paranoid, your own attempts to shield yourself (or others) from danger can become a danger itself. In this age of color-coded alerts, it gives you a warm sense of *Schadenfreude* when you hear that the mastermind behind the Capitol's new fail-safe antiterrorism system was hoisted by his own petard.[4]

We can chuckle a bit because George M. White, who helped design a $725,000 security system, only suffered a bloody nose when a hydraulic barrier skewered his 1987 Mercury Marquis. The three-foot-high metal barrier hadn't fully receded beneath the pavement when the chauffeur clanged over it. The front tires and undercarriage were damaged, and the vehicle had to be towed. White was treated by the attending physician at the Capitol.

■■

Less fortunate was Ricardo Gonzalez, a Cuban immigrant who floated on an inner tube to South Florida in 1992. He settled into a trailer near Fort Lauderdale, but the neighborhood was not the safest. First, his bike was stolen. A few weeks later, a group of teenage bullies attacked him, so he started carrying a sack of homemade explosives in order to

---

[4] A petard was a medieval battering ram with an explosive head. To be hoisted meant to be lifted or blown up. Thus to be hoist with one's own petard is to be blown up by one's own weapons.

protect himself from muggers (like you do). Unfortunately, one of the bombs in his bag exploded. He tried to take another grenade out of the bag, and it exploded in his hand. He was arrested, and the bomb squad was called to detonate the two remaining grenades.

■■

Rita Rupp of Tulsa, Oklahoma, had perhaps watched too many episodes of *CSI: NY*. She was so worried about the teeming crime she was likely to encounter on a cross-country drive that when she and husband Floyd set out for New York for a wedding, she prewrote a note that she could drop if there was an emergency. It said, "Help Kidnaped Call Highway Patrol. My Ford Van Cream and Blue Oklahoma" and finally her name and phone number.

She put the note in her purse and forgot all about it. But when the couple made a pit stop in Auburn, Massachusetts, Rita accidentally dropped the note. Police issued an all points bulletin, and the story was splashed all over the news. The next day Floyd called his office to check messages and told a coworker, "I'm sitting here enjoying a view of the ocean."

"You have no idea what's going on, do you?" the manager replied.

■■

But don't assume that paranoia is simply a product of our post-September 11 culture. There have always been people who should have had the sense to fear fear itself. Thomas Nuttall was a pioneering British botanist, ornithologist, and zoologist who traveled to North America in 1808 to study the previously undocumented flora and fauna of much of the U.S. Northwest. His talent for botany was, unfortunately, not well matched by his talent as an explorer.

He was nicknamed "Old Curious" and was a little obsessive about finding new species. Occasionally he would wander away from his group while collecting plants and become lost. His colleagues often had to light beacons to help him get back to camp. One time,

> There have always been people who should have had the sense to **fear** fear itself.

he wandered so far that a search party was sent to look for him, but when Nuttall spotted them he assumed they were Indians and tried to escape. The would-be rescuers were forced to pursue him through the bush for three days. Eventually, they had chased him around in a circle long enough that he accidentally wandered into camp himself.

■ ■

Official security has been known to create comical overreactions as well. This next one sounds like something from the movie *Airplane*, but indeed it happened. Flight controllers at Oakland International Airport in Waterford, Michigan (which in spite of its fancy name is a small field catering primarily to private pilots) were speaking with a corporate Gulfstream jet over the radio in the year 2000 when they clearly heard someone in the background saying "hijack."

They called the FBI and police. The plane, which had just taken off, was ordered to return, and armed SWAT teams were there waiting for the plane. It took a little while to sort out what had happened. What the tower controllers had heard was a passenger greeting a friend, who happened to be named "Jack." Everyone had a good laugh, and the plane was allowed to continue on its way.

■ ■

Sometimes you've just got to go, and you generally don't want to draw too much attention to yourself when you use the toilet. You certainly don't expect to end up in handcuffs. In the post-September 11 world, however, anything has the potential to set off a security alert when you travel by air. In February 2002 a Delta Airlines passenger flying from Los Angeles to Salt Lake City decided he just couldn't wait to use the restroom even though the aircraft was only twenty-five minutes from touchdown and the "Fasten Seatbelts" sign was on. After relieving himself, he was scolded by an air hostess and ordered to take his seat. He gave a triumphant "thumbs up" sign to another passenger. Two air marshals saw the gesture, thought it was suspicious, and took him into custody. Just to be sure no one tried anything, they ordered all the

> Sometimes you've just got to go.

other passengers on the flight to put their hands on their heads until the plane had safely landed.

But mistaking urination for terrorism didn't begin in 2001. Back in 1983 Johan Peter Grzeganek, a twenty-three-year-old German who spoke little English, was jailed for making a bomb threat because he had to go to the bathroom. A few minutes after the plane took off from the Hollywood–Fort Lauderdale Airport, Grzeganek realized that he would not be able to hold it until the "Fasten Seatbelts" sign was turned off. He asked the flight attendant for permission to go. She told him to stay in his seat. He objected, saying that his bladder would explode and "the roof will fly."

Although the flight attendant spoke German, she misinterpreted the slang expression and assumed he was threatening to blow up the plane. Crew members wrestled him to the floor, turned the plane around, and made an emergency landing. He was taken to jail, where he stayed for ten months, unable to make the $10,000 bond. Finally U.S. District Judge Norman Roettger cleared up the confusion. "It's a disgrace he's been in jail this long," he said. "Do you see anything that happened that couldn't have been remedied by letting this man go to the bathroom?"

■ ■

A number of years ago I was ready to board an airplane. I had done my share of traveling, and I anticipated the gate clerk's questions. I set my bag on the scale and announced, "I packed my bags myself. No one unknown to me has given me anything to take on board the flight."

The clerk paused, then said, "I have to ask you anyway. Did you pack your bags yourself?"

Of course, it was all I could do to keep from answering, "No."

Recently, when the federal government revamped airport security, they realized that the questions they'd been asking for years were not really going to root out terrorists. The obvious reason? A person who actually intends to blow up an airplane is not going to tell you so just because you ask. Liars lie. At least that is what I thought until I read the following story.

Now far be it from me to offer advice to potential terrorists, but I am probably not revealing any huge national security secrets when

I say that smuggling weapons is much more successful if you do your best to avoid customs screenings.

An entire plot to overthrow the military regime that rules the Seychelles archipelago in the western Indian Ocean came undone because of a curious lapse on the part of one of the conspirators. In 1981 Colonel Mike Horare, a mercenary whose 1960s exploits during the war in the Belgian Congo were dramatized in the film *The Wild Geese*, hatched a plan to seize Victoria, the capital city of Seychelles. He assembled a team of forty-seven soldiers who entered an airplane posing as a vacationing rugby team.

> I am probably not revealing any huge national security secrets when I say that smuggling weapons is much more successful if you do your best to avoid customs screenings.

Being a nation made up of 176 square miles of mostly beaches and ocean, with tourism, coconut exports, and fish canning its main sources of income, security at the Seychelles Airport was not what you would find in, say, Israel. In fact, it was basically run on the honor system. Most of the would-be conquerors smuggled their AK-47s in golf bags and suitcases. One of the mercenaries, however, was concerned about something he was carrying. He had stashed several litchi fruits that he thought might violate agricultural import regulations. So he decided to enter the voluntary custom inspections line. The customs inspector wasn't nearly as concerned about the fruit as he was the AK-47.

The battle started prematurely as security guards pulled their weapons and some of the mercenaries pulled theirs. Most of the group were captured, but a few hijacked a plane back to South Africa, where they were promptly arrested.

■■

By far, the ultimate example of someone held captive by his own attempts at security was Hiroo Onoda, who continued to fight World War II until March 9, 1974. In 1944 Onoda was stationed on the island of Lubang in the Philippines with orders to organize Japanese troops to fight off the invading Americans.

Onoda was not prepared for the carnage that came with the U.S. invasion. As he described in his book, *No Surrender*, the American soldiers brought overwhelming force and their own sense of proportion. He saw U.S. Marines take down a single soldier with a five-inch cannon. They walked over terrain littered with Japanese bodies, chewing gum and dropping the wrappers as they went.

> The American soldiers brought overwhelming force and their own sense of proportion.

Onoda and four Japanese survivors headed for the hills. They struggled to survive with a little rice, bananas, and coconut milk. When those ran dry they "liberated" supplies from the islanders. Onoda never lost hope because his superior officer had assured him, "Whatever happens, we'll come back for you." Years went by.

One day leaflets rained from the sky announcing the war was over, but the four soldiers would not be fooled. It was all clever U.S. propaganda. In 1949 (four years after the war had officially ended), a weak-willed member of the quartet surrendered. Another was killed in a skirmish in 1954.

By now the remaining two holdouts, Onoda and another named Kozuka, were completely and utterly convinced that the Americans would stop at nothing to flush them out of the jungle, and they would not waver. Onoda's family left personal letters and photos on the island. They left stacks of newspapers showing the day's peaceful headlines, but they were taken as further evidence of the Americans' shrewdness.

When Onoda's brother stood in a clearing calling to him over a loudspeaker, Onoda hid in the jungle, thinking that it was an uncanny impersonation. In 1972 Onoda's last ally was killed, and he was left to fight World War II alone. Finally Onoda stumbled upon a Japanese camper, Norio Suzuki. Suzuki struck up a conversation with Onoda and began to persuade him that there was peace in Japan. Even though Onoda seemed convinced, he wouldn't leave unless he was ordered to do so by his commanding officer. On March 9 his former CO, Major Yoshimi Taniguchi, now a bookseller, traveled to Lubang.

When Onoda saw him, he saluted and said, "Lieutenant Onoda, sir, reporting for orders." The retired major ordered him to stop fighting and return to his family. The war was finally over for Lieutenant Onoda.

Onoda returned to Japan as an amusing folk hero, but he found it all a little embarrassing. "For thirty years I had thought I was doing something for my country," he wrote. "But now it looked as though I had just caused a lot of people a lot of trouble."

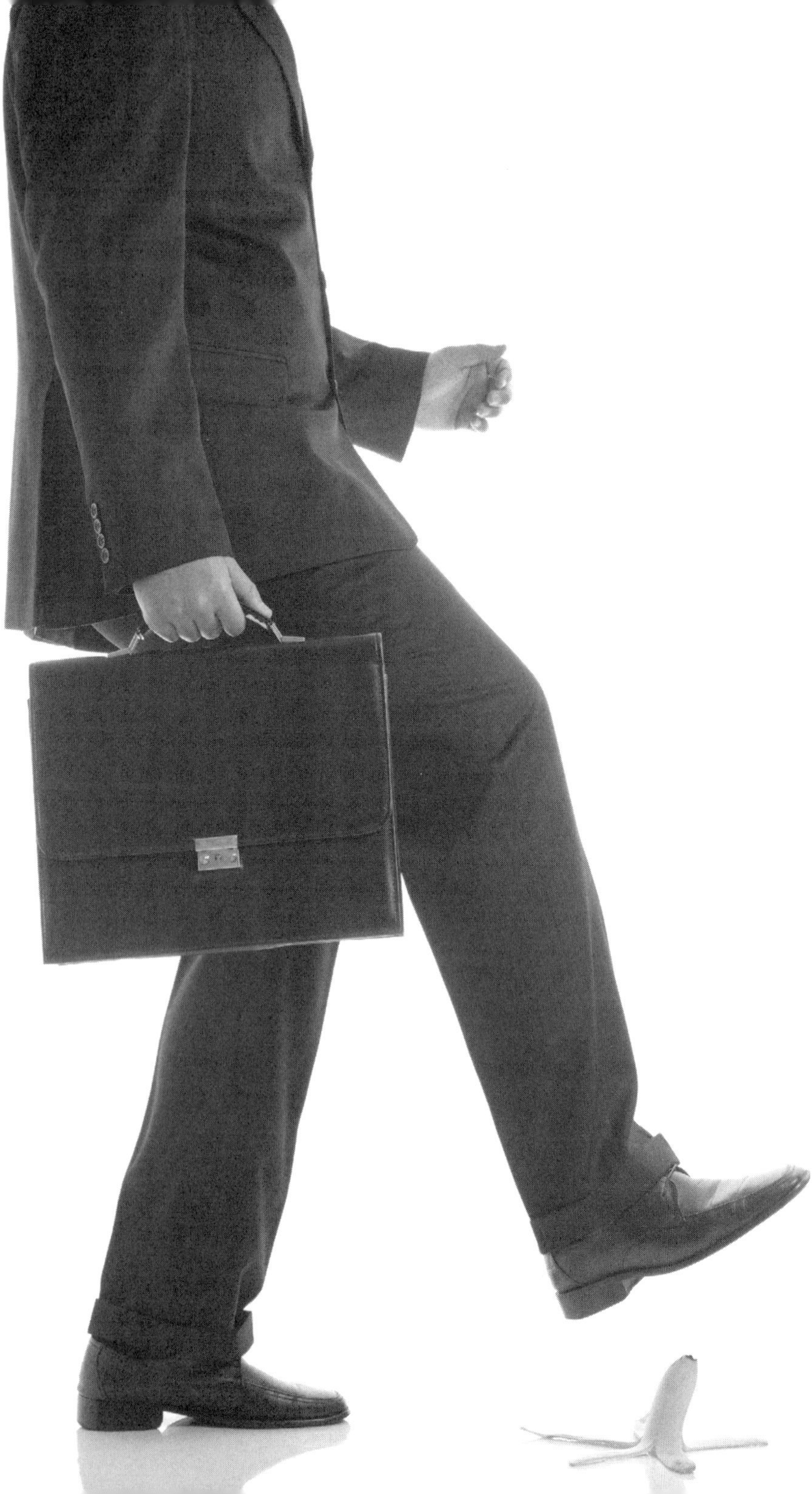

XI.
Cartoonish Accidents

Sometimes an accident or a mishap creates a visual image reminiscent of a cartoon. It's no fun for the person who actually suffers, but it just strikes a chord that makes you laugh.

Random Acts *of* Cartoonness

Take the case of the ninety-one-year-old German man (the Reuters news service didn't name him) who needed a rescue after he slipped while repairing his roof and somehow glued himself in place. He was recoating the roof with bitumen when he fell and got stuck "like a beetle on its back." Local firemen detached him using ropes and ladders. He was unharmed, but sticky.

■ ■

You remember the song about the old woman who swallowed the fly? Life imitates art. Mustafa Kaya, a Turkish farmer, accidentally swallowed a fly. He was afraid it would lay eggs and multiply inside him, so he took a big swig of insecticide to kill it. It may have killed the fly, and it came very close to killing Kaya. "I never knew just a bit of insecticide could do me harm," he said from his hospital bed.

> "I never knew just a bit of insecticide could do me harm," he said from his hospital bed.

From the 1989 British book *That's Life* (it seems to have written itself, as no author is listed) comes the story of a Swedish professor who literally lost his audience. He must have been a very important guest, for they had him address a full house in the best lecture hall at a university in California. The hall was fully automated with a splendid desk with an array of buttons. The buttons could be used to dim the lights, change slides, draw the blinds and so on.

As the lecturer became engrossed in his subject matter, he leaned forward, placing both forearms firmly on the row of buttons. There was a grinding noise, and within seconds the audience sank out of sight and a dance floor closed over their heads. The professor was quite alone.

> There was a **grinding** noise, and within seconds the audience sank out of sight and a dance floor closed over their heads.

Sports Shorts

Of course, we take even more pleasure when an accident comes as the result of a foolish stunt, as it did when Tim Hurlbut decided to streak at an NHL ice hockey game in Calgary, Canada. The twenty-one-year-old college student needed money to buy new textbooks, so when two strangers offered him $200 to jump over the boards wearing only his red socks, he was game.

But there is a reason you find so few streakers at hockey games: the ice is slippery, not to mention cold. Hurlbut stumbled over the boards and landed unconscious on the ice. There he lay for six minutes as God made him as the medical staff was called to attend to him. He was arrested and charged with public drunkenness. The judge criticized the young man for making a "pathetic spectacle of yourself splayed naked on the ice...."

The $200 bet would have come in handy in paying the $2,500 (Canadian) fine, but the men who dared him to perform the stunt were long gone. A nightclub, the Cowboys Dance Hall, staged a fund raiser to help recoup the money.

"Come down and lend your support for a man who brought so much joy into our lives with a simple pair of red socks," said the Cowboys manager.

∎ ∎

A helpful hint for would-be daredevils: if you plan to bungee jump, don't scrimp on the cost of the elastic cord. Eric Barcia, a twenty-two-year-old from Virginia, had always wanted to try bungee jumping, but not knowing where to get a cord, he decided to make one himself. He collected a bunch of elastic cords with hooks on the ends and connected them to each other with electrical tape. Next, he fastened his homemade bungee to a railroad trestle and jumped. You're probably expecting me to say that the cord came apart. In fact, it did not, but this is only because Barcia failed to measure the distance from the trestle to the ground. The cord he'd assembled was longer than the distance he was to travel, so he hit the ground at full speed.

∎ ∎

In the early 1970s, bowling centers started using a new, harder finish to coat the lanes on the pro tour. The new coating was more durable, but the ball tended to skid more. Bowlers came up with a chemical solution; they found that if they soaked a bowling ball in a chemical solvent overnight, it would soften the surface and the ball would grab the lane better. There was only one drawback: the solvent they used, methyl ethyl ketone, was toxic and flammable. It could burn your lungs and even cause brain damage, but those are small considerations when you're trying to bowl a perfect game.

One night in 1973, fourteen bowlers were staying at an Illinois motel during a PBA tournament. When guests started complaining to the management of a strange odor emanating from nearby rooms, the owner decided to investigate. He was not pleased to discover bowling balls soaking in tubs of dangerous solvent. He told the bowlers in no uncertain terms—either they got the chemical vats out of the room or they would have to leave.

The bowlers lugged their pails of soaking balls out into the parking lot. Late that night a weary traveler pulled into what he thought was an empty parking space and crashed into the pails, knocking them over. The motel, as luck would have it, was at the top of a hill. Gravity did its work, and soon bowling balls were plowing into cars, trees, and lampposts. Guests were treated to a display of dozens of bowlers in their nightclothes chasing bowling balls around the lot. Some of the balls were a block away when they finally came to rest.

That was the end of the line for soaking bowling balls. Companies started making presoftened bowling balls soon after, and the bowlers put the explosive chemicals away.

■ ■

We close this section with the only person so bad at golf that he managed to destroy a nation's entire air force. Admittedly, destroying the air force of the West African republic of Benin was not quite as difficult as it might sound. In 1987 the entire air force consisted of five jets. Nevertheless, it has to rank up there as a stunning achievement in the world of sports.

Mathieu Boya of Porto-Novo, Benin, liked to relax when he finished his shift in a cotton-processing plant with a few practice swings. Because Benin had no golf course, Boya whacked at the balls in a nearby field, which happened to be beside the Benin Air Base. Given these conditions, it's not surprising that his shots could be a bit wild. On this particular afternoon, Boya's shot flew straight over the barbed-wire fence and up into the air, where it crashed into a large bird. The stunned creature tumbled out of the sky. As it happened, the bird had been flying directly above a trainer jet that was taxiing into position with its canopy open. The bird smacked into the pilot's helmet, and the disoriented pilot lost control of his craft. It veered off the runway and right into the row of parked planes. They fell into each other like so many dominoes and exploded into a dramatic fireball.

Meanwhile, Boya was standing in stunned disbelief with the golf club still in his hand. He was arrested and charged with hooliganism. He was given the option of making restitution, but since the airplanes were worth about $40 million and he earned slightly less than that (about $275 a year), he decided to take the jail time.

Jangled Out *of* Tune

Being a rock star is all about the image. A cartoonish accident can quickly deflate that sexy, swaggering style and bring a *Schadenfreude* snicker to the lips. I risk revealing my age by sharing this item clipped from a fan magazine in the 1980s (the things we do for our art): At the 1985 San Remo song festival, the lead singer of Duran Duran, Simon LeBon, accidentally knocked over his microphone and had to improvise. He lip-synched the last chorus of "The Wild Boys" into the handle of his walking stick, which he was using because he had broken his toe in Italy.

About a decade later, Jon Secada, the Cuban-born Grammy Award winner who got his start as a backup singer with Gloria Estefan, was given the honor of appearing as part of the opening ceremonies for the World Cup. He made his grand entrance and immediately slipped into a hole on the stage that had been covered with a white sheet. The band had already started the first song, so he had no choice but to sing from the hole with only his head above stage level. Afterwards he was taken to a nearby hospital and treated for a dislocated shoulder.

■■

Classical musicians have their share of cartoon accidents as well. In the United States Tchaikovsky's *1812 Overture* has become a Fourth of July staple for orchestras. Why this would be is a bit unclear. It was written to commemorate Napoleon's defeat in Russia. Its popularity at patriotic celebrations outside Russia can't be because of its triumphant acclamation of "Lord God, Protect the Czar." It's got to be the cannons. Tchaikovsky's score is one of the few ever written to include percussion by cannons. There are five shots in the beginning and eleven blasts in the finale. It is a popular work with orchestras worldwide. If nothing else, it keeps audiences awake. The English have even produced a version performed by sheep and chickens, which led author Margaret Atwood to quip, "Generals screw up, their fiascoes get made into art and then the art gets made into fiascoes. Such is the march of progress."

Here's another example of that march of progress. In 1999 Paolo Esperanza, the honored bass trombonist of the Simphonica Mayor de Uruguay, decided that firing a real cannon wasn't quite exciting enough. He came up with a plan to spice things up a bit at an outdoor children's concert. Paolo, who was presumably more talented at music than physics, placed a large lit firecracker—equivalent to a quarter stick of dynamite—into an aluminum straight mute, which he put into the bell of his double-valve bass trombone.

> "I thought the bell of my trombone would shield me from the explosion and would focus the blast outward," he later said from his **hospital bed.**

"I thought the bell of my trombone would shield me from the explosion and would focus the blast outward," he later said from his hospital bed. When the firecracker went off, the mute shot like a cannon through the woodwind and viola players, finally striking the conductor and knocking him into the audience. The folding chairs started to collapse like so many dominoes. The sound of falling audience members drowned out the music. Meanwhile, back on stage, a burst of superheated gas surged through the trombone. The bell split and peeled back on itself, the mouthpiece fused to the lead pipe, and Esperanza suffered third-degree burns to the mouth and face. Not only did he tumble backwards off his seat, he also let go of his instrument. The hot slide shot out and hit the third clarinetist on the head, knocking him unconscious.

■■

In his *(Incomplete) Book of Failures*, Stephen Pile recounts the tale of an unnamed "promising American pianist" who gave a concert at the Erewan Hotel in Bangkok in the early 1970s. The pianist had been playing for only a few seconds when it became clear that there was going to be a problem. Due to the humidity in the room, the D key was sticking. This would have been a problem for any pianist, but it was especially annoying in this case because the artist was to perform a program comprised of Bach's D Minor Toccata and Fugue and his Prelude and Fugue in D Major. What is more, as a reviewer in the *Bangkok Post* noted, the piano stool had been greased within an inch of its life, and during one climactic moment, the pianist found himself swiveling around to face the crowd.

The frustrated musician gave up on the Toccata in D and decided to try Liszt's Fantasia in G Minor, at which point the G key started to stick. To free the keys as he played, he took to kicking the lower section of the piano with his foot. The old instrument's leg soon gave way, and the whole thing started to tilt about thirty-five degrees.

At this point the musician rose, bowed, and left the stage. The audience politely applauded. He returned with a fire axe and started to smash the piano. Hotel security had to wrestle the axe from the virtuoso's hands and drag him from the stage.

On Stage

Edmund Kean, who lived from 1787 to 1833, was regarded as one of the greatest actors of his day, but his first appearance on stage was an unmitigated disaster. Perhaps it was the curse of *Macbeth*. So much misfortune supposedly strikes during productions of that Shakespeare tragedy that superstitious actors won't speak its name in the theater. They call it "the Scottish Play," but the bad-luck demons see right through that.

A 1796 production was directed by Jack Kemble, who wanted to make the production a real spectacle—and succeeded beyond his wildest dreams. In act 4, scene 1, Macbeth creeps back into the cave of the Three Witches to have his fortune told for a second time. Normally, to provide the requisite creepiness, various ghosts float around in the background. But Kemble wanted to do something special. He envisioned a horde of disheveled and downtrodden-looking children chained and manacled and marching through the cave.

If you did the math from Edmund Kean's birth year, you will note that he was nine years old at this time, but he had already done a lot of living. He had run away to sea at age seven and then found that he didn't much like being forced to work while manacled in leg braces. So he managed to escape and found himself cast as a ghostly orphan in the production.

The child chain gang looked sufficiently depressing, but the dramatic effect quickly unraveled as the kids started shuffling around the stage. It was just not as easy to get a group of children to walk at a uniform pace as the director had assumed. Kemble, who had cast himself as Macbeth, was just coming to the scene's climax where he fell back, awestruck by the prophecies of the witches, when young Kean lost his balance and fell over.

The other children to whom he was tethered predictably followed like so many dominoes. The great tragedy was instantly transformed into a slapstick comedy. Audience members' eyes welled as they gave in to peals of uncontrollable laughter. And the comedy had only just begun. Once the kids were chained together on the floor in a disordered heap, they couldn't get back up. Each time one boy managed to get himself upright, another kid would try to get up and pull the first guy down again. The various ghosts waiting for their entrances were trapped in the wings because they couldn't get past the mound of manacled moppets.

∎∎

Stage hypnotists have suffered their share of mishaps as well. Ann Hazard—yes, that's her real name—was put under by a stage hypnotist at Glasgow's Pavilion Theater. While under hypnosis, Ann asked the hypnotist, Robert Halpern, if she could go to the lavatory, and he told her to "go by the quickest exit." She went to the front of the stage and fell off, breaking her right leg in two places. She later sued the theater for £80,000 in damages. She didn't sue the hypnotist because variety acts aren't known for their deep pockets.

Car Trouble

Vehicles, of course, are a great source of unintentionally comic misery. Take, for example, the accidental thrill ride race-car driver Buddy Baker got at the Smoky Mountain Raceway in 1968. His Dodge blew a tire, spun out of control, and crashed into a cement wall. He was helped out of his car and had suffered broken ribs and a concussion.

Fortunately, they kept a vehicle at the raceway in case they needed to speed an injured driver to the hospital. Unfortunately, it was an old retired hearse. The medics strapped Baker onto a stretcher with wheels and loaded him into the back of the hearse. When they closed the door, it didn't latch.

As the driver hit the gas, the back door flew open, and Buddy rolled right out. The gurney started its own lap around the racetrack. The real race cars were under a caution flag, but they were not going slowly enough for a wheeled stretcher to outrun them. Baker's life began to flash before his eyes. He was sure that his obituary the next morning would read "Race Car Driver Killed in Gurney Accident."

Thankfully, Don Naman, the fast-thinking pace-car driver, waved the cars as close to the wall as he could. The drivers couldn't help but chuckle as they saw Buddy rolling past them with the ambulance drivers in hot pursuit.

The medics finally caught up with the stretcher and wheeled it back to the hearse, but Buddy had had enough adventure for one day. He leaped off the stretcher and sat in the front seat with the drivers. After he was treated and released, they offered to take him back to the speedway in the hearse, but he said no way!

Demonstrations Gone Wrong

A special brand of cartoonish accident is the one that begins with someone saying, "Here, I'll show you...." Demonstrations gone wrong can sometimes produce snickers instead of sympathy. One example from Hollywood star Eleanor Powell. She was in a class by herself when it came to screen tap-dancing stars. Her style was the polar opposite of Fred Astaire, with whom she was paired in the film *Broadway Melody of 1940*. Where Fred was graceful and smooth, Eleanor was a high-energy powerhouse.

In one of the numbers in the film, she was paired with George Murphy. The "Between You and Me" sequence was described by *Action Magazine* as "ending with swirling, partnered spin-outs, a galloping tap pattern scooting the breadth of the stage." The construction of the sets for this number was of utmost importance. Everything had to be designed to allow her to move freely and safely. Unfortunately, the dancer was not consulted before the building started.

During rehearsals, Eleanor realized that the ramp on which she and George Murphy were to slide was too high and she asked to have it adjusted.

    The technical expert, Arnold Gillespie, didn't want to make any time-consuming changes. He told the star, "Watch me do it. It will be fine." So she stood aside and watched as Gillespie did a few taps on the ramp . . . and twisted his ankle. The crew made the adjustment.

■■

In 1871 the highly regarded defense attorney Clement Vallandingham was defending a man named Thomas McGehan, charged with shooting another man in a barroom brawl. Vallandingham planned to argue that the victim had accidentally shot himself while drawing his pistol. "I will show you in half a second," Vallandingham said. He picked up a revolver, put it in his right pocket, drew it out, and in the process snapped the hammer. He had picked up the wrong gun and didn't realize he was demonstrating with a loaded weapon. It went off and shot Vallandingham in the abdomen. Twelve hours later he was dead. His client was acquitted.

■■

In 1918 Chung Ling Soo asked two people to shoot at him. They did. He died. No surprises there. Unfortunately, this was not how it was meant to be. Soo was a magician, a contemporary of Harry Houdini, and he was a sensation in Europe. He performed in silk robes and had his head shaved except for one long braid in back. Londoners loved the exotic magician.

    The incident was part of a magic trick called "Condemned to Death by the Boxers." The bullets were supposed to go into a dummy chamber in a trick gun, and he would miraculously catch the bullets in a plate. Instead, a flaw in the plug in the gun sent the real bullet into the gun's real barrel and inevitably into the illusionist's chest. The most remarkable story was yet to come. Soo, who billed himself as "The Marvelous Chinese Conjurer," performed in silence because he ostensibly did not speak any English. When the bullet tore into his body, however, Soo instantly gained the ability to speak without any trace of a Chinese accent.

"Oh my god!" he cried. "Something's happened. Lower the curtain."

It turns out that Chung Ling Soo was really Willian Robinson of Westchester County, New York. His Chinese assistant Suee Seen was Olive Path. She was born in Cleveland. What is more, she was Robinson's second wife—he had forgotten to divorce the first. He also had a mistress on the side.

Robinson had worked as an assistant to the great magicians Alexander Hermann and Harry Kellar but failed to make a name for himself until he stole someone else's. That unfortunate was a real Chinese magician named Chung Ling Foo. Robinson traveled to Europe and was so popular that by the time the real Chung Ling Foo made it over, people thought he was a fraud.

Perhaps Robinson's death was not worthy of *Schadenfreude* at all. Lee Warren, who wrote an opera about The Original Chinese Conjuror that was staged in 2006, thinks his on-stage death ensured his place in history. "If he hadn't died on stage," he said, "nobody would have remembered him." Perhaps, but I'm guessing he would have preferred a few more years with his various wives to immortality as the guy whose bullet-catching trick went wrong.

> He would have preferred a few more years with his various wives to immortality as the guy whose bullet-catching trick went wrong.

■ ■

"I worshiped Jesus Christ. I knew Jesus Christ. Pastor, you're no Jesus Christ."

In August 2006 evangelist Franck Kabele of Gabon, West Africa was so filled with the spirit that he told his congregation he'd had a revelation that anyone with faith could walk on water just like Jesus Christ.

The thirty-five-year-old took his congregation to the beach, saying he would walk across the Komo estuary, which usually takes twenty minutes to cross by boat. He walked into the water, which soon engulfed him. He never returned.

Another tale of motivation gone wrong comes from the world of sports. In 1974 Coach Butch Morgan made a special effort to fire up the Cagers, the basketball team of the College of St. Joseph the Provider in Rutland, Vermont. They were going up against their more powerful rival, Castleton State College.

Morgan selected a special poem for the occasion and had copies of "Don't Quit" printed up to give to each player as he read aloud. The four-stanza poem, by an anonymous author, contains the lines "Don't give up, though the pace seems slow; You might succeed with another blow." Morgan was clearly impressed with the bit about the slow pace. After the players had had time to read the poem, he asked them to respond to it. He gave them some time to study it and talk about it.

Meanwhile, the fans in the gym were getting restless. The referee was getting antsy, and he kept peeking into the locker room and asking, "Are you done yet?" Morgan felt that what he was doing was more important than anything that might happen on the gym floor. When the team finally emerged, the officials assessed them five technical fouls—one for each starting player—for delaying the game. The motivational speech cost them dearly. They lost 79–78.

Accidents *of* Enormous Scale

Then there are the cartoonish accidents of an enormous scale. For example, the one that made an entire lake disappear. This bizarre situation occurred in 1980. The entire lake spun away in a whirlpool like a bathtub when the plug is pooled. The thirteen-hundred-acre coastal lake, eight tugboats, nine barges, a mobile home, greenhouses, and a visitor's center all disappeared down the drain.

The neighbor that caused this curiosity was Texaco, which had located oil reserves beneath the lake. The company erected two platforms and started drilling. They never struck the oil, but when they reached a depth of 1,228 feet, they broke into a salt mine beneath the lake, owned by the Diamond Crystal Salt Company. Once they'd broken a passage into the chamber, the result was inevitable. The drilling rigs, incidentally, were sucked into the mine as well. A few days later, the lake began to refill, and the nine missing barges popped back up to the surface.

Imagine that you are sitting in a municipal building on your lunch break, eating the sandwich your wife packed in a brown paper bag, when off in the distance you hear a great rumble, and next thing you know you're swimming for your life in a rolling quagmire of molasses.

Fate had this sticky situation in store for the unsuspecting people of Boston on January 15, 1919. The initial disaster was ordinary, as disasters go. There was an explosion in a tank owned by the Purity Distilling Company of Cambridge. It toppled over and crushed a number of neighboring buildings. What happened next was far from ordinary. The tank contained about two million gallons of molasses, which coursed through the city in a mighty stream. It covered the streets with a river three inches thick. About fifty horses were engulfed. The goo sucked up a house owned by a Mrs. Clougherty and shook it from its moorings. The owner was thrown through a window and killed, one of twenty-one people drowned in molasses that day. Legend has it that on a hot summer day in Boston's North End you can still smell the molasses.

> Next thing you know you're swimming **for your life** in a rolling quagmire of molasses.

It wasn't the first time something like this happened. On October 17, 1814, in the small London parish of St. Giles, nine people drowned and two homes were destroyed when a tidal wave of beer flooded the neighborhood. The cause of the alcoholic river was the explosion of a vat containing thirty-five hundred barrels of beer. Rescuers waded into beer up to their waists to find victims who had been swept away, slammed into walls, and pinned under debris.

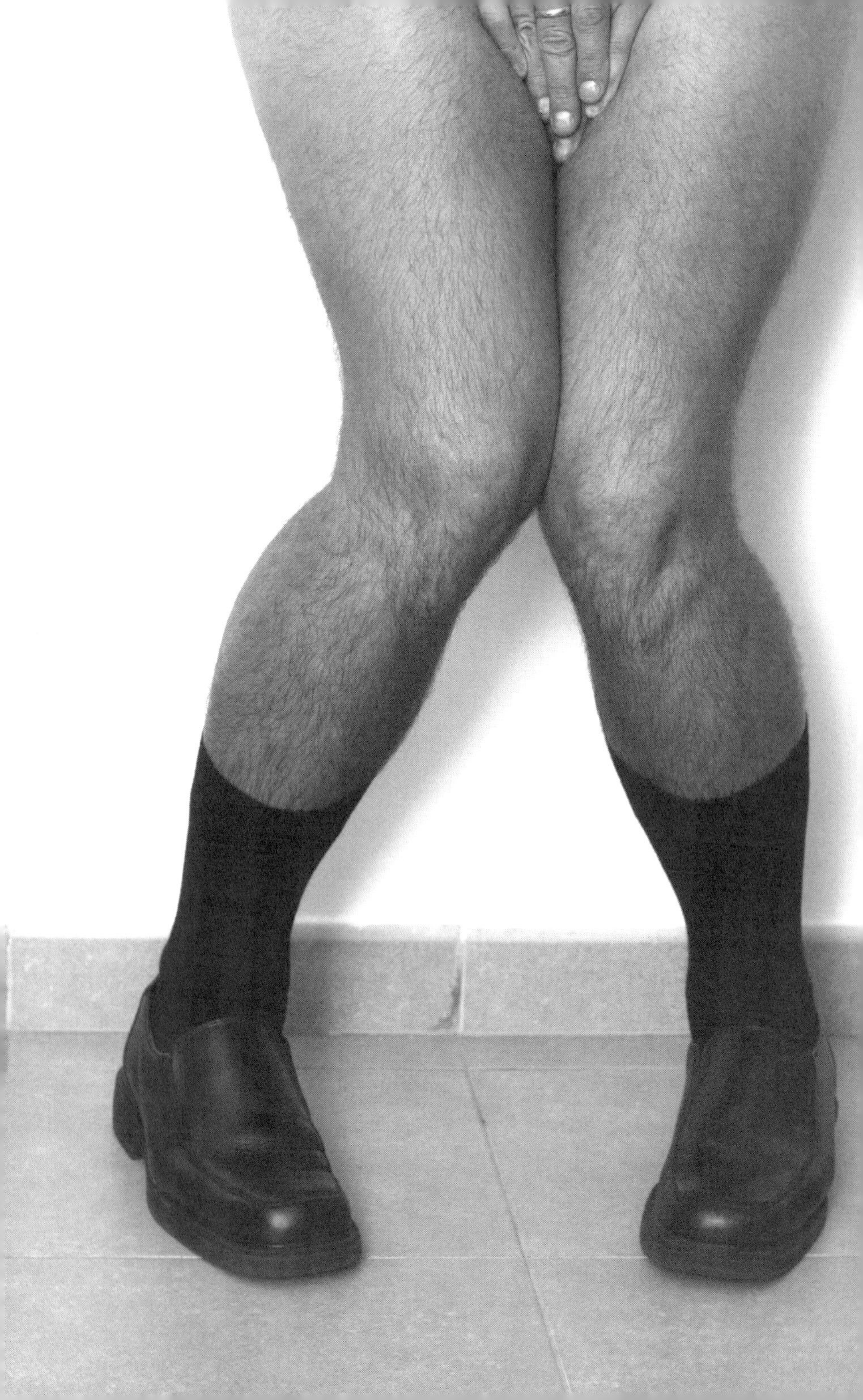

XII. Embarrassing Moments

Everyone has suffered an embarrassing moment, and they're always good for a laugh, especially when they happen to someone else.

Embarrassing Adventures *with* Technology

In 1994 a woman, whom the newspapers were tactful enough not to name, was woken by the telephone. When she picked it up, she heard heavy breathing and thought it was an obscene phone call. She hung up, but it rang again. This time she heard groaning, and she recognized the voice of her daughter crying, "Oh, my god!"

The terrified mother quickly called the police and reported that someone was attacking her daughter a hundred miles away. When the panicked mother tried to call her daughter again, all she got was a busy signal.

Police officers were immediately dispatched to the daughter's home to investigate. They found the young woman, and a man, but there was no attack. It seems during the heat of passion the couple pressed the automatic redial on the telephone at the bedside with a toe. The last number that had been dialed was the woman's mother.

A police spokesman said, "If you're going to indulge in this sort of thing, move the phone."

∷

Technology has changed life in many ways, not the least of which is the new ability to embarrass yourself at long distances with one click of the "Send" button. For whatever reason, the British seem to especially relish this form of technological voyeurism. When a juicy e-mail makes the rounds, the British media are quick to pick it up and ferret out the individuals involved.

Before we present the awards for the greatest e-mail bumbles, I humbly recommend the following additions to the twenty-first-century dictionary.

time-lapsed judgment: A force that causes you to write an angry message to someone for not answering your e-mail, when you do not know if they have logged on and seen it or not.

dumbopause: (n) The moment between hitting "Send" to send an electronic message and realizing that you wish you hadn't sent it.

the It's-Out-There Effect: An uneasy feeling in the moments between dumbopause and e-mendment.

e-mendment: (n) The electronic message you write as a correction to the original message you wish you hadn't sent.

e-ingziety: (n) The realization that the e-mendment only emphasized how dumb the original e-mail message had been.

releef: (n) What you feel when you receive your reply and learn that the recipient was not offended.

> **e-mendment:** (n) The electronic message you write as a *correction* to the original message you wish you hadn't sent.

Now the grand champion of e-mail embarrassment—Claire Swire. Claire was a serious, button-up kind of gal with an upper-crust British accent, sensible glasses and long dark hair, not that people who read her e-mail would know that.

One day in 2000 the twenty-six-year-old was sitting at her office, a little bored, and she started exchanging e-mails with her twenty-seven-year-old boyfriend, Bradley Chait, a lawyer at the firm Norton Rose. First, she sent him a joke about a robbery at a sperm bank, and he replied "cute."

A few minutes later, Claire e-mailed a graphic account of performing what the papers of the day called "a Monica Lewisnky–type sex act" on him. Brad the cad couldn't resist sharing this praise of his manhood with a few friends. He hit forward and added the line "Now THAT'S a nice compliment from a lass, isn't it?" Three minutes later, one of his friends passed it along to eleven of his closest buddies. They forwarded it to their buddies, and next thing you know, Claire's antics were being downloaded to office cubicles from Moscow to Johannesburg.

So many curiosity seekers tried to discover the lovers' identities that they caused the Norton Rose Web site to crash. Next thing you know, the media were camped out on Swire's door and parts of the e-mail, with phrases blacked out, were run in the newspapers.

Claire wrote back to some of the strange men who eventually e-mailed her directly, "What do you care about my social life? Shouldn't you all be working?" But it was to no avail. The genie was out of the bottle, and there was no containing it. Now whenever a similar e-mail gaffe makes Internet lore, the British papers call it "pulling a Claire Swire," although in all fairness it really should be called "pulling a Bradley Chait." If you want to avoid Clair Swire Status, here are a few tips.

1. Use caution when forwarding messages. In 2002 investment banker Tripp Murray met accountant Mary Callahan, an employee at PricewaterhouseCoopers. A week later he decided to send her a friendly e-mail asking what her plans were for the weekend. When she got the message, Mary decided to forward it on to a friend, along with her own comments. She talked about how her date the night before had fallen asleep during sex and revealed perhaps more than she intended about how some women's minds work.

"Ok first—here is the e-mail I received from Tripp, the new guy I met last week," she wrote. "If you want to go out, perhaps we can get him to pay for drinks at Park. Since we have not slept together, he will of course be trying to impress me and will, therefore, do anything I ask. Unlike John, who fell asleep during sex last night. I went over to his place last night around 11:30. We started having sex. When I noticed his eyes were closed for a little too long, I said 'John wake up.' At which point he shot up saying 'what'd I miss.' Yes, I think that is a new low."

But instead of clicking on "forward" to send the whole thing to her friend, she hit the "reply" button and sent the message to Tripp. He found the gaffe pretty amusing and sent the misdirected e-mail to some of his friends with the comment "you will love this." They were also amused, and Mary's e-mail zipped around the Internet with the speed of a fake virus warning.

    PricewaterhouseCoopers decided that Mary had suffered enough humiliation and didn't discipline her for the incident.

2. **If you are fond of "porn parties," be especially careful with your e-mail list.** Rachel Fountain of Brighton, England, found this out the hard way. She meant to send an e-mail invitation to watch an episode of *Sex Tips for Girls* to a friend, who happened to have the same name as her boss, the finance director at American Express. The wires got a little crossed, and the invite, which featured a picture of a naked man and a bunny-girl, went to the boss by mistake. Rachel lost her job.

3. **If you don't want your girlfriend to know about it, it's best not to put it in writing.** Trevor Luxton, age twenty-two, asked the rhetorical question, "Am I the worst boyfriend in the world?" in his sleazy e-mail. Thousands of people would soon be answering "yes."

    The subject of the e-mail was "Story Time." It said, "last night I was all geared up for a night in front of the telly watching football while Jo's still away. Suddenly I get a text from my mate's ex which says 'I'm coming round'. She comes round, we get chatting, then we start kissing and fondling (as you do). Then I find myself sitting in the armchair with a beer in one hand, remote in the other, West Ham on the box and her on her knees. Then the phone rings and it's Jo who was bored at the airport."

    He went on to report that during the conversation the girl stopped and "looked up at me, winks and whispers 'say hello to Jo for me' and then gets back to the job at hand." His "story" went out to five friends, one of whom thought the tale worthy of sharing. One of the second-tier friends forwarded it with the message, "I think we should get this dirty love rat in as much trouble as possible by sending it around the city."

    The campaign was more effective than that forwarder could have imagined. Next thing you know, the e-mail has landed in the inbox of newspapers, and "Clever Trevor" T-shirts, featuring the infamous e-mail, were on sale on the Internet. Luxton was suspended from his well-paid London job with the French bank Crédit Lyonnais over the incident, but amazingly, he didn't lose his fiancée, nineteen-year-old Jo. Jo was a travel agent and was on a business trip in Corfu when the e-mail went out. Trevor told her that the story was fiction, and she believed it.

"I know it was a joke," she told the *Daily Mirror*. Why was she talking to the press? Her mother, Brenda, took bids for the rights to her story. She was reportedly offered £10,000 but said that she wanted three times that much.

4. **If you are dating several women at one time, and you send them all the same romantic e-mail, be sure to use the blind-carbon-copy feature and not "cc."** Mark Ridgewell, a forty-four-year-old divorcé whose description on an Internet date site said he was "totally faithful" and "extremely loving and sincere," was dating at least four women in 2003. In order to avoid messing up their names, he called them each "Princess." That was also a big time saver when it came to e-mail correspondence. He could write a saucy e-mail to "Princess" and send it to all the women at once. Unfortunately, the CC feature, which showed the e-mail addresses of all the recipients, gave him away. The women decided to turn the tables on him. One of the women invited Mark to the pub. He was shocked when the other three burst in with local news cameras in tow.

5. **Be wary of the "Reply all" feature.** Sharon Dyson, who was on a business trip in Australia, was one recipient of an e-mail her boyfriend Alex had sent to her and thirty friends. She decided to write back to him, and instead of hitting "Reply" she hit "Reply all," and her message was zapped to everyone on the list. This would have been no more than a minor annoyance had her message not contained lurid details of the couple's phone sex sessions. Soon everyone Alex had ever met knew exactly how his girlfriend

pleasured herself while thinking of him and what she planned to do with him and a bottle of massage oil when she got home to London. To make matters worse, she also included unfavorable remarks about her firm's clients. "I have to write a sucky 'thank you' email to clients now," she said.

6. **Listservs are different from personal e-mail.** The Republican New York assemblyman Willis Stephens was reading an online discussion board frequented by his constituents in June 2005. Stephens was normally what you could call a "lurker." He monitored the conversations but didn't post. The listserv was created by a Democratic village trustee who was a longtime political adversary.

Stephens decided to send a message about what he was reading to aide Beth Coursen. "Just watching the idiots pontificate," he wrote. Unfortunately, instead of sending the message to his aides, he sent it to the listserv's mailing list of nearly three hundred constituents. Realizing fairly quickly that calling your constituents "idiots" is hardly a page out of Emily Post, Stephens sent out a red-faced follow-up.

"To all who read and post on this group, I honestly enjoy reading most of what is exchanged on this site and do not direct my indiscreet characterizations to anyone in particular or to the group in general. In fact, now I most closely resemble the type of poster I described."

Pratfalls by People *in* Power

This is a good lead-in to a special category of embarrassing moment, pratfalls by people in power. It must be hard to be a world leader and to have every utterance recorded and analyzed. You're expected to be articulate and appropriate at all times. That's tough, especially when you're dealing with a foreign language, culture, and protocol. Which is not to say that we're willing to cut our world leaders any slack when they put their foot in it.

From George W. Bush calling out "Yo! Blair" (an even deeper embarrassment for Blair than for Bush) and winking at the Queen to the translation gaffe that had Jimmy Carter saying he "desired the Poles carnally," diplomatic faux pas are usually more entertaining than they are truly damaging. Thus we can rehash them here for our amusement.

When Bill Clinton was given a Romanian flag as a gift, he noticed that it had a big hole in the middle. The hole was there to symbolize the 1989 revolt that brought the country to democracy. The U.S. president hadn't been briefed on this factoid, so he sent a note to Romania thanking them for the "poncho." The White House PR team excused the gaffe by saying that Mr. Clinton was only "joking" and that it was a "light-hearted comment."

In 1999 Clinton ruffled some feathers with another "light-hearted comment" when, during a speech on cultural tolerance, he compared the two sides in the Irish peace process to "a couple of drunks" who can't leave the bar. His remarks fed into the stereotype of the Irish drunk, and he was forced to issue a standard Clinton apology: "I used a metaphor which was inappropriate, and I am sorry," he said.

■ ■

We all have family dramas and embarrassing relatives. (Before you get smug about it, the corollary to this is that we are all somebody's embarrassing relative.) When you're president of the United States, family dramas shine on a monumental scale.

The award for the absolutely greatest achievement in familial embarrassment goes to first brother Billy Carter. From releasing a beer that tanked to urinating in public to judging and participating in a world-championship belly-flop competition, Jimmy's little brother was the comic relief to the president's straight man. During the Carter presidency, Billy Carter, thirteen years Jimmy's junior, held court at his Plains, Georgia, gas station cracking wise.

"I'm a George Wallace Democrat who voted for Jimmy Carter only because he's my brother," he said. You never knew what was going to come out of his chain-smoking, beer-chugging mouth next, and reporters swirled around, hoping to capture something outrageous. Billy was happy to play it up. He made himself available for personal appearances such as ribbon cuttings, judging beauty pageants, and basically anything that would pay him his $5,000 fee. His income from such appearances was estimated to be more than twice his brother's presidential salary. And it was worth every penny in those pre–reality-TV days to see him swig beer in the hotel where matrons of the temperance union were gathering for a national convention or to watch him dressed in a white tuxedo and top hat flying away in a hot-air balloon or to hear him blasting "damn Yankees" or call the IRS "SOBs."

His attempt at entrepreneurship was "Billy Beer," a foamy swill that was generally undrinkable and disappeared from the shelves as soon as the novelty wore off. Most people who bought the stuff did so for the cans rather than the content, thinking they'd be swell collectors items. Because everyone else did this as well, a six-pack of Billy Beer, which sold for $1.75 in the day, fetches about as much today on eBay.

Big brother Jimmy tried not to interfere with his brother's business, which is just as well, because if he did, Billy said, "I'd tell him to kiss my ass." But the president had to have wished Billy would tone it down just a bit.

There was, for example, the time when he met an African-American city council candidate, Carter Gilmore, who quipped that they were both "Carters" and maybe they were related. Billy Carter replied, "Every family has a nigger in the woodpile." Carter Gilmore demanded a public apology, but Billy refused.

But his pièce de résistance when it came to embarrassing the White House occurred when he accepted a $220,000 loan for representing Libya's interests and got a federal investigation aimed at him just in time for Jimmy's reelection campaign. When the younger Carter died of pancreatic cancer at age fifty-one, Rev. Dan Ariel said of him, "Those of us who knew him well and cherished his friendship could begin a long list with the words 'Billy Carter was the only person I have ever known who . . .' and you can fill in the blank." That's a good summation for the rest of us as well.

■■

Problems with diplomacy are not an American invention. In fact, a British royal may be—to choose a metaphor—the king of gaffes. Prince Philip, the husband of Queen Elizabeth II, accompanies her majesty on her diplomatic travels. This cannot have been easy for a tough, no-

nonsense ex-naval officer who distinguished himself in World War II. Let's just say political correctness is not his strongest suit. In fact, an entire book was published celebrating his unscripted remarks around the world. It's called *Duke of Hazard: The Wit and Wisdom of Prince Philip* and was compiled by Phil Dampier and Ashley Walton.

Here are some of the greatest hits: Once in Cardiff, Wales, when addressing young members of the British Deaf Association who were standing close to a band playing steel drums, he said, "Deaf? If you are near there, no wonder you are deaf." In Scotland he asked a driving instructor how he managed to "keep the natives off the booze" long enough to pass the driving test. In Hungary he told a British man he must have arrived recently because he hadn't yet "got a pot belly." He asked Aborigines in Australia if they still threw spears at each other. At a Hindu temple in London he asked priests if they were Tamil Tiger terrorists. He once told a thirteen-year-old schoolboy that he was too fat to fulfill his dream of becoming an astronaut, and most infamously of all, in 1986 he told British students in Beijing, China, that "if you stay here much longer you'll all be slitty-eyed."

■■

At least Prince Philip never stole anything, which is more than can be said for Russian president Vladimir Putin, proud possessor of a Super Bowl championship ring. At a meeting of American business executives and Putin, New England Patriots owner Robert Kraft decided to show his diamond-encrusted 2005 ring to the former KGB agent. The ring, which had 124 diamonds, was worth more than $15,000. Putin apparently misunderstood Kraft's offer to examine the ring. He looked it over, admired it as he modeled it on his hand, then put it in his pocket and walked away. When the story of the stolen ring started to make international headlines, it was time for Kraft to perform some diplomacy of his own:

"I showed the president my most recent Super Bowl ring," Kraft said in a press statement. The Russian president "was clearly taken with its uniqueness. At that point, I decided to give him the ring as a symbol of the respect and admiration that I have for the Russian people and the leadership of President Putin."

Putin, ever cool, had "nyet comment" about the gaffe. The Super Bowl ring was deposited in the Kremlin library.

■ ■

Getting back to our current commander in chief, in international situations he often seems to relish acting out the stereotype of Americans as backslapping cowboys. His laid-back, folksy style plays well in the heartland, but it has not always played well on ceremonial occasions. While Tony Blair (much to the dismay of the British populace) seemed comfortable being addressed as "Yo! Blair," the German chancellor Angela Merkel reacted less warmly when the American president tried to give her an unsolicited back rub during the 2006 G-8 Summit. Merkel, who was named by *Forbes* magazine as the most powerful woman in the world, violently shrugged the commander in chief's hands off her shoulders with an alarmed look on her face that any would-be Romeo will recognize as the "don't touch me" stare. The German press loved this one. They called it "Bush's Love Attack on Merkel!"

■ ■

But the greatest political pratfall of all was committed by George W's father, President George H. W. Bush. It may have been through no fault of his own, but losing your lunch on the lap of the Japanese prime minister, Kiichi Miyazawa, during a 1992 state dinner ranks about as high as it gets on the diplomatic embarrassment scale.

It was amusing to Americans—Dana Carvey did an obligatory skit based on the incident on *Saturday Night Live*, but to the Japanese it was comedy gold. They had a variety act that became a show-biz sensation over there. It was a monkey trained to throw up and faint at the command "Bush-san! Bush-san!" (We can only assume this is funnier if you're Japanese.) The Japanese coined a new term for a humiliating episode of public vomiting, *bushusuru*, which translates loosely as "pulling a Bush."

A *Baltimore Sun* reporter gave an example of the expression used in context: It takes place in the Roppongi nightclub

> The Japanese coined a new term for a humiliating episode of **public vomiting,** *bushusuru,* which translates loosely as "pulling a Bush."

district between a man in a trench coat and a companion in a dark suit.

Trench coat (pointing to sidewalk): "Abunai yo!" (Hey, watch out!)

Dark suit (looking down): "Jaa, dare ga Bushushita, ne!" (Jeez, somebody did a Bush, didn't they?)

The expression stuck because they needed such a word. It is a feature of Japanese nightlife that men often deliberately get as drunk as they can as fast as they can and then lose their stomach contents in inappropriate places.

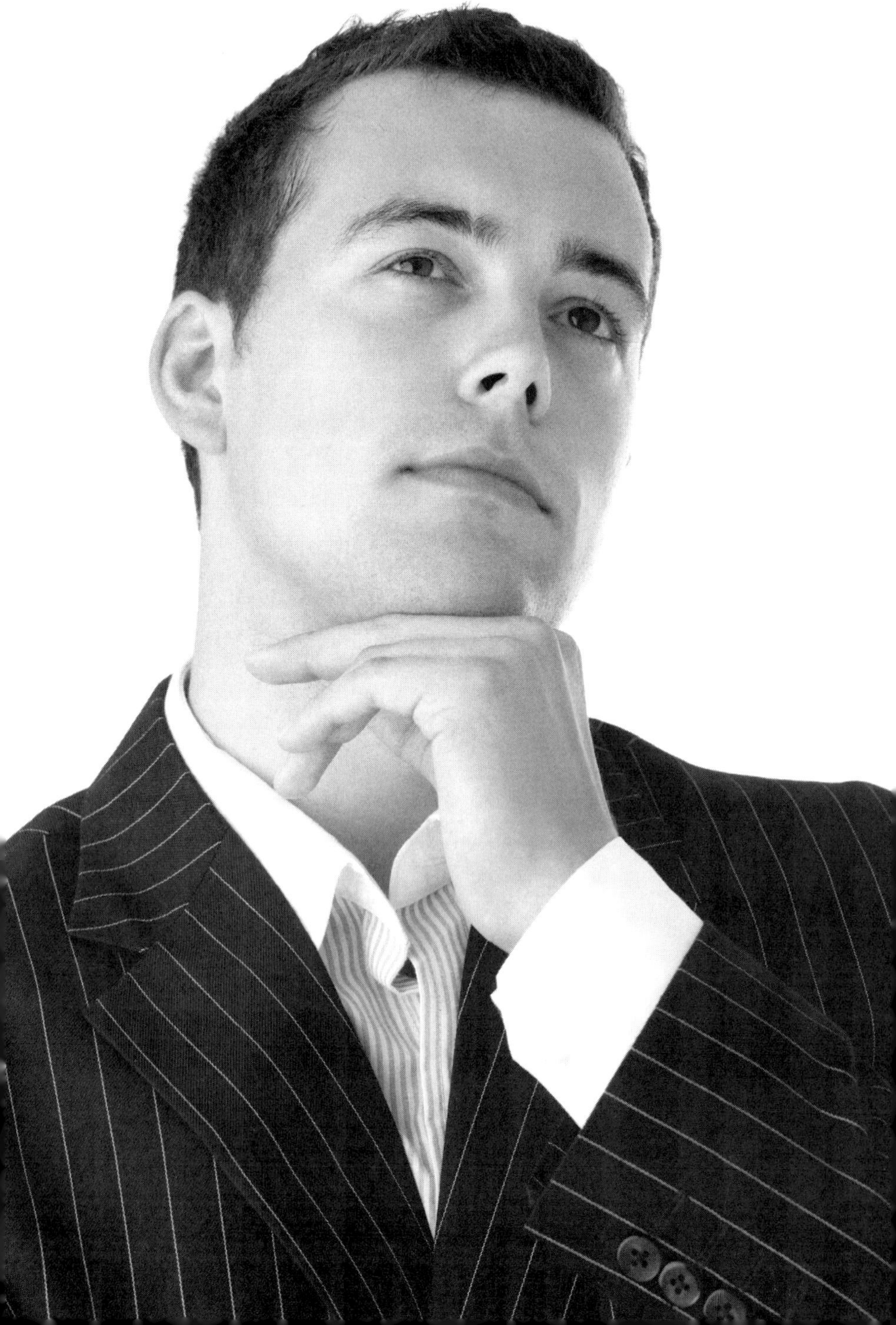

XIII.
Unappreciated Ideas

My favorite type of *Schadenfreude* is the affectionately dark humor that you feel when reading about the lives of quixotic dreamers with big plans that anyone else can see are clearly doomed. You can't help but root for this underdog even as you laugh at his rather predictable failure.

If You Build It, *Schadenfreude* Will Come

One thing about visionaries and dreamers is that they tend not to be too keen on the details. Jimmy McQuat came to Canada from Scotland in the mid-1800s when he was thirty-one years old. His plan was to set up a farm, work hard, meet a beautiful Canadian woman, and settle down. The first part of his plan went quite well. If there was anything Jimmy McQuat knew how to do it was work. No one could call him lazy. He started with forty-five hectares in Emo in Northern Ontario. Soon he had two more farms. For some reason Jimmy didn't manage to find his bride; perhaps he was just too sweaty from all that farming. Whatever the reason, without a wife Jimmy became restless and decided to go west in search of gold.

He had no more luck finding gold than he'd had finding a bride. His hard work had come to naught, so he decided to head into a remote area outside Atikokan called White Otter Lake and live out his days as a near hermit. If you wanted to be a hermit, this was definitely the place to be. Even today it is accessible only by boat, plane, and snowmobile during winter.

Jimmy was haunted by a memory from his childhood. Once he and a friend had played a prank and thrown a corncob at a man. The man shouted at Jimmy, "You'll never do any good! You'll die in a shack!" Jimmy was determined not to live out that prediction, and being a hermit, he had some time on his hands.

The five foot seven Scotsman single-handedly built his dream cabin. One by one he cut red pines and dragged them to the foundations. It took him seventeen years, but when he was done he had his very own log castle, three stories tall with a four-story tower. It was at this point that it occurred to him that he might want to own the land on which he'd single-handedly built his castle. He applied for ownership—and was turned down. The devil is in the details.

> The **devil** is in the details.

Another great builder was William Henry Schmidt, known by the nickname "Burro" for reasons which will become apparent. Burro was born in Woonsocket, Rhode Island; a sickly child, he nevertheless outlived six of his brothers and sisters who died of tuberculosis. He thought the dry climate out West might do him some good, so he joined the prospectors seeking their fortunes in California.

He arrived in California in 1894 and dug around the El Paso Mountains. He made a lucky strike in Copper Mountain, near Randsburg, then realized that the quickest route to the nearest smelter was straight through the mountain. So in 1906 he started to dig. Working with only a pick, a hammer, a hand drill, and a pack of burros, he chipped away day and night. He limited himself to one two-cent candle each day and used dynamite only when absolutely necessary. To save money, he cut the fuses as short as possible. As soon as they were lit, he had to run for his life and throw himself on the ground.

At some point he became so obsessed with his tunnel that he forgot all about prospecting. He struck several veins of gold, silver, iron, and copper deep in the mountain, but he just kept on tunneling. He was never married—except perhaps to his dream of finishing the tunnel—and lived most of his life underground.

In 1938, after thirty-two years of digging, sixty-six-year-old Schmidt broke through to daylight at the other end of the 1,872-foot tunnel. The tunnel, originally created to facilitate the transportation of ore, was finally finished. By this time, however, an overland road and rail links between the mountain's north and south sides had been built, and the tunnel was unnecessary. Burro Schmidt died in January 1954 at the age of eighty-three.

Military Intelligence

Louis Feiser, the inventor of napalm, came up with another brilliant military strategy that, alas, failed to gain acceptance. In 1943 Feiser proposed gathering millions of bats and keeping them in the cold, which would induce a state of hibernation. Then the army could attach a small incendiary device on each bat. The bats would be released over Japan, and as they fell they'd warm up and start hanging under the eaves of buildings, setting fire to them. The plan was abandoned after test bats flew into the rafters and set fire to a U.S. Army hangar and to a general's car.

The Americans weren't the only ones to train animals to deliver bombs. During World War II, the Russians invented the dog mine. Ever since Pavlov, Russians have had a knack for getting dogs to do what they want. So they trained a bunch of the animals to associate food with the underside of tanks. Next they strapped antitank mines to their backs and let them loose into the path of the advancing enemy. What they had failed to consider was that the dogs didn't know whether a tank was Russian or German. Since they'd been trained on Soviet tanks, and they were closer, they headed straight for them, causing an entire Russian division to retreat.

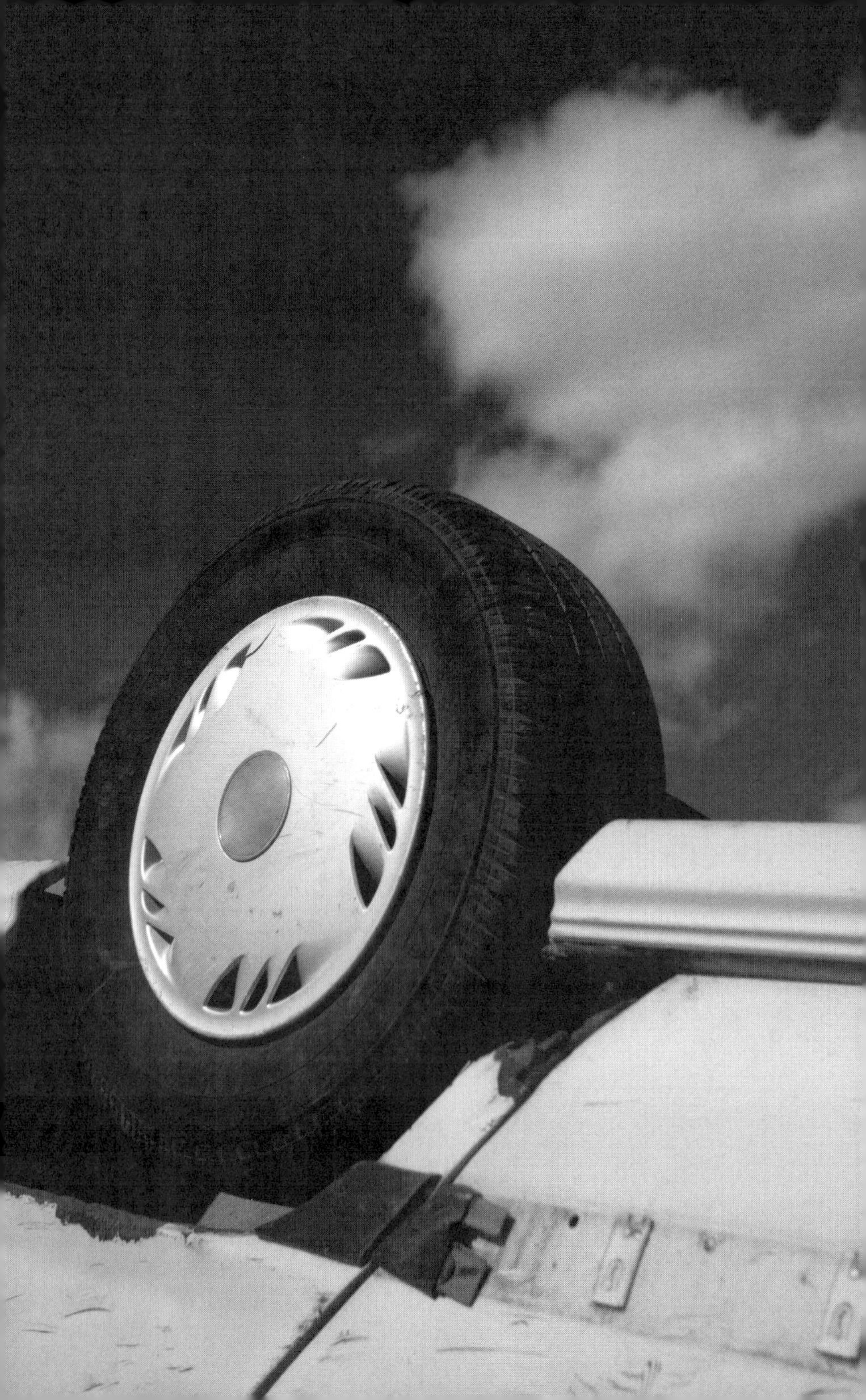

XIV.
Really Bad Days

You've probably had one of those experiences yourself—one thing goes wrong, then another, then another. You stub your toe getting into your car and because your foot hurts, you don't hit the brake quickly and you rear-end a car, and the guy gets out, and he's six foot seven, two hundred pounds, angry . . . and he has a law degree. You're late for work, spill your coffee on your new khaki slacks, and the copier eats your report. Your boss fires you, and when you go home early, you catch your wife in bed with your best friend. They're so startled they knock a candle over and set the house on fire.

One misfortune may not make you giggle, but stack enough of them up, and there's nothing you can do but laugh. Sometimes you need a little distance before you can see the humor in the situation. That's why it's especially easy to laugh when it's happening to someone else!

Bad Days *with* Vehicles

In August 1981 John Jenkins of North Kent Coast, England, decided to take his family fishing. They piled into their four-wheel-drive truck and headed for some nearby mud flats. About a mile out, the Dodge got stuck. Jenkins walked out to the road, called back to the farm, and had someone bring out one of his tractors so they could pull it out.

As the tractor was driving toward the truck, it too got stuck in the mud. Since the Dodge had not been dislodged, the family got out and headed back to the road. They watched helplessly as the tide rolled in and the truck and tractor disappeared beneath the water. There was nothing they could do, so they had someone take them home. The next day Jenkins headed back to the scene with a second tractor. He hitched this tractor to the first one and extracted it from the muck. He and his farmhand then drove the two tractors toward the truck. Both got stuck. Jenkins was undeterred. He still had one tractor left. He went back home and got it, and it was not long before it was mired, too.

This time when the tide rolled in, it flooded all four of his vehicles. By Saturday, word of Jenkins' ordeal had spread, and the flats were covered with onlookers as the farmer returned with a mechanical digger. He started digging and managed to get one of the tractors out. He then drove it back to pull out a second tractor. This time the digger got stuck. As the tide rolled in, it, too, sank beneath the water. The next day Jenkins returned with the tractor he had rescued. He tried to pull the digger out but only succeeded in getting the tractor stuck again. With all of his vehicles buried in the muck, he finally gave up.

■■

Bob Finnegan of Belfast, Northern Ireland, must hold the record for the least successful street crossing. The twenty-two-year-old steelworker was crossing the Falls Road one Friday night in 1975 when a taxi struck him and flung him over its roof. The driver didn't stop. Next another car ran him over, pushing him into a gutter. The second driver didn't stop either. An amazed crowd gathered to gawk at Finnegan's misfortune. As they stood, a van plowed through and injured four people—one of them was Finnegan. As a fourth vehicle came down the road, everyone who could move scattered out of the way. Only one man was hit—Finnegan. After being struck by four vehicles within two minutes, he was admitted to the hospital with a fractured skull, broken pelvis, broken leg, and other injuries but amazingly, he survived.

> After being struck by four vehicles within two minutes, he was admitted to the hospital with a fractured **skull,** broken pelvis, broken leg, and other injuries.

■■

Not so lucky was Biagio di Crescenzio. On May 24, 1974, he was driving near Fondi just outside Rome, Italy, when he lost control of the car and crashed into a tree. A Good Samaritan put the injured motorist in his car and drove him to the Fondi Hospital. The physicians on staff could tell that Crescenzio's injuries were beyond anything they could treat, so they loaded him into an ambulance, which speeded toward the larger hospital in Rome.

The ambulance got only a few miles, however, before it collided with an oncoming car. One of the drivers who witnessed the accident put the patient in his car and sped to the hospital in nearby Latina.

Crescenzio's injuries were beyond the means of the hospital in Latina, so they loaded him into another ambulance bound for the hospital in Rome. Ten miles from Latina, the ambulance swerved into oncoming traffic. Biagio di Crescenzio was killed.

■■

And don't you hate it when someone rear-ends you in traffic, injures your back, and turns you gay? I know I hate it when that happens, and so did Carmon Leo, who sued in Wayne County Circuit Court, claiming that his back injury robbed him of his masculinity. As he explained it, during the six months he was laid up, he couldn't support his wife, so he felt emasculated. The only logical thing he could do when he got better was to start hanging around in gay bars and reading gay porn. The jury was understandably sympathetic and awarded him $200,000. They also awarded his wife $25,000.

When *Your* Bad Day Is *Your* Wedding Day

Those fairy tales with their "happily ever after" endings are cruelly misleading. Even if you do make it to the church, there's no guarantee that everything is going to go smoothly with your life from then on.

First, there is the wedding itself, with all those petty stresses—in-laws who don't get along, dresses that don't quite fit, trying to get all the details just right. If your hair was a disaster, your heel fell off your shoe, and your uncle got drunk at the reception, you'll be gratified to know that your big day was absolute perfection compared to some others. Here are a few wedding disasters that make bad catering seem like a cause for celebration.

The beautiful bride, nineteen-year-old Adrienne, shared her "I do's" with twenty-one-year-old Marine reservist David Samen. The reception was held at the scenic Mill on the River Restaurant in South Windsor, Connecticut. Situated on the shores of the Podunk River, the Mill on the River has been voted "the most romantic restaurant in Connecticut." The eighty or so guests enjoyed the "lush manicured lawns" and Garden Gazebo and generously partook of beverages from the open bar.

There was the traditional tossing of the bouquet, the cutting of the wedding cake, and the ride in the police cruiser with the lights flashing. Oh, wait, perhaps that last one is not out of Martha Stewart.

The bride, who also enjoyed the open bar quite a bit, "flipped out" when the bar closed at 4:00 p.m. and was carried out by family members. In the parking lot she smashed flower vases, threw a tier of her wedding cake, spit on her wedding ring, and, in the words of a restaurant spokesperson, "Said awful things involving body parts she does not own."

When the groom tried to drive away from the blushing bride in his Chevy Blazer, she threw herself onto the hood of the car. Police caught up with her as she was walking along the highway in her wedding dress. She gave the cops a salute involving only one digit, kicked at the police cruiser's windows, and tried to bite a cop. The handcuffs were a nice accessory to her wedding gown. All that wedding cash came in useful when it came time to cover the $1,000 bail.

> If your hair was a disaster, your heel fell off your shoe, and your uncle got drunk at the reception, you'll be gratified to know that your big day was absolute **perfection** compared to some others.

"I'm sorry to certain people," Samen later said, "like my family and some of the police officers." The "other" officers had no comment.

■ ■

Alcohol played a part in the wedding of Willard Roberts of Nashville, Tennessee. He decided he just couldn't marry his intended, Lisa. In order to get his courage up to break the news, he consumed two gallons of beer. When he tried to explain, undoubtedly with great diplomacy, she knocked him down and sat on him until he agreed to go through with the wedding after all. After only a month of married life, Willard filed for divorce.

■ ■

Daniel and Susan Stockwell of Basingstoke, England, are in the running for the shortest-married-bliss award. At the reception Daniel started talking to an ex-girlfriend, and Susan, as one guest said, "blew her top."

"It's a mistake," she said. "I want a divorce." The groom agreed, "I must have been mad to go through with it. I'm better off without her."

■ ■

The night before her wedding, a Greek bride-to-be, who was not named in the newspaper stories, was enjoying her bachelorette party with some friends. The bride couldn't wait to show off her wedding gown, so she took a couple of friends home for an advance showing. She got quite a show. The gown was there, just as she expected. What she did not expect was that it would be on the body of her fiancé or that her cross-dressing fiancé would be in the arms of his best man. The bride suffered a nervous breakdown and was taken to a clinic for treatment. The wedding was canceled.

> What she did not expect was that her cross-dressing fiancé would be in the arms of his best man.

■■

There is a scene in the movie *In & Out* in which Kevin Kline's character gets to the part of the wedding where he is supposed to say, "I do," and instead he says, "I'm gay." If you think that couldn't happen in real life, think again. A man named Martin Chapman reportedly got up on a chair at his wedding reception and asked everyone to be silent. As the family members stood, expecting a toast to the beautiful bride, Chapman announced, "I cannot live with a woman. I'm gay." Then he opened his shirt to show hickies he'd gotten the night before from another man. The bride added a few injuries of her own to the groom's upper body before consulting a lawyer on how to get an annulment.

■■

Peter Amalembiye of Kenya got quite a bit more than he bargained for at his 2001 wedding. He arrived at the Shibale Church of God in Mumias prepared to wed Lilian Anyango. He was surprised to find a second bride, his ex-girlfriend Esther Atieno. She was dressed for the occasion and came with an entourage of supporters who felt that she should have the main role in the ceremony.

"Either Amalembiye marries Atieno or there will be no wedding at the church," shouted one man. Amalembiye expressed his objection by smashing the man over the head with a chair. The wedding devolved into a giant fistfight that was eventually broken up by the police.

■■

The winner of the award, however, for sheer outrageousness and style must go to Stuart and Jane Torrance. The couple had been together for eight years and had two children when they finally decided to take the plunge. Everything was planned to the last detail—the hall, the reception—and Stuart's brother Campbell was honored to be the best man. Jane also thought he was the best man. During the reception, she slipped away with Campbell and made love to him on a bathroom floor. "I will never forgive Jane and Campbell for doing this to me," Stuart said. "I have lost a brother and a wife, and I hope they have miserable lives." The wedding was annulled on the grounds that it wasn't consummated, and Stuart burned the "Jane" tattoo off his arm with a lighter.

But here's the thing: Stuart did forgive Jane and Campbell. In fact, after Stuart lost his job as a forklift driver, he found himself homeless and moved in with Campbell and new girlfriend Jane. The happy couple were planning to be married and asked Stuart to be the best man. Best of luck.

Bad Days *of the* Criminal Types

In his book *Legal Blunders,* Geoff Tibballs tells the story of an Italian bank robber who had a very bad day. He charged into the bank, hoping to make an impression. That he did: He tripped over a doormat and went flying. His mask slipped and his gun went off, but only his pride was wounded. He got up, started toward the cashier again, and tripped on the slippery floor. In the process he dropped his gun. He realized this was not his lucky day, and he gave up on his plan, walked out of the bank, and bumped into the policeman who had just written him a parking ticket.

■■

It can really get your goat when you can't even get the police to stop laughing at you as they haul you off to jail. That was Filbert G. Maestas's argument. He went before the Colorado Court of Appeals to argue that his constitutional rights were violated by giggling police officers. You see, Maestas and an accomplice had stolen several boxes from a meatpacking plant. They assumed they'd absconded with enough sides of beef to provide steaks for months to come. What they had actually taken were rennets. Rennets are inedible beef tissue used in curing cheese. In plain language, Maestras and his

> It can really get your goat when you can't even get the police to stop **laughing** at you as they haul you off to jail.

buddy had filled their car with cow rectums. The police were more than happy to share this tidbit, and they couldn't stop laughing. "If I go to jail for stealing beef assholes, I'm going to be really mad," the beef thief reportedly said. That is exactly what happened. The Court of Appeals let the conviction stand.

Bad Days *That* Defy Description

You ever have that feeling that no matter what you do, and no matter how hard you work, you just can't dig out from under? Well, you've got nothing on a Romanian civil engineer who, in 1978, showed up for work one day to find his entire excavation for a new subway station had disappeared. That's right, the whole hole, twelve thousand cubic meters' worth, was nowhere to be found.

There had certainly been a big hole in the ground when he clocked out at 7:00 p.m., but when he returned, all he could see was a park with benches and trees. He was certain he was in the right place, but there was no trace of his team's work. He was ready to check himself into the loony bin when someone finally explained what happened.

Nicolae Ceausescu, the totalitarian leader of Communist Romania, was going to give a speech to new students at Bucharest's Polytechnic University. He thought the park would be a nice backdrop for his welcoming words. When someone sheepishly pointed out that the park no longer existed because they were building a new subway station there, Ceausescu ordered that the park be put back. Overnight hundreds of laborers worked to restore the park to its former glory. Trees and soil were taken from other parts of the city and planted in the former hole. By the time the civil engineer in charge of the project returned to work, there was no evidence that he or his team had ever been there.

■■

Sometimes there is a story of a person who has just had enough, and he decides to end it all, but the poor guy can't even get that right. Joerg Mueller of Berlin was such an individual. He chose what he must have thought would be a fitting, dramatic conclusion to his life. He drank a bottle of plum brandy, then climbed a fence at the Friedrichsfelde Nature Park, and jumped naked into the pool in the bear exhibit. He expected to be eaten. The three well-fed bears were not interested. If being snubbed by three fat bears wasn't bad enough, the police pulled him out of the compound, saying, "Come on, Goldilocks, time to go home."

FREAKSHOW

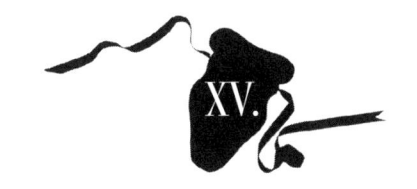

XV.
The Joy of Gawking and Other Weirdness

Sometimes a misfortune is so grand that you can't help gawking at it like an accident at the side of the road—or Mike the headless rooster. Not familiar with Mike? In 1945 he was quite the celebrity, kind of a sick version of Rin Tin Tin or Mr. Ed. Mike certainly didn't intend to become an animal celebrity, and if he'd been asked, I'm sure he'd have been just as happy to peck anonymously around the yard of Lloyd and Clara Olsen's farm as he had been doing on the morning of September 10.

That's when he was selected, along with several chickens, to be sacrificed to the dinner table. If you've ever been on a farm, you know that the birds' reflexes cause them to move after they are decapitated. They start to run around like . . . hmmm, I wish there were an apt metaphor. Most chickens eventually fall down and die like good little main dishes but Mike was different. He kept running around the yard as if his head were still attached. The next morning he was still running around. The Olsens decided to conduct a little experiment to see just how long Mike could survive without his head. They started feeding him by dripping crushed grain and water down his throat.

> Most chickens eventually fall down and die like good little main dishes.

Mike kept on doing all the normal chicken things. He climbed onto perches, tried to crow, and even tried to preen his feathers with his phantom head. Word of the headless wonder reached a theatrical promoter, who smelled gold. He put Mike on display next to a jar with a preserved rooster head. (It wasn't actually Mike's own head. The cat had eaten that.) People paid 25¢ each to see Mike, and his promoter took in about $4,500 a month. That would be a staggering $44,000 or so in today's money.

Other would-be carnival stars tried to replicate Mike by chopping off the heads of their own roosters, but alas, they couldn't make it work. The Olsens had by chance hit Mike in just the right spot to remove the head but preserve enough of the brain stem to keep the bird alive. Nothing lasts forever, though, especially decapitated birds. Mike mercifully died eighteen months after he'd met the axe.

Outrageous Misfortune

Many stories of misfortune are so outrageous that they are a human version of Mike the Headless Rooster. It's kind of disturbing, but we can't help looking. Take the story of Lance Grangruth, a Duluth, Minnesota, carpenter who failed to notice that he'd been shot in the head with a nail gun until he tried to take his hat off and found it was nailed on.

Grangruth was working on a garage when his coworker, perched on a ladder above him, lowered his arm. He didn't realize Grangruth was standing below. The nail gun had a built-in feature that won't allow it to fire unless it is pushed against a surface. Unfortunately, the device couldn't distinguish between a wooden board and a carpenter's head. Grangruth heard the nail gun go off but didn't feel the nail penetrating through his skull and about an inch and a half into his brain.

Amazingly, the wound didn't bleed. Grangruth just sat on the couch talking, with the nail sticking out of his head, as he waited for the ambulance. Any day that ends with a doctor pulling a nail out of your skull has to count as a bad one, but it could have been much worse. Somehow the nail managed to penetrate in just the right spot to avoid doing any functional damage to the brain.

"I've had worse headaches," the lucky carpenter told reporters.

Metaphorical Headless Mikes

Then there are the metaphorical headless-Mike stories, the ones that would seem unbelievable if they were written into a soap opera. When a couple wants a baby, and has trouble conceiving, they will go to almost any lengths to get their bundle of joy.

Demetrius Soupolos, a twenty-nine-year-old Greek guest worker in Stuttgart, Germany, was devastated when medical tests revealed he was sterile. He convinced his wife, a blonde beauty queen named Traute, that the only solution was to find someone who looked like her husband and ask him to father the child. Demetrius approached his neighbor, Frank Maus, and offered to pay him $2,500 to have sex with his wife three nights a week. Frank and his wife, Hilde, had two children of their own. Hilde, for some reason, was not quite as keen on the idea as her husband was. "I don't like this any more than you," he told her. "I'm simply doing it for the money."

What could she say? They did need the money. Somehow, things started to unravel for poor Frank after that. After six months of performing his contractual duty with Traute, she was still not pregnant. Demetrius was getting impatient with the whole thing and asked Frank to undergo a medical exam. The result? Frank Maus was also sterile. In fact, the doctors said, Frank had always been sterile.

Frank was incredulous. It simply wasn't possible; after all, he was the father of two children. This is when Hilde raised her hand. "Well, actually, about that. . . ." Frank, it turns out, had not fathered Hilde's children at all. As if that weren't enough bad news, Demetrius filed a lawsuit against Frank for breach of contract.

■■

Speaking of paternity problems, with modern DNA testing, it's rare that a single mom can't identify who did the deed. But there are exceptions. A three-year-old girl in Missouri will probably never know who her daddy is. She can at least narrow it down to two. Four years ago her mother, Holly Marie Adams, was in town for the rodeo and had relations with two men, Raymon and Richard Miller on the same day. Nine months later, there was a new child in the world. Why can't they just do a genetic test? Because Raymon and Richard are identical twins with identical DNA.

One of the boys is the uncle, and one is the father, but neither one wants to be a man and support the child. Now the courts are trying to straighten this one out. The mother chose Raymon as the father. Raymon pointed his finger at his mirror-image brother and then suggested the state of Missouri pick up the child-support tab.

The brothers' mom was quoted as saying, "I felt like I had gained a granddaughter but lost my sons."

■ ■

When Britney Spears leaves the house to go clubbing with Paris Hilton and forgets to wear underwear under her miniskirt, or when Martha Stewart is sent to jail, there is a sideshow quality to it, and CNN is the new carnival barker.

The craziest sideshow in recent years has to be that of astronaut-from-hell Lisa Nowak. We have always thought of astronauts as an elite group of highly trained and stoic individuals. Just listen to the Apollo 13 crew's mission tapes as they describe, with a measured monotone, malfunctions that could leave them floating frozen in a damaged space capsule for eternity. They seem almost superhuman. During the Cold War space race, astronauts were certainly trotted out in front of the cameras as examples of our nation's best and brightest.

On the other end of the control scale, you have a woman playing out her own version of the film *Fatal Attraction*. She speeds across the country with an angry look on her face, dressed in a trench coat and wig, and—best of all for stand-up comedians—an adult diaper so she won't have to deal with those pesky rest stops. Clearly this person is no rocket scientist. Oh, wait, she is a rocket scientist?

> Clearly this person is no rocket scientist. Oh, wait.

A mission specialist on the Discovery space shuttle's July 2006 flight, Lisa Nowak seemed like the perfect example of the NASA corps. She was brilliant and excelled in her job. She looked polished and scrubbed in her orange NASA space suit, but her emotional life was clearly another story. Seeing such a person unravel is tragic and yet so shockingly incongruous with the image we have of astronauts that the public couldn't help but gawk.

Nowak, a married woman, was allegedly involved with space shuttle pilot Bill Oefelein. She described the relationship as "more than a working relationship but less than a romantic relationship." Nowak drove a thousand miles from Houston to Orlando on February 5, 2007, to confront and possibly kidnap her romantic rival Air Force Captain Colleen Shipman at the Orlando airport's long-term parking lot. According to police, Nowak stalked Shipman as she picked up her bags, then followed her into the parking lot. Next she banged on Shipman's car window. When Shipman rolled the window down, Nowak doused her with pepper spray. Shipman then drove away and called the police.

When police got to the parking lot, they found Nowak dumping a garbage bag that contained a BB gun, a steel mallet, rubber tubing, and a folding knife. Her car contained latex gloves, e-mails from Shipman to Oefelein, a love letter from Nowak to Oefelein, and handwritten directions to the airport and Shipman's house. The astronaut was arrested and charged with attempted kidnapping and burglary and later with attempted murder.

The whole thing came as a gift to late-night talk-show hosts, who branded her the "astro-nut" and said, "This is one small step for man, one giant leap to the nuthouse."

■ ■

While we're on the subject of sideshows, there is one entertaining case of a misfortune that befell an actual carnival attraction. Sideshows of the nineteenth century were not always what they seemed. This became hard to hide when Miss Stevens, the Pig-Faced Lady, escaped from the Camberwell Fair in 1837.

Miss Stevens was actually a performing bear whose face and paws had been shaved. It was dressed in a Victorian lady's gown and special lace gloves that hid its claws. A boy hid behind the animal and prodded it with a stick so that it would grunt whenever someone asked it a question. The showman would draw people in by shouting, "Hear what they say! Hear what they say about Madame Stevens, the wonderful Pig-Faced Lady!" Then onlookers would buy a ticket and come in and ask "Miss Stevens" if she was happy, if she planned to marry, and if she had been born in Lancashire. Each time the boy prodded the bear, and it gave a grunt in reply. Then the showman would shuffle the group out and call another group to come in.

Trouble came one evening when Madam Aurelia, the Fat Lady, attacked the Pipe-Smoking Oyster, thereby upsetting Miss Stevens. In the confusion she ran away and had to be captured by animal-control authorities. Fortunately, they got her back just in time to make her the star attraction at the Hyde Park Fair. It celebrated Queen Victoria's coronation in 1838 with the type of solemnity you'd expect for such an auspicious occasion.

The Curse *of the* Winning Ticket

We may not like to admit this ugly truth, but one of the main things that makes us feel *Schadenfreude* is jealousy. Most of the time, your own life isn't that spectacular. You pay the minimum balance on your Master-Card bill with a handy Discover Card check. You have just enough to make the minimum on your *other* MasterCard. You're left with so little cash that you need to use your Visa to buy groceries. It can sometimes seem you're allergic to money. Be grateful that it's only metaphorical in your case.

There are people who are physically allergic to the stuff. The irritant in question is nickel, which not only shows up in the coin of that name but also in paper money. An article in the August 1991 issue of the *Journal of the American Academy of Dermatology* reported that people with nickel allergies can get stubborn rashes from handling legal tender.

So you're broke. You think you've got an original problem here? You're going to have to try a bit harder. Most Americans are drowning in credit-card debt. Americans now owe 99¢ for each dollar we earn. Before you Canadians start to gloat, you should know that you're not much better. Canadian household debt is now 97.4 percent of household income. According to a poll taken by ACNielsen in May 2005, Americans are the most cash-strapped of any nation. The survey of people in thirty-eight countries found that 28 percent of Americans say they have "no spare cash" after covering their living expenses. By comparison, only 5 percent of Russians said they had no spare cash at the end of the month. (Russians earn about $303 a month. The average American makes $926 a *week*.)

People who want to be millionaires outnumber millionaires by a comfortable margin. There are roughly 288 million more nonmillionaires in America than millionaires. Oh, and your odds of winning the lottery? About 2 and a half billion to one against. That's why tales of lottery winners having a "curse" evoke a particular *Schadenfreude* reaction all their own. In fact, the black humor of someone having the ultimate stroke of luck (a lottery windfall) followed by the ultimate string of bad luck became a regular story line for one of the characters on the hit television drama "Lost." But that character is disqualified from inclusion here on the grounds that he is fictional. We don't need him. There are too many real-life cases of lottery fortunes and misfortunes to tell.

Take the case of William (Bud) Post of Oil City, Pennsylvania.[5] In 1988 he won the $16.2 million jackpot in the Pennsylvania state lottery. Bud thought all his prayers had been answered, but then again, so did his brother. His brother hired a hit man and plotted to kill him and his wife in order to claim the winnings for himself. After that, things just got worse. Post's wife—his sixth—walked out. Then his landlady sued him for a third of the winnings and won. During the lawsuit, the funds were frozen, and Post lost his business and the gas was turned off at his home. By 1996 Post was in bankruptcy court, where he auctioned off the remainder of his lottery jackpot to a company that pays winners a lump sum for future payments. They paid him a little more than half of the remaining jackpot.

"I want to be rid of the lottery, believe me, Your Honor," Post said. "It's really been a pain." Post was living off social security when he died in January 2006.

■ ■

---

5 Perhaps Bud Post was haunted by the "Gold into Lead" ghost of Edwin Drake lurking around Oil City. Oil City was so named because it was the site in 1859 of the first oil well, and Edwin Drake, an employee of Seneca Oil, was the first lucky man to strike oil—280 times more oil than had ever been gathered in a single day in history. When word of his discovery leaked out, the region was flooded with oil-hungry neighbors who bought up the surrounding property and started tapping into the reserves, quickly draining them. The owners of Seneca Oil, meanwhile, rewarded Drake for his find by firing him seven months later. Drake sold his stock for a pittance and eventually found his way to New York, penniless, dressed in shabby clothes and nearly unrecognizable. He died in 1880 at the age of sixty-one. No one from the oil industry attended his funeral, although they did erect a $100,000 statue in his honor in 1904. Too late to help Drake.

You want more? Jack Whittaker, who won the largest single jackpot in U.S. history, liked to gamble. (Why do you suppose he bought a lottery ticket in the first place?) And $314.9 million can buy a lot of betting slips. It can also buy a lot of trouble, especially when folks know you're loaded. Whittaker was sued by an employee of a bookmaker who said he assaulted her. He was also charged with threatening to kill the manager of a bar and with drunken driving. His car was broken into, then his house, and he was drugged at a strip club so employees could make off with $500,000. (He carried that much so he could make some big bets).

■ ■

And it just gets worse. Alex and Rhonda Toth of Florida were down to their last $24 when they won $13 million in 1990. What did they get with their money? Some trinkets, a car, and a lot of trouble. Their newfound riches led to bitter family squabbles. At one point Rhonda Toth filed an injunction against her nineteen-year-old son and his girlfriend, who allegedly killed the family dog and burned the Corvette. They were then sued by the IRS for filing fraudulent income tax returns and ended up in bankruptcy court. An odd aside to this story is that they also made headlines when Bertie Higgins, who wrote the hit song "Key Largo," crashed his Chrysler into Rhonda's daughter's car. It doesn't have much to do with the lottery, but it is odd.

■ ■

A man in Meiningen, Germany, won a national lottery of $921,000 in 1997 but had squandered it away by 2003. He started breaking into homes and cars to steal money because he was too ashamed to go to the welfare office and admit the money had run out.

Stephen Perisie of Riverside, Ohio, won the lottery twice, once in 1990 for $3 million and then again in 1992 for $100,000. His wife, Kim Kay, thought she might enjoy the millions a bit more if she had them all to herself, so she hired a hitman. She agreed to pay the hired gun, an undercover police officer, as it turned out, $500 for the killing and gave him a down payment of $25. Kay pled guilty and faces up to twenty-five years in prison, but amazingly, Stephen Perisie said he wants her back.

"You don't wash twenty-two years under the bridge," he said.

A lottery win can even be a curse to the town at large. After Rebecca Jemison won $67 million, her husband Sam Jemison closed the bar that had been the gathering point of their Ohio neighborhood. The bartenders and waitstaff joined the ranks of the unemployed, and local restaurants saw business drop off. And representatives of the city complained to the *Plain Dealer* that they were spending thousands of dollars on extra police and to take calls from people all over the country who wanted to share in the instant wealth.

Incidentally, if you want to reap the rewards of a lottery windfall without shelling out the $1 to buy a ticket, you should think twice. Ask Tyrone Bennett of Paterson, New Jersey, or Julius Day of Victorville, California. Both were arrested in separate cases of similar stupidity. They showed up with big smiles on their faces to cash in their winning lottery tickets. The tickets had been stolen in break-ins at convenience stores. Here's the thing: the tickets have serial numbers on them—how do you suppose they know if they're real or not? Cashing the ticket was like saying, "Hi, I'm the burglar you've been looking for!"

Even game shows have been known to produce misfortune along with fortune. Raymond Taylor, who won $81,000 in cash and prizes on *Wheel of Fortune* in 1993, was so moved by the experience that he wouldn't leave. The producers of the show had to file a lawsuit demanding he stop "stalking" the set.

"I wanted to have a life with the show," Taylor said. "I loved the show enough to be a part of it." But the show was a fickle mistress.

". . . when we're done with [contestants], we're done with them," said producer Marki Costello.

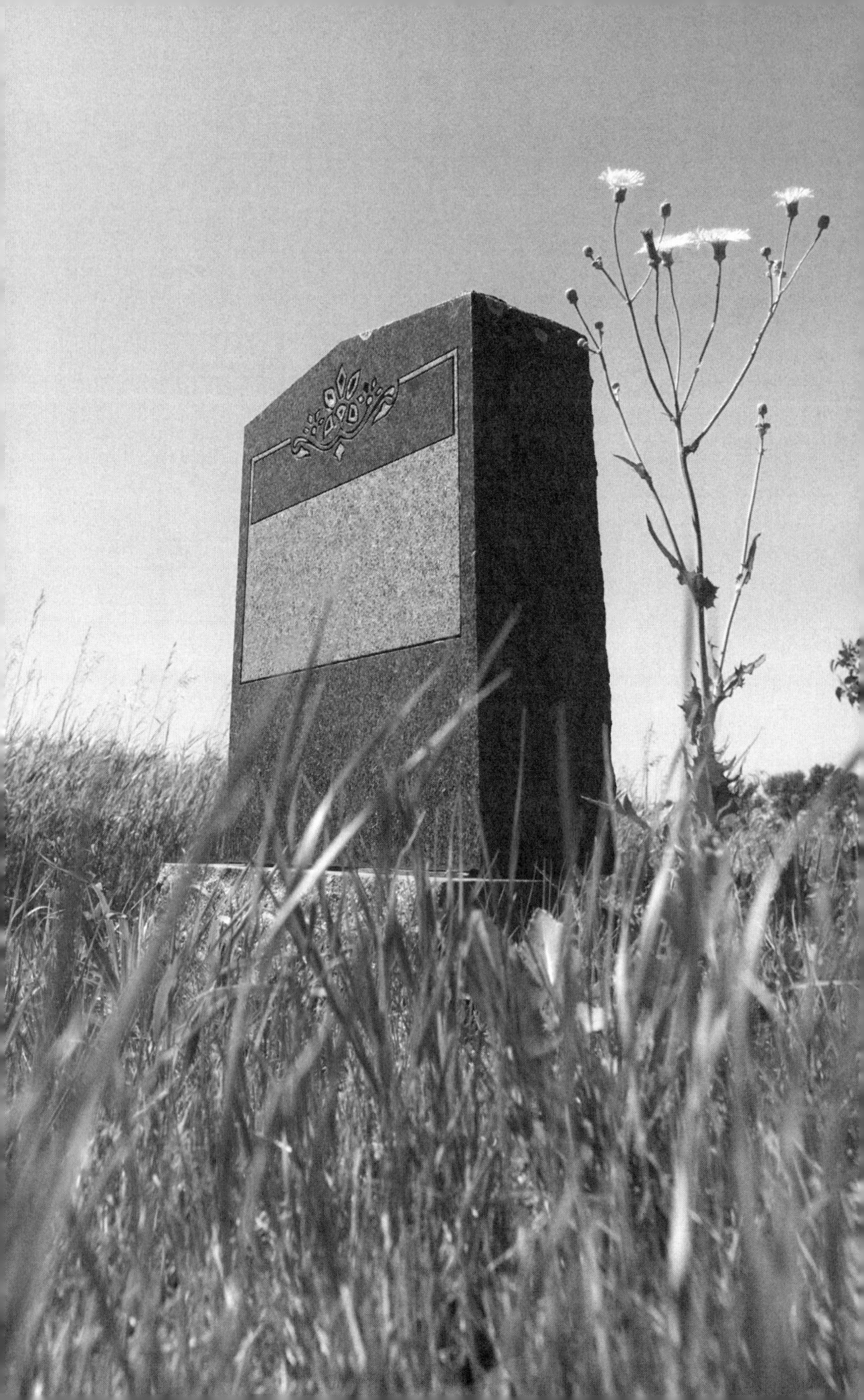

XVI.

How Will You Be Remembered?

What are those people saying about you over at the watercooler and behind the office door? Don't you hate those hushed voices? Well, if you think your name has gotten a bad rap, look at the beating some other poor saps have gotten.

When Jim Ferrozzo, the assistant manager of San Francisco's Condor nightclub, imagined his obituary, he probably never envisioned it would be printed under the headline "Exec in Topless Club Dies in Freak Mishap with Piano, Woman." Let this be a lesson about the dangers of sex in the workplace. One night in 1986, the club was closed, and the patrons had gone home. Ferrozzo and his girlfriend decided to take the opportunity for a little fun on top of the piano. Unfortunately, the piano was mounted on a hydraulic lift. In their passion, they somehow turned the lift on but failed to notice the motion. They were found the next morning pinned to the ceiling. The woman suffered minor bruises, but Ferrozzo had been smothered between the piano and his girlfriend. It took the rescue team three hours to pry them loose.

Here's one from the "Boy Named Sue" file: Shirley Povich, a popular sportswriter from the *Washington Post*, was honored by being included in *Who's Who of American Women*. Povich would have been more honored by this if he were a woman. Mr. Povich, despite his confusing first name, is a man. This is something the editors failed to notice, even though the entry correctly stated that Povich was married to a woman named Ethel.

You remember Edward Everett, don't you? No? He was *the other guy* who made a speech at Gettysburg. A former Massachusetts congressman and president of Harvard, he was considered the greatest orator of his day. He crafted every word of his speech, spoke for two full hours, and finished to great applause only to become a historical footnote. Abraham Lincoln's address, which contained the line, "The world will little note, nor long remember what we say here . . . ," was panned by reporters, but you won't find Everett's speech carved in stone.

If you're forgotten entirely, your legacy will be downright stellar compared to that of poor James Challis. The nineteenth-century thinker is recorded in the *Encyclopedia Britannica* as the "British clergyman and astronomer, famous in the history of astronomy for his failure to discover the planet Neptune."

By the way, while we're on the subject of failing to discover large land masses, the explorer George Vancouver generally does not deserve a place in this book. He was the first European to see many North American locales and gave many their present names: Mount Baker, Mt. Rainier, Port Orchard, and Puget Sound are just a few. The city of Vancouver in Canada and another Vancouver in Washington State were named *for* him, not *by* him. But Vancouver is celebrated in Ocean Shores, Washington, for one thing he failed to see. When Vancouver was sailing along the Northwest coast, he never stopped at the site of their fair city. Each year the people of Ocean Shores gather to celebrate "Undiscovery Day." They have a huge party and finish the evening by wading out into the ocean and shouting "Hey, George!" The annual celebration was established in 1973.

Here's one from the "Thanks-for-the-honor-but-next-time-send-money" file: Henry Shrapnel was born in 1761 in Bradford-on-Avon, England. He became a British soldier and served in Gibraltar, the West Indies, and Newfoundland. In 1784, as a second lieutenant in the British Royal Artillery, Henry Shrapnel had an idea that would change the nature of war and give the British an edge over Napoleon at Waterloo. He spent his own money to develop a new type of shell that would be filled with musket balls and gunpowder. The canister would explode in flight, spreading metal fragments for hundreds of yards. The soldier was never paid for his invention, nor reimbursed for his expenses in developing it. His only payment was immortality in the form of the word *shrapnel*.

Shrapnel may have preferred a less violent fate for his name, but he did invent a weapon, after all. How would you like to see your humanitarian efforts turned into a word for an instrument of death? That's what happened to French physician Joseph Guillotin. He favored the use of a beheading machine as a more humane method of execution than the gallows. Guillotin did not invent the device that removes one's head from one's shoulders; such devices were known to have been used as early as 1307 in Ireland. But he was instrumental in convincing the powers that be during the French Revolution that if they were going to kill, they should at least try to be humane.

So the machine he advocated came to be known as the *Guillotin*. There is a persistent tale that Guillotin met his demise in his own invention. Although that is a much better story than the truth, Guillotin died of natural causes. The Guillotins were deeply troubled by how their name was being used, and after Guillotin's death, his children petitioned the French government to change the name of the blade, but it was too late. Their petition was not granted, and they changed their own name instead.

Some people's names have terrible connotations through no fault of their own. Before you get too critical of Adolf Hittler's parents, you should know that they gave him the name in 1937 before the reputation of the other guy was cemented. Still, it is a problem getting people to take your reservation without hanging up if you share a name with history's most reviled Fascist leader. Then there are the calls at all hours of the night from giggling pranksters and their funny genocide jokes.

Hittler hasn't changed the name, he says, because it would be an insult to his parents, but he's not insulted himself that one of his sons uses his ex-wife's maiden name. Before the war, the name "Adolf" was not that common. It was at the peak of its popularity in 1937. About 1.7 percent of German men were Adolfs. During his reign, Hitler (the one with one "t") forbade his countrymen to name children after him. After the war most "Adolfs" and "Hitlers" disappeared. The ones burdened with the name already rushed to change it, and new Adolfs were rarely christened.

Adolf Hittler of Austria is a coach driver. Sometimes when he takes tours his employer asks him to come up with an alternative name.

> It is a problem getting people to take your reservation without hanging up if you share a name with history's **most reviled** Fascist leader.

When he is taking an Israeli tour group, for example, he tells them his name is Adrian Heller. In 1998 Hittler had the pleasure of meeting Heinrich Himmler, a bricklayer born in 1941. They met at a conference in Braunau, Austria, of people with names connected to the Nazi past.

And there are few eponyms less flattering to their originators than the one derived from poor Derrick. He was an executioner at London's Tyburn prison in the seventeenth century; during his illustrious career, he was responsible for more than three thousand executions. He served in the Earl of Essex's expedition against Cadiz. During the conflict Derrick was found guilty of rape, and the executioner was, himself, sentenced to death. The Earl of Essex thought Derrick's services were too valuable to let him die. So he pardoned Derrick, only to find himself brought before the executioner he had spared. That's a decision you have to regret.

> Besides a sudden death, hanging often had another side effect that was a real crowd pleaser. Because of the surge of hormones and blood, it was not uncommon for a criminal to get an erection as he was suddenly strangled.

The word *derrick* came to be associated with the gallows and later with any hanging apparatus or scaffolding. This is where many history books conclude the story, but Derrick's name lives on in one more familiar term. In the days before television talk shows and Quentin Tarantino films, people looked forward to executions as a form of entertainment. Besides a sudden death, hanging often had another side effect that was a real crowd pleaser. Because of the surge of hormones and blood, it was not uncommon for a criminal to get an erection as he was suddenly strangled. The voyeuristic onlookers kept a watchful eye out for protrusions that they jokingly nicknamed "derricks," a term that over time was shortened to *dick*. If your name is only synonymous with jamming up the photocopier, be grateful.

Bibliography

Achenbach, Joel. "Pee-wee's Nightmare: The Kiddie Star and the Ancient Taboo." *Washington Post*, July 31, 1999.
Adams, Cecil. "What Was the Deal with Jimmy Carter and the Killer Rabbit?" The Straight Dope (syndicated column), November 19, 1995.
"Addenda." *Washington Post*, April 6, 1995.
Adler, Bill Jr., and Julie Houghton. *America's Stupidest Business Decisions*. New York: Quill, 1997.
Allen, Jenny Lee. "Choking Man Checks into Mental Hospital." *Sarasota Herald Tribune*, March 12, 2003.
Aloff, Mindy. *Dance Anecdotes*. New York: Oxford University Press, 2006.
"And the Bride Wore Handcuffs." *People*, September 1, 2003.
"And the Police Officer Just Laughed and Laughed." *Greeley (CO) Daily Tribune*, January 21, 1977.
Asay, Paul. " 'There Are No Secrets'; The Rise of the Rev. Ted Haggard Was as Dramatic as His Plummet into Scandal." *Gazette*, January 7, 2007.
"Assemblyman Calls Constituents 'Idiots.'" *Associated Press*, June 29, 2005.
"Author, Runner Appears as Lehigh University Lecturer." *Doylestown (PA) Intelligencer*, March 4, 1984.
Bacon, Richard. "Snorting Coke in a Toilet Was So Seedy." *Mirror*, December 11, 1998.
Bainbridge, Jim. "Columbus Would Object to His Try." *Colorado Springs (CO) Gazette*, May 23, 2001.
Baker, Chris. "Tirades of Baghdad Bob Give Voice to Action Figure." *Washington Times*, April 19, 2003.
Baldwin, Paul. "Thongs of Praise!" *The People*, July 5, 1998.
"Barr's Defamation Suit Dismissed." *United Press International*, June 15, 2004.
Bastel, Joan. "Banzai!" *Doylestown (PA) Daily Intelligencer*, September 25, 1981.

Bates, James. "Get-Rich-Quick Author Albert Lowry Files for Bankruptcy." *Washington Post*, June 4, 1987.
"Battered by Four Vehicles." *Stevens Point (WI) Daily Journal*, July 26, 1975.
Bean, Matt. "Winona Ryder Convicted of Theft, Likely to Get Probation." *Court TV News*, November 7, 2002.
"Bears Eat Keeper Who Took Their Bile." *BBC News*, October 11, 2005.
"The Best and Worst Bosses in America." *Redbook*, September 1, 1996.
"The Best and Worst of Everything." *Parade*, December 28, 2003.
"The Best and Worst of Everything." *Parade*, December 18, 2005.
"Big Winner Has a String of Bad Luck." *Associated Press*, March 13, 2004.
"Billy Beer Debuts, but Hard to Find." *Hayward (CA) Daily Review*, November 1, 1977.
"Billy Carter Laid to Rest without Any Formalities." *Chicago Sun-Times*, September 27, 1988.
"Billy James Hargis Obituary." *Economist*, December 18, 2004.
Blackhurst, Chris. "How the Man Who Lost It All Is Starting to Sparkle Again." *Evening Standard*, March 24, 2004.
"Blue Peter Presenter in Drugs Sacking." *News Letter* (Belfast, Northern Ireland), October 19, 1998.
Boggan, Steve. "Stagecoach Executive Called Its American Passengers Riff-Raff, Magazine Claims." *Independent*, May 27, 2002.
Bohannon, John. *Kickers: All the News That Didn't Fit*. New York: Ballantine, 1998.
Bombaugh, Charles C. *Facts and Fancies for the Curious*. Philadelphia: J. B. Lippincott Company, 1940.
Boston Police Department News. Daily Incidents for January 5, 2007. www.bpdnews.com.
"Brazilian Brewmaster Says Lifetime of Beer Tasting Made Him Alcoholic." *Modern Brewery Age*, April 3, 2000.
Broadhead, Rick. *Dear Valued Customer, You Are a Loser*. Kansas City, MO: Andrews McMeel, 2004.
"Brother Dies, to Live Alone." *Canandaigua (NY) Daily Messenger*, April 27, 1936.
Brown, Jonathan. "Lawyer in Row Over £4 Ketchup Stain Quits Firm." *Independent*, June 22, 2005.

Brunvand, Jan Harold. "Cactus Victim Got the Point." *Syracuse Post Standard*, November 23, 1987.
Buncombe, Andrew, "When the Rules of the Game No Longer Apply," *Independent*, March 27, 2001.
"The Burger that Conquered the Country." *Time*, September 17, 1973.
Burnett, Jim. *Hey Ranger!* Dallas, TX: Taylor Trade, 2005.
Burro Schmidt Tunnel Information. www.burroschmidttunnel.org.
"The Busiest Busybody." *Syracuse Post Standard*, April 11, 1979.
Butler, Mark. "Heroes Led by Fools." *Australian*, February 12, 2005.
"Captain Calamity Loses Touch." *BBC News*, August 9, 2001.
"Captain Calamity Returns to Sea." *BBC News*, July 21, 2001.
Carr, Rebecca. "A Week of Crisis." *Atlanta Journal-Constitution*, December 20, 1998.
Carter, Mike. "London Pornographer First Ever Sentenced for Commercial Kiddie Porn." *Associated Press*, November 19, 1998.
Cassingham, Randy. *This Is True: Deputy Kills Man with Hammer*. Boulder, CO: Freelance Communications, 1999.
———. *This Is True: Glow in Dark Plants Could Help Farmers*. Boulder, CO: Freelance Communications, 1997.
———. *This Is True: Pit Bulls Love You, Really*. Boulder, CO: Freelance Communications, 1998.
"Cat Swims—Man Drowns." *Burlington (NC) Daily Times-News*, September 21, 1949.
Cavett, Dick, and Christopher Porterfield. *Cavett*. New York: Harcourt, Brace, Jovanovich, 1974.
"The Cheating People vs. Larry Flynt." *Glasgow (Scotland) Daily Record*, December 19, 1998.
"Christian Bookstore Robbery Goes Awry." *USA Today*, May 10, 2006.
"City Banker's Lewd Emails Do Rounds," *Independent*, January 20, 2006.
Clancy, Paddy. "Stolen Trawler Lost and Found." *Irish Voice*, May 4, 2007.
"Club Takes Up Cause of Would-Be Streaker." *Miami Herald*, February 16, 2003.
"Cold Cash Motivates Poor Red Socks Fan." *San Diego Union Tribune*, November 12, 2002.
Collier, Aldore. "Milli Vanilli: Creating Controversy and Platinum Records." *Ebony*, July 1, 1990.

Connelly, Joel. "Hypocrisy at Home in Both Poltical Parties." *Seattle Post-Intelligencer*, October 4, 2006.

Contemporary Authors Online. Gale, 2007. Reproduced in Biography Resource Center. Farmington Hills, MI: Thomson Gale, 2007.

Cook, Helen. "Flopeye the Sailor Man." *Mirror*, August 23, 2001.

Cooper, Glenda. "Religious Teacher by Day, Horned Devil by Night." *Independent*, July 6, 1998.

Cooperman, Alan. "Minister Admits to Buying Drugs and Massage." *Washington Post*, November 4, 2006.

Cote, Neil. "As You Were Saying." *Boston Herald*, February 2, 2003.

Cull, Nicholas J. "Obituary: Vaughn Meader; Ill-Fated Mimic of John F. Kennedy." *Independent*, November 24, 2004.

Cunniff, John. "Dream of Wealth through Real Estate Has Become Smudged." *Journal Record*, March 14, 1986.

Curriden, Mark. "Dallas Computing Firm Settles Lawsuit by Worker Fired for Jury Duty." *Knight Ridder/Tribune Business News*, February 13, 1999.

Currie, Tyler. "Zip Code 00000." *Washington Post*, April 2, 2003.

Dahl, Melissa. "Cheney in Comics' Sights after Shooting Accident." *Sacramento Bee*, February 14, 2006.

Darman, Jonathan, and Andrew Murr. "Morality Tale: A Pastor's Fall from Grace." *Newsweek*, November 13, 2006.

Davies, Huw. *Pedestrian Safety Expert Gets Hit by Bus.* Kansas City, MO: Andrews McMeel, 2005.

Davis, Phil. "Couple Cursed by Jackpot Is Indicted." *St. Petersburg Times*, April 13, 2006.

Davis, Skippy. "Getting Even." *Macon Telegraph*, May 26, 1999.

"The Day the Lake Went Down the Drain." *Elyria (OH) Chronicle Telegram*, November 21, 1980.

"Death of Hon. C. L. Vallandingham." *Portsmouth (OH) Times*, June 24, 1871.

"Death of Vallandingham." *Elyria Independent Democrat*, June 21, 1871

Degregory, Lane. "Run-In with a Bird Spoils Fabio's Busch Gardens Visit." *Virginian Pilot*, March 31, 1999.

———. "Supermodel Warns that New Coaster Is Not Safe." *Virginian Pilot*, April 17, 1999.

Delevett, Peter. "E-mail Bragging Gets Worker Fired." *San Jose Mercury News*, May 22, 2001.

Denniston, Lyle. "Who Is Gary Hart?" *Syracuse Herald American*, March 25, 1984.
"Did Not Own His Body." *Greeley (CO) Daily Tribune*, January 4, 1938.
Dobson, Roger. "Warning: A Rude Boss Is Bad for Your Heart." *Sunday Mirror*, April 1, 2001.
Donaldson, William. *Brewer's Rogues, Villains, Eccentrics*. London: Cassell, 2002.
Dorrell, Oren. "Good Lottery Luck Can Go Bad Fast." *USA Today*, February 27, 2006.
"Dozen Killed, 50 Hurt, as Tank of Molasses Burst." *Bridgeport (CT) Standard Telegram*, January 16, 1919.
"Drink-Drive Shame for Road Boss." *Mirror*, September 29, 1996.
Elston, Laura. "Archive: Private Man Who Still Speaks His Mind." *Birmingham Post*, June 10, 2006.
"Email Claire and Her True Blue Cousin." *Evening Standard*, December 20, 2000.
"Equality! We're Having as Many Affairs as Men." *London Sun*, February 12, 2003.
"Evangelist Accused of Bisexual Affairs." *Elyria (OH) Chronicle-Telegram*, February 11, 1976.
"Exploding German Just Had to Urinate." *Syracuse Herald Journal*, October 22, 1993.
"Exposed: E-mail Embarrassment Reaches New Lows." *London Sunday Business*, June 10, 2001.
Fallowfield, West. "School Employee, Girlfriend to Be Arraigned." *Philadelphia Inquirer*, September 25, 2001.
Farquhar, Michael. *A Treasury of Great American Scandals*. New York: Penguin, 2003.
Felton, Bruce. *What Were They Thinking?* Guilford, CT: Globe Pequot Press, 2003.
"Fighter Kayoed without a Blow." *Nevada State Journal*, April 11, 1943.
"Fixx Dies of Heart Attack." *Elyria (OH) Chronicle Telegram*, July 22, 1984.
Fleet, Michael. "Handcuffed Juror Halts Court Case." *Daily Telegraph*, January 31, 1998.
Flynn, Bill. "Harry Heitman Rochester's Iron Man of 1918." Red Wings Baseball History, www.redwingsbaseball.com/history/heitman1918.html, accessed February 23, 2007.

"Ford Awarded Six Cents as Damage Against Tribune." *Lima (OH) Times Democrat*, August 15, 1919.

Foster, Freling. *Keep Up with the World*. New York: Grosset & Dunlap, 1949.

Francis, Don. "In the earliest days of the oil field, the big bang wasn't a theory." E&P, www.eandp.com, accessed March 14, 2007.

Frank, Jeffrey A., and Lloyd Grove. "The Raging Battles of the Evangelicals; Swaggart Confirms Investigation of Bakker." *Washington Post*, March 25, 1987.

Frauenfelder, Mark. *The World's Worst*. San Francisco: Chronicle Books, 2005.

Friedman, Philip. *Washington Humor*. New York: Citadel Press, 1964.

Frusha, Roy. "U.S. Has History of Politicians Faking Service." *Daily Advertiser*, April 5, 2007.

Gabbay, Alyssa. "A Devil of a Mess for Congregation: Pastor Accused of Trying to Kill Wife Fingers a Demon in Human Form." *Philadelphia Daily News*, November 25, 1994.

Galloway, Jim. "Scandal Repair Task." *Atlanta Journal-Constitution*, April 30, 2001.

Gardner, Lyn. "How Not to Catch a Bullet." *Guardian*, June 9, 2006.

Gardner, Martin. "Oral Roberts on Jim Bakker." *Free Inquiry*, June 22, 1994.

Garfield, Ken. "Minister to Step Down after Hooters Remarks." *Charlotte Observer*, December 5, 1995.

Gary, Chris. "Final Blow to Captain Calamity as Winds Force Him to Abandon Voyage," *Independent*, June 20, 2001.

"German Police Rescue Man Glued to Roof." *Reuters*, March 14, 2007.

Gilbey, Ryan. "Cover Story: How to Keep Your Nose Clean." *Independent*, February 16, 2004.

Gill, Charlotte. "Lover Lets Her Fingers Do Too Much Talking." *Daily Mail*, March 10, 2004.

Gilmore, Commander. "Another Case of Bambi's Revenge." *Shooting Industry*, January 1, 2000.

———. "Busted Again." *Shooting Industry*, December 1, 2006.

———. "He's the Top Gun in the Symphony Orchestra." *American Handgunner*, September 1, 1999.

———. "A Master of Keen Observation." *Shooting Industry*, March 1, 2007.
Goldberg, M. Hirsh. *The Complete Book of Greed*. New York: William Morrow and Company, 1994.
Goldstein, Richard. "Persecuting Pee-wee." *Village Voice*, January 15–21, 2003.
———. "The Wrong Way to Enter History." *International Herald Tribune*, December 27, 2003.
Gorski, Eric. "Christ Gives Drag Queen, Lesbian New Life." *Colorado Springs (CO) Gazette*, November 6, 1999.
"Governor's New Grandchild: What's-Her-Name." *San Jose Mercury News*, August 1, 1996.
"Gown-Wearing Groom Forces Bride's I Don't." *New York Daily News*, August 14, 1998.
Graham, Caroline. "Ryder in the Storm." *Mail on Sunday*, August 25, 2002.
Great American Trials Vol. 1. http://law.jrank.org/collection/10/Great-American-Trials.html
"Greenpeace Just Kidding about Armageddon." *Washington Post*, June 2, 2006.
Greenwood, Chris. "Party Girl's E-mail Goes Round the World." *Independent*, August 26, 2006.
Gregory, Leland. *Idiots in Love*. Kansas City: Andrews McMeel, 2006.
Gregory, Leland H., III. *Great Government Goofs*. New York: Dell, 1997.
Grimes, William. "Magician's Persona One of His Best Tricks." *New York Times*, August 28, 2005.
Gumbel, Andrew. "The Accused." *Independent*, November 3, 2002.
Gysin, Christian, and Tania Shakinovsky. "Am I the Worst Boyfriend in the World?" *Daily Mail*, October 4, 2002.
Hale, Beth. "Basting Banker Faces Email Inquiry." *Daily Mail*, January 20, 2006.
Hall, Allan. "The Man Who Tried to End It All by Feeding Himself to the Bears." *Mirror*, June 30, 2001.
Hall, Kristin. "Investors Say Oilman Swindled Them Out of Millions, Then Turned Up on MTV's Sweet Sixteen." *Associated Press*, June 1, 2007.
Hammel, Sara. "Bribery Charge for Girls Gone Wild's Joe Francis." *People*, April 13, 2007.

———. "Girls Gone Wild Founder Joe Francis Indicted for Tax Evasion." *People*, April 12, 2007.

Hanania, Ray, et al. "Capone Rubs Out TV Competition." *Chicago Sun-Times*, April 23, 1986.

"Hargis: Sex Report from Pagan Press." *Lincoln (NE) Journal Star*, February 22, 1976.

"HarperCollins Fires Regan." *Oakland Tribune*, October 16, 2006.

Harris, Art. "Jim Bakker, Driven by Money or Miracles?" *Washington Post*, August 29, 1989.

Harris, John F. "Ark. Panel Supports Disbarring Clinton." *Washington Post*, May 23, 2000.

Hartlaub, Peter. "Pee-wee May Be Heading Back to His Playhouse." *San Francisco Chronicle*, January 24, 2007.

"Hearing Aid Fitted to the Wrong Ear." *Bucks County (PA) Courier Times*, March 7, 1978.

Hempel, Carlene. "E-mail's Reach Can Make a Few Ill-Chosen Words Come Back to Haunt the Sender." *Raleigh (NC) News and Observer*, February 20, 2002.

Henderson, Paul, et al. "She Believes Him . . . but Would You?" *Mail on Sunday*, October 6, 2002.

Hendrickson, Robert. *QPB Encyclopedia of Word and Phrase Origins*. New York: Facts on File, 1997.

Henican, Ellis. "Suit: Women's Boss Videotaped Toilet." *Newsday*, July 28, 1997.

Hermann, Andrew. "Girls Creator to Pay Teens." *Chicago Sun-Times*, April 12, 2007.

Hiassen, Carl. "Hypocrisy Did In Member of 'God Squad.'" *Miami Herald*, March 3, 1996.

Hill, Crow. "Mink Are on the Run, and the Fur Is Flying." *Philadelphia Inquirer*, August 12, 1998.

"Historical Slave Foe Was a Resident of Winooski." *Sheboygan (WI) Press*, February 28, 1931.

Hoekstra, Dave. "Down-to-Earth Actor Wallows in the Mud." *Chicago Sun-Times*, August 12, 1994.

Hoffman, Claire. "Joe Francis: 'Baby, Give Me a Kiss.'" *Los Angeles Times*, August 6, 2006.

Hopkirk, Elizabeth. "How a Serial Seducer Was Snared in Love Trap." *Evening Standard*, October 8, 2003.

"How Chung-Ling-Soo Died." *Gleaner*, May 1, 1918.

"How Low Can You Go?" *Newsweek*, November 26, 2006.
"Huge Internet Demand to See Birth of Sean." *Birmingham Post*, June 17, 1998.
"Human Resources Column." *Sacramento Bee*, April 1, 2002.
Humane Society of the United States. http://www.hsus.org.
Hunter, Jennifer. "Shelving Ted Haggard's Marital Advice." *Chicago Sun-Times*, November 22, 2006.
Hyena, Hank. "Crippled Masturbator Sues and Wins!" *Salon*, November 29, 1999.
"I Was an Idiot, Admits 'Crap' Speech Ratner." *Birmingham (England) Post*, April 28, 2005.
"IBM Credits Success to Treating Customers and Employees Well." *Penton*, September 23, 1999.
"In Brief." *Daytona Beach News-Journal*, December 23, 2001.
"Internet Birth Mother Caught in Police Web." *Birmingham Post*, July 2, 1998.
Ispen, Beth. "Woman Charged after Man Stabbed in the Buttocks." *Fairbanks Daily News Miner*, October 31, 2001.
Jagger, Suzy. "Email Chauvinist." *Daily Mirror*, October 4, 2002.
———. "Oops! Unsexy Mary Does a Claire Swire." *Mirror*, September 13, 2002.
Joyce, Mike. "Milli Vanilli." *Washington Post*, April 23, 1990.
"Jude Compliments Winona Ryder's Performance During Probation." *CourtTV News*, December 15, 2003.
Kallestad, Brent. "Got a Bad Boss? You've Got Company." *Chicago Sun-Times*, January 2, 2007.
Kamen, Al. "In Frozen North, Cold Shoulder from '69." *Washington Post*, November 10, 1999.
"Kansas City, MO/Software Company CEO's Harsh E-Mail Affects Stock Price." *Knight Ridder*, March 24, 2001.
Kelbie, Paul. "Captain Calamity Has to Be Rescued Once Again." *Independent*, August 23, 2001.
Kennedy, Sean. "Son of a Preacher Man." *Advocate*, December 19, 2006.
Kettermann, Steve. "Why Publishing Needed Judith Regan." *San Francisco Chronicle*, December 31, 2006.
Kim, Rose. "Settlement in Toilet Taping." *Long Island (NY) Newsday*, August 8, 1997.
Kinnell, Peter. *The Complete Illustrated Encyclopedia of Erotic Failure*. London: Futura, 1989.

Kirby, David. "After the Fall." *Advocate*, November 21, 2000.
Kirchner, Paul. *Oops!* Los Angeles: General Publishing, 1996.
Klein, Karen. "Super Password Winner Gets 5-Year Prison Sentence." *Daily News of Los Angeles*, May 3, 1988.
Kleinberg, Howard. "God Squad Member Busted with Hooker." *Wichita Eagle*, March 6, 1996.
Knott, Tom. "Al-Sahhaf, Answer and a Few Antiwar Absurdities." *Washington Times*, April 10, 2003.
"Laguna Niguel, Calif., INS Workers Indicted in Document-Shredding Case." *Knight Ridder/Tribune Business News*, January 31, 2003.
Lawless, Annette. "Column: Women Have Gone Too 'Wild.'" *Kansas State Collegian*, April 18, 2007.
"Lawmaker Caught with Prostitute Resigns." *St. Petersburg Times*, March 2, 1996.
Lee, Albert. *Henry Ford and the Jews*. New York: Stein and Day, 1980.
Lee, Laura. *Blame It on the Rain*. New York: HarperCollins, 2006.
———. *The Elvis Impersonation Kit*. New York: Black Dog and Leventhal, 2006.
———. *100 Most Dangerous Things in Everyday Life*. New York: Broadway, 2004.
———. *The Pocket Encyclopedia of Aggravation*. New York: Black Dog and Leventhal, 2001.
Lefley, Jack. "Owner Blows £2.7 m Building so His Ex-Wife Couldn't Get It." *Evening Standard*, July 11, 2006.
"Lewd E-mail Lawyers to Keep Jobs." *Birmingham Post*, December 22, 2000.
Lines, Andy. "All I Said Was 'Hi, Jack.'" *Mirror*, June 8, 2000.
"Lip Sync Scam Sinks Milli Vanilli." *Chicago Sun-Times*, November 16, 1990.
Loh, Jules. "Why Has Roy Sullivan Been Zapped 7 Times?" *San Mateo Times*, October 22, 1977.
Lord, Lewis. "The McHistory of America." *U.S. News & World Report*, December 27, 1999.
Lowther, William. "Dick Cheney Blasts Friend in Accident on Bird Shoot." *Daily Mail*, February 13, 2006.
"Lucky Escape for Captain Calamity." *BBC News*, August 22, 2001.
Lundry, Sarah. "Former Astronaut Lisa Nowak's Attitude Cost Her Mission." *Orlando Sun Sentinel*, May 2, 2007.

Lyons, Douglas C. "The Richest Black Lottery Winners." *Ebony*, February, 1990.
Macdonald, Marianne. "Lovers Dial M for Maximum Embarrassment." *Independent*, July 2, 1994.
Mandel, Miriam B. "A Reader's Guide to Pilar's Bullfighters: Untold Histories in *For Whom the Bell Tolls*." *Hemingway Review*, Vol. 15, Issue 1, 1995.
Mann, Judy. "Flynt's Assault on the Hill." *Washington Post*, January 15, 1999.
Mark, Jon. "In Arizona, Cactus-Nappers Beware!" *Daily Oklahoman*, February 23, 1986.
Martin, Patrick. "Who Is the Unluckiest Man Ever to Have Lived?" *The Times (UK)*, February 10, 2006.
"Mayerling Extends Language of Dance." *Bennington Banner*, March 16, 1978.
"McDonald's Founder Dies." *San Mateo Times*, December 13, 1971.
McKellar, Wiley Rowland. "Bushusuru: What's Funny in Japan Remains Puzzling to Us." *Harrisburg (PA) Patriot-News*, February 1, 1992.
McKeon, Clare. "Just Practising." *Sunday Mirror*, November 3, 2002.
McKinnon, Jim. "Man Held in Wielding of Turtle Is Freed." *Pittsburgh Post-Gazette*, July 13, 1994.
McKittrick, David. "Europe: Return of the Wayward Bishop." *Independent*, February 2, 2006.
Millar, Chris. "City Woman in Ketchup Email Row." *Evening Standard*, June 21, 2005.
Miller, Matt. "Man Says He Didn't Plan Sex with Girls." *Harrisburg (PA) Patriot-News*, June 30, 2007.
Mills, James. "A Female, an Email and the Tale of a Lover Caught Napping." *Daily Mail*, September 14, 2002.
"Miracle Is Sunk." *Daily Record*, August 30, 2006.
"Miss Ike Raises Cane and Burglar Ends Up in Pokey." *Memphis (TN) Commercial Appeal*, March 22, 2002.
Mitchell, John. *Eccentric Lives and Peculiar Notions*. Secaucus, NJ: Citadel Press, 1984.
"Moleman Exits." *Syracuse News Herald*, April 13, 1977.
Montes, Duardo. "Couple in Debt Gets $11 Million Revenge." *Chicago Sun-Times*, August 25, 1995.
Morgan, Helen. "Milk Protest Turns Sour." *Scotsman*, October 12, 2002.

Morgansen, Andy. "Running Turned Him Around." *Oakland Tribune*, November 22, 1977.

Mueller, Norm. "Sports Fans, I Bet You Didn't Know." *Oshkosh (WI) Daily Northwestern*, May 15, 1972.

Mueller, P. S. "Philip Van Munching, The Devil's Adman—Ellen Fein Divorcing Husband." *Brandweek*, May 14, 2001.

"Mugger Goes from Robber to Robbed." *Reuters*, June 19, 2007.

Murdock, Deroy. "Overzealous Regulators Exposed." *Human Events*, October 2, 1998.

Murray, Raphael. "Beware the Curse of *Schadenfreude*." *Art Business News*, January 1, 2003.

"Music Makes You Smarter? Second Installment." *Music Trades*, July 1, 1999.

"Nail Hits Carpenter on the Head—Literally." *Daily Herald*, October 11, 1989.

Nash, Bruce, and Allan Zullo. *The Baseball Hall of Shame*. New York: Pocket Books, 1985.

———. *The Baseball Hall of Shame 2*. New York: Pocket Books, 1986.

———. *The Baseball Hall of Shame 3*. New York: Pocket Books, 1987.

———. *The Baseball Hall of Shame 4*. New York: Pocket Books, 1990.

———. *The Fishing Hall of Shame*. New York: Pocket Books, 1991.

———. *The Golf Hall of Shame*. New York: Pocket Books, 1989.

———. *Gutter Humor: Outrageous but True Bowling Stories*. Kansas City, MO: Andrews and McMeel, 1994.

———. *The Sports Hall of Shame*. New York: Pocket Books, 1987.

Nash, Jay Robert. *Zanies*. Piscatawny, NJ: New Century Publishers, 1982.

Noah, Timothy. "PR Tips for Mohammed Al-Sahhaf." *Slate*, April 7, 2003.

O'Connor, Michael. "Yo, Vladi, About that Ring . . . ." *Boston Herald*, June 29, 2005.

O'Neil, Frank. *The Mammoth Book of Oddities*. New York: Carroll and Graff, 1996.

"Organic Food Advocate Rodale Dies." *Long Beach (CA) Independent/Press Telegram*, June 8, 1971.

O'Sullivan, Jack. "Shiny Happy People: Children's TV Is Fronted by Squeaky-Clean Paragos." *Independent*, October 20, 1998.
"Other Top Company Clangers." *Mirror*, April 3, 2004.
"The Outing of Jim West." *Economist*, May 14, 2005.
Padawer, Ruth. "Rules Girls vs. Code Guys in Battle of Wiles." *Bergen County (NJ) Record*, January 5, 1997.
Parkes, Adam. "A Sense of Justice: Whistler, Ruskin, James, Impressionism." *Victorian Studies*, Vol. 42, Issue 4, 2000.
Parris, Matthew. *The Great Unfrocked*. London: Robson Books, 1998.
Parrish, John. "Motoring People: Driving Mad." *The People*, July 30, 2000.
"Payback Time for Drunk Diamond Thief." *Reuters*, November 21, 2006.
"People, etc." *Elyria (OH) Chronicle Telegram*, December 6, 1981.
Perry, Loran. "Rambling Reporter: The Human Mole." *Pasadena (CA) Independent*, October 24, 1968.
"Perry Mason Loses a Case," *Fresno Bee*, September 5, 1963.
Pile, Stephen. *The (Incomplete) Book of Failures*. New York: Dutton, 1979.
Plotz, David. "Rep. Bob Barr." *Slate*, February 22, 1998.
Pochna, Peter. "Chemist Confesses in IDEXX Spy Case." *Portland (ME) Press Herald*, July 23, 1999.
———. "Trade Secrets Trial Begins in Portland." *Portland (ME) Press Herald*, August 10, 1999.
"Porn Party Sacking." *Daily Post*, November 23, 2002.
"Portrait of a Jet-Set Family." *Evening Standard*, January 25, 2002.
Postman, David. "Even the Mayor Wonders: Who Is the Real Jim West?" *Seattle Times*, December 2, 2005.
Potter, Deborah. "At What Price Publicity?" *American Journalism Review*, March 1, 2002.
Powell, Mark. "Billy Beer Sales Go Flat." *Bucks County (PA) Courier Times*, May 16, 1978.
"Prince Philip: His Life of Gaffes." *Sunday Mirror*, September 28, 2003.
"Protest Problem." *Seattle Post-Intelligencer*, March 20, 2003.
Prugh, Jeff. "Billy Carter: A Hot-Air Buffoon in a Hot Air Balloon?" *Winnipeg Free Press*, August 31, 1977.
Pryke, Chris. "Travel: Call of the WILD." *Birmingham Post*, February 17, 2001.

Quintanilla, Michael. "The Fashion World Is Falling Hard for Higher and Higher Heels." *San Antonio (TX) Express News*, November 15, 2006.

"Rantering about Rubbish." *Economist*, April 27, 1991.

Rawling, Gerald. "Swindler of the Century." *History Today*, July 1, 1993.

Regan, Geoffrey. *Historical Blunders*. London: Carlton, 2002.

———. *The Past Times Book of Military Blunders*. London: Guinness Publishing, 1991.

Reid, T. R. "Video Shows Entire Bush Collapse." *Washington Post*, January 11, 1992.

Reilly, Jerry. Telephone interview by author, December 7, 1997.

Reinhard, David. "John and Anne: Out of Homosexuality." *Oregonian*, September 8, 1996.

Reinstein, Mara. "I Don't Deserve This." *Us Magazine*, May 21, 2007.

"Remarkable News of 1910." *Washington Post*, December 4, 1910.

Reusse, Patrick. "Wrong-Way Run and Unhappy Memory." *Minneapolis (MN) Star Tribune*, January 24, 1999.

"A Rich Vein of Humour; Answers to Correspondents." *Daily Mail*, May 30, 2001.

Richmond, Randy, and Tom Villemaire. *Colossal Canadian Failures*. Toronto, ON, CA: Hounslow, 2002.

Rising, Gerry. "The Odd History of the Little-Known Pig War." *Buffalo News*, June 18, 2001.

Rock, Lucy. "He Is a Brad Boy." *Mirror*, December 16, 2000.

Roeper, Richard. "Pee-wee's X Adventure Is the Last for Kids' Star." *Chicago Sun-Times*, July 30, 1991.

Rosellini, Lynn. "Of Rolexes and Repentence." *U.S. News & World Report*, March 7, 1988.

Ross, Bonnie. "More Bride, Less Zilla." *Syracuse Post Standard*, September 7, 2003.

Rudd, Andy et al. "I'll Stand by Worst Boyfriend in World." *Daily Mirror*, October 5, 2002.

Rudenstein, David. "Did Elgin Cheat at Marbles?" *Nation*, May 29, 2000.

Ruffin, Steven A. *Aviation's Most Wanted*. Washington, D.C.: Potomac Books, 2005.

"Rules Author Sued for Defamation." *Associated Press*, January 30, 2007.
"Russia's Putin Pockets Super Bowl Ring." *Associated Press*, June 29, 2005.
Ruth, Daniel. "Geraldo Rivera Vaults Back to TV on Capone Show." *Chicago Sun-Times*, April 21, 1986.
"Santa Gets Smashed—Window Two." *Chicago Sun-Times*, December 6, 1994.
Sawer, Patrick. "Ketchup Email Leaves Lawyer's Reputation Stained." *Evening Standard*, June 17, 2005.
Schaverien, Tracy. "Is This the Unluckiest Man in Britain?" *Sunday Mirror*, April 20, 1997.
Schlosser, Joe. "We Sued, Yadda, Yadda, Yadda, We Lost." *Broadcasting and Cable*, June 28, 1999.
Schoonover, Kelley. "A Riches-to-Rehab Story." *Newark (NJ) Star-Ledger*, December 14, 2004.
Schwartz, Donald M. "Vault Blast a Bust." *Chicago Sun-Times*, April 22, 1986.
"Seattle Man Charged in Bizarre Duck Case." *Associated Press*, April 17, 2007.
"Security Video Premieres at Winona Ryder Trial." *CourtTV News*, October 31, 2002.
"Self-Proclaimed Psychic No Match for Soviet Train." *Chicago Sun-Times*, October 2, 1989.
"Sharp Student Just Says No to Pencil's Message." *Washington Post*, January 9, 1999.
Shattered Dreams: 100 Stories of Government Abuse. 4th ed. Washington, D.C.: National Center for Public Policy Research, 2003.
Shaw, Karl. *The Mammoth Book of Oddballs and Eccentrics*. New York: Carroll and Graff Publishers, 2000.
Shepherd, Chuck. "News of the Weird." *Chronicle-Telegram*, July 5, 1992.
Sherman, Mark. "Election '92: U.S. Senate." *Atlanta Journal-Constitution*, July 7, 1992.
Simmons, Ian. *The Fortean Times Book of Bizarre Behaviour*. London: John Brown Publishing, 1998.
Singh, Rob. "Vile Sex Email that Could Cost Banker His Job." *Evening Standard*, January 20, 2006.

Slack, Donovan. "Putin Has Super Ring Goof." *Salt Lake City (UT) Desert News*, June 29, 2005.

"SLF: Citizen's Motion to Disbar Attorney Clinton Moves to National Stage." *US Newswire*, May 20, 1999.

Smith, Doug. "Paddles and Portage—An Atikokan Journey." *Scouting Magazine*. www.scoutingmagazine.org/issues/0410/a-padd.html, accessed April 2, 2007.

Smith, Ken. *Raw Deal: Horrible and Ironic Stories of Forgotten Americans*. New York: Blast Books, 1998.

Sorkin, Andrew Ross. "An E-mail Boast to Friends Puts Executive Out of Work." *New York Times*, May 22, 2001.

Spence, Clark. *The Rainmakers: American Pluviculture to World War II*. Lincoln, NE: University of Lincoln Press, 1980.

"Spirit World." *Salt Lake Tribune*, January 18, 2003.

Srivastava, Mehul. "Think Your Boss Is Bad? Think Again—Meet the Worst." *Sacramento Bee*, August 12, 2006.

Staple, Arthur. "World Cup Talk." *Bergen County (NJ) Record*, June 18, 1994.

Steinberg, Neil. *Complete and Utter Failure*. New York: Doubleday, 1994.

Steiner, Wendy. "A Pot of Paint: Aesthetics on Trial in Whistler v. Ruskin." *Art in America*, January 1, 1993.

Stevenson, Richard W. "Get-Rich-Quick Artist Lowry Now Reduced to Rags." *Seattle Post-Intelligencer*, July 13, 1987.

Steyn, Mark. "So Much News, So Little Sense." *Chicago Sun-Times*, May 27, 2007.

"Streaker at NHL Game Ordered to Donate to Charity." *Associated Press*, February 12, 2003.

Stringer, David. "Book Chronicles Britain's Prince Philip's Gaffes." *Associated Press*, May 29, 2006.

Strouse, Chuck. "Christmas in Prison." *Broward Palm Beach New Times*, December 20, 2001.

Suggs, Ernie. "Glavin Pleads Guilty to Public Indecency." *Atlanta Journal-Constitution*, October 13, 2000.

"Teacher Banned for Hitler Comment." *Associated Press*, February 8, 2000.

Teitell, Beth. "Travelers Put Their Worries Into Overdrive." *Boston Herald*, June 17, 1997.

"This Problem Is Too Big a Load for City Folks." *Lincoln Journal Star*, January 13, 2005.

Thomas, Dana L. *Lords of the Land*. New York: G. P. Putnam's Sons, 1977.

Thomas, Evan. "The Shot Heard Round the World." *Newsweek*, February 27, 2006.

Thompson, Clay. "Tale is True: Man Killed by Saguaro's Arm." *Arizona Republic*, November 21, 2005.

Thornton, Jeannye. "Stones Fly in the TV Temple." *U.S. News & World Report*, June 8, 1987.

Tibbals, Geoff. *Legal Blunders*. New York: Carroll & Graf Publishers, 2000.

Tinsley, Jesse, and Lila J. Mills. "Misfortune Trails on Heels of Lady Luck." *Plain Dealer*, January 25, 2004.

Tomlinson, Gerald. *Speaker's Treasury of Political Stories, Anecdotes and Humor*. New York: MJF Books, 1990.

Torkelson, Jean. "Purity of Pastors Questioned: Christian Authors Cite Studies that Many Watch Porn." *Rocky Mountain News*, November 18, 2006.

"TV Actress Held in Vegas Video Store Robbery." *Associated Press*, March 3, 1991.

"TV Appearance Leads to Arrest." *Associated Press*, July 16, 1999.

"20,000 Pounds for Hypnotism Victim." *Independent*, November 4, 1994.

"2 Brides plus 1 Groom Equals Trouble." *East London (South Africa) Dispatch*, December 18, 2001.

"Unlucky Ticket Sold." *Doylestown (PA) Intelligencer*, September 29, 1996.

Usborne, David. "Bakker's Back." *Independent*, June 15, 2003.

"Vandals Attack Elevator—It Fights Back." *Orlando Sentinel*, May 9, 2007.

"Vasectomy, Abortion Fail Disease-Plagued Family." *Modesto Bee*, April 24, 1977.

Vozzella, Laura, and Nicole Fuller. "A Little Quip, A Big Uproar." *Baltimore Sun*, May 11, 2007.

Walsh, Charles. "A Situation in Which Rules Are Made to Be Broken." *Connecticut Post*, March 25, 2002.

Walsh, Lawrence. "Shared Thanks, Troubles Don't Dampen Rossis' Hospitality." *Pittsburgh Post-Gazette*, November 24, 1995.

Ward, Stephen. "Terrified Thief Foils Terrorist Bombers." *Independent*, July 22, 1994.

Warda, Mark. *Neighbor vs. Neighbor: Legal Rights of Neighbors in Dispute*. Clearwater, FL: Sphinx Publishing, 1991.

Warren, Marcus. "*Rules* Author Blames Divorce on Dental Work." *Chicago Sun-Times*, September 29, 2004.

Watson, Traci. "Astronaut Posts Bail After Being Charged with Attempted First-Degree Murder." *USA Today*, February 7, 2007.

"The Ways of Misers." *Syracuse (NY) Sunday Herald*, May 5, 1889.

"Weak-Bladdered Plane Passenger Released." *Albany (NY) Times Union*, October 26, 1993.

Weir, Kytja. "911 Calls Land Woman, 86, in Jail." *Charlotte Observer*, May 24, 2005.

"When to Terrorise the Talent." *Economist*, February 22, 2003.

Wicks, Ben. *Ben Wicks' Book of Losers*. Toronto, ON, CA: Seal, 1979.

Willa, Brendon. "Hymn and Errs Sale at Church." *Mirror*, April 25, 2003.

Wimmer, Adi. "The Intolerable Burden Father Gave Me." *Jerusalem Post*, October 13, 1998.

Winberry, Jen. "Commentary: Behind the Music Captures Prime Moments in Pop Culture." *University Wire*, April 27, 2006.

"Woman, 85, Beats Burglar with Six-Pack." *San Jose Mercury News*, July 13, 1991.

"Woman in Hiding After 'Smutty' E-mail Goes Global." *United Press International*, December 16, 2000.

Wyatt, Kristen. "Indecency Charges Throw the Legal Foundation Into Turmoil." *Macon Telegraph*, October 6, 2000.

York, Anthony. "Bob Barr's Emotional Distress." *Salon*, April 8, 2007.

Zacks, Richard. *An Underground Education*. New York: Doubleday, 1997.

About the Author

Michigan native Laura Lee has enjoyed an eclectic career in publishing and performing arts. Not only is she perhaps the only corporate speech writer in America who once worked as a professional mime and improvisational comedian, she has also written a dozen books on topics ranging from poetry and ballet to Elvis impersonation and annoying things. Her titles include *The Pocket Encyclopedia of Aggravation, 100 Most Dangerous Things in Everyday Life and What You Can Do About Them, Bad Predictions, A Child's Introduction to Ballet,* and *The Elvis Impersonation Kit.*

Currently she divides her time between her writing career and touring with the artistic director of the Russian National Ballet Foundation of Moscow. She has not yet achieved the kind of success that makes people secretly root for her downfall, but she hopes with enough work and persistence to get there some day.